TEN YEARS IN THE RANKS
U.S. ARMY

*This is a volume in the
Arno Press Collection*

THE AMERICAN MILITARY EXPERIENCE

Advisory Editor
Richard H. Kohn

Editorial Board
Bernard Brodie
Edward M. Coffman
Morris Janowitz
Russell F. Weigley

*See last pages of this volume
for a complete list of titles.*

Ten Years in the Ranks U. S. Army

AUGUSTUS MEYERS

ARNO PRESS
A New York Times Company
New York • 1979

973.74
M613t

Editorial Supervision: RITA LAWN

Reprint Edition 1979 by Arno Press, Inc.

Reprinted from a copy in the State Historical Society of Wisconsin Library

AMERICAN MILITARY EXPERIENCE
ISBN for complete set: 0-405-11850-3
See last pages of this volume for titles.

Manufactured in the United States of America

89-4189

Library of Congress Cataloging in Publication Data

Meyers, Augustus, 1841-
  Ten years in the ranks, U.S. Army.

  (American military experience)
  Reprint of the 1914 ed. published by Stirling Press, New York.
  1. Meyers, Augustus, 1841-   2. United States. Army. Army of the Potomac--Biography. 3. United States--History--Civil War, 1861-1865--Personal narratives. 4. United States. Army--Military life. 5. United States--History--Civil War, 1861-1865--Regimental histories--Army of the Potomac. I. Title. II. Series.
E601.M623   1979   973.7'41'0924 [B]   78-22387
ISBN 0-405-11864-3

Ten Years in the Ranks
U. S. Army

BY

AUGUSTUS MEYERS

NEW YORK
THE STIRLING PRESS
1914

COPYRIGHT, 1914
BY AUGUSTUS MEYERS
NEW YORK

Preface

THIS narrative of ten years' service in the United States Army on the frontier and during the Civil War at an early period of my life is written mainly from memory after an interval of more than half a century. I have endeavored to describe in a simple manner the daily life of a soldier in the ranks while serving in garrison, camp and field.

AUGUSTUS MEYERS.

Table of Contents

PART I.	Enlistment and Service on Governor's Island, New York Harbor, in 1854 . . .	1
PART II.	At Carlisle Barracks, Pa., in 1855 . .	33
PART III.	Journey from Carlisle to Fort Pierre Nebraska, Territory, in 1855	49
PART IV.	Fort Pierre and the Sioux Indians, 1855-1856	71
PART V.	Establishing Fort Lookout, 1856-1857 .	109
PART VI.	Service at Fort Randall, Campaigning in Kansas and Expiration of My Enlistment, 1857-1859	127
PART VII.	Re-enlistment and Return to Frontiers, 1860	157
PART VIII.	Service in Washington and Georgetown, D. C., 1861-1862	177
PART IX.	The Peninsula Campaign, 1862	197
PART X.	The Seven Days' Retreat, 1862	225
PART XI.	Harrison's Landing to Fredericksburg, Va. 1862-1863	257
PART XII.	Chancellorsville to Winter Camp of 1863-1864	287
PART XIII.	In Grant's Campaign, 1864	311
PART XIV.	Departure from the Field and Last Days of Service, 1865	341
REFLECTIONS	. . . .	351
ADDENDA	. . . .	353

PART I.

ENLISTMENT AND SERVICE ON GOVERNOR'S ISLAND, NEW YORK
HARBOR, IN 1854.

ON March thirty-first, 1854, with the consent of my widowed mother, I joined the United States Army. I enlisted for a period of five years, as a musician in the general service, at the recruiting office, at No. 115 Cedar Street, New York City. My age was twelve years and nine months. I was of slender build, but in good health and passed the medical examination. After being sworn in at a notary's office in Nassau Street, I was conducted by the recruiting sergeant to the Governor's Island boat landing at the Battery; there he placed me in charge of Sergeant John Brown, cockswain of the eight-oared barge manned by soldiers from the Island. As this was then the only way for passengers to reach the Island, I had to wait a long time for the next trip of the barge, and it was late in the afternoon when we started.

There were but few passengers besides myself, a woman, a civilian or two and a few soldiers returning from "pass," more or less hilarious. After a struggle with the swift currents of the East River and considerable pitching and tossing, we landed at the Island dock near the Guard House, where I was taken in charge by a corporal of the guard who conducted me to the South Battery on the east side of the Island opposite Brooklyn, where the boys learning music were in quarters. We reported to Sergeant Hanke, who was in charge of all the non-commissioned officers and music boys in that battery.

Sergeant Hanke, after looking me over, asked whether I desired to learn to be a drummer or a fifer. When I expressed a preference for the former, he made some remarks about my slim and very youthful appearance, and advised me to think it over for a day or two. He called for Corporal Butler, who conducted me to Room No. 1 on the ground floor, to the south of the sally-port, of which he had charge.

On my entrance into the room there arose a cry of "Fresh fish" from the boys who were present. They surrounded me, asked my name, where I lived and many other questions and demanded to know whether I had any money or tobacco, taking no pains to hide their disappointment when I confessed that I had neither. The corporal, who had left the room, fortunately returned soon and relieved my embarrassing position. He assigned me to "bunk" with the only boy in the room who had no bedfellow or "bunkie."

The corporal's presence diverted the boys' attention from me for a while and gave me time to examine my surroundings. I found myself in a room with two windows that overlooked the parade ground and one facing inward towards the interior of South Battery. There were six iron double bedsteads in the room and a single bedstead for the corporal in a corner next to a window. The double bedsteads were made so that one-half could be folded up over the other half when not in use. This in a measure relieved during the day the very crowded condition at night when all the beds were down. The beds consisted of a bedsack stuffed with straw, which was rolled up in the day time, and a pair of blankets, neatly folded, laid on top. There were no sheets nor pillows for the boys—the corporal was the only one who enjoyed these luxuries, and he had provided them himself. The boys slept on the bedticks and covered themselves with their blankets when it was cold, or used one of the blankets to lie on when it was warm enough, folding up a jacket or some other piece of clothing as a substitute for a pillow.

A wide shelf around the room above the beds provided space for knapsacks, extra shoes, drums, fifes, and other objects, and on hooks under the shelf were hung the overcoats. There was a coal fire burning in the grate. A few wooden benches and a chair for the corporal in charge; this, with a water pail and a tin cup on a shelf behind the door, completed the furniture of the room.

After a while I heard a drum beat, which was the first call for "retreat." Ten minutes later, the "assembly" sounded to form ranks on the parade outside of the sally-port. The boys formed in two ranks, those who were proficient with their drums and fifes on the right. The command, "parade rest," was given by one of the sergeants, and the "retreat" played by the musicians as prescribed in the regulations. Then came the command, "Attention," and a roll call, at which each boy present answered, "Here." Some special orders were read and then at the command, "Break ranks, march," the boys rushed back to their quarters, to deposit their instruments and adjourn to the mess room in the basement for supper.

I was directed to follow, and found the mess room large enough to hold the entire company of boys at one sitting. There were long pine tables and benches without backs, all scrubbed clean. At each boy's place was a thin plate, containing a small portion of stewed dried apples, a large stone china bowl filled with black coffee (sweetened but without milk) and a slice of bread about four ounces in weight. There were iron spoons, knives and forks, and a few dishes on the table containing pepper and salt.

I asked one of the boys if they had the same kind of a supper every day, and was informed that sometimes they got molasses in place of the dried apples. As the boys finished their meager supper they left the mess room without any formality and returned to their quarters or went out to have a smoke in some place unobserved. I went back to my quarters and sat on a bench, chatting with some of the boys, who told me many things about their daily duties and the treatment they received. They all wished to leave the Island, and hoped to be sent soon to join a regiment somewhere. Some were reading books by the feeble tallow candle light, some played checkers on home-made checker boards, or amused themselves with other games.

Thus passed the evening until nine o'clock when the call for "Tattoo" sounded. There was considerably more music than at "Retreat," otherwise it was the same. There was another roll call and dismissal to quarters, where the beds were let down and the blankets spread. With a little skylarking, the boys undressed and lay down. The orderly covered the fire in the grate with ashes, "Taps" were sounded by the drummer detailed for that purpose, lights were extinguished, and all were supposed to be silent. But there was whispering and smothered laughing, which ceased only after some vigorous language and threats of reporting by the corporal.

I lay down alongside of my strange bedfellow, who kindly shared his blanket with me, my head pillowed on my jacket. There was a glimmering light from the fireplace, by which I could make out the forms of my companions and that of the corporal stretched out on his more comfortable bed in the corner. Soon all seemed to be asleep except myself. I remained awake a long time, thinking of the circumstances that had brought me here, the strange company I was sharing, and wondering what my future would be. At last, weary with the day's unusual experiences and excitements, I also fell asleep. And thus ended my first day as a soldier in the United States Army.

I was awakened next morning at daylight by a drummer beating the first call for "Reveille," and the corporal's voice shouting, "Get up! you lazy fellows," to some who were slow to respond. The boys, who slept in their underclothing, hastily put on their pants, stockings and shoes. Then each grabbed a tin wash basin from its hook in the hall, went out of doors to a pump and filled the basin, which he carried into the hall, and, placing it on a bench, performed his ablutions, drying himself on a roller towel. In the warm season this performance took place out of doors. It was a cold, raw morning, and it made me shiver as I followed the others outside; but I concealed my distress to avoid being laughed at.

We finished dressing, and soon heard the drum beat the "Assembly," and the corporal's call to "Turn out and fall in." Ranks were formed, as at "Retreat" and "Tattoo," and the roll was called. The fifers and drummers played the "Reveille," which was a much longer performance than either "Retreat" or "Tattoo." It consisted of perhaps a half dozen tunes, commencing with a piece called "Three Camps," then "Slow Scotch," "Austrian," "Dutch," "Quick Scotch," 'Hessian," etc. Some of these pieces were played in slow time and others in quick time; they and the regular calls were the same as were used at the time of the American Revolution and had never been materially changed since.

Immediately after we were dismissed, we went to breakfast which consisted of a small piece of boiled salt pork—cold—a piece of bread and a large bowl of black coffee. There was also some grease in a dish, saved from the boiling of the pork, which some of the boys spread on their bread as a substitute for butter, seasoning it with pepper and salt.

Soon after breakfast "Doctor's Call" sounded, and those who felt unwell were conducted to the hospital to be examined by the surgeon. The boys now became busy making up their beds, cleaning their shoes, brushing their clothes and polishing their brass buttons with the aid of a brush and what was called a "button stick." Some pipe-clayed or chalked the white braid on their jackets. The room orderly, who was changed daily, swept the floor, replenished the fire and everything in the room was put in order for the daily inspection made by Sergeant Hanke.

At eight o'clock came the call to "fall in" for guard mounting, ranks were formed and after a critical inspection as to cleanliness by the sergeant, the company marched to the main parade ground in the center of the Island. About the same time we heard a band playing as it left the main garrison followed by the guard detail for the day. The lines were formed, the adjutant and the officer of the day took their places. Then the arms, accoutrements and clothing were inspected. An orderly for the commanding officer was selected from the guard and one from the boys for the adjutant.

The entire interesting ceremony of the Guard Mount was performed according to regulation, the band playing at intervals. The guard passed in review, marched off to their station and relieved the old guard. The boys were marched back to the South Battery where, shortly after their arrival, a call for "School" sounded at nine o'clock. As I was in citizen's clothing I did not have to take part in any formation of ranks. I was simply a spectator until I was uniformed.

At eleven o'clock school was over and practice on the fife and drum continued until noon. The drummers, twenty-five or more in number, went outside and made a great racket under the east wall of the South Battery, which could be heard on the other side of Butter Milk Channel in Brooklyn. They were in charge of their instructor, Sergeant Moore, who was called the drum major and had Corporal Butler as an assistant. I watched the boys practicing and noted how difficult it seemed to be for some to hold the drum-sticks properly and beat the first exercise, called "Mammy-Daddy," without hitting the rim of the drum as often as the drum-head, which would bring down upon them a reprimand from the instructor, or in some cases a rap across the knuckles for some persistently awkward boy. When I took note of the exceedingly large and heavy drums used in the service at that time, which the drummers were obliged to carry, I resolved to become a fifer, as I considered it more genteel and a step towards acquiring some knowledge of music.

While the drummers were practicing outside of the Battery, Sergeant Hanke, the fife-major, and a corporal were instructing an equal number of fifers in the school room that was filled with a shrill din as each tried to play a different tune.

At noon musical instruction ceased, and we went to the mess room for dinner. The menu consisted of a bowl of rice soup containing some desiccated vegetables, a small piece of boiled beef and the usual piece of bread. I was told that about three times a week there was bean soup served with boiled salt pork or bacon and, at rare intervals, one or two boiled potatoes.

After dinner there was nothing to do until two o'clock when school opened again for two hours. At four o'clock in the afternoon drill commenced. The boys were instructed in what was called the "School of the Soldier"—facing, marching, etc. They drilled singly at first, then in squads and finally by company according to Scott's Tactics, always without arms. Drill was over at five o'clock when there was a rest until "Retreat." This was the daily routine of duties, except on Saturdays, when they ceased at noon.

On Saturday afternoons some of the boys were detailed in turn to scrub and holy-stone the floor of our quarters and the benches, which consumed some hours. The remainder of the boys were free to do as they pleased.

On Sundays we attended guard mounting at eight in the morning and at ten-thirty we marched in a body to the Episcopal Chapel, a short distance from our quarters. The chapel was a frame structure, seating about two hundred besides the music boys. The services were attended by some of the officers and their families, soldiers' wives and their children and such of the soldiers and recruits as wished to attend. There was no regular post chaplain; I do not think there were any in the army at this time. A minister from New York or Brooklyn conducted the services. I do not remember whether any collections were taken up—if there were I am sure it was fruitless so far as the boys were concerned, unless the Sunday immediately succeeded a pay day.

The interior of the chapel was very plain, only one aisle had cushioned seats and they were not for our use. There was a small organ and a few wooden tablets were hung on the walls. One of them was much larger than the others. It commemorated the wreck of the steamer *San Francisco,* bound for California, and the drowning of a number of soldiers and music boys, whose names were on the tablet. This always interested me, and if the sermon was dull or I felt sleepy, I would read it over and over again until I could repeat all the names by heart.

On Sunday afternoon we were free to roam about the island as we pleased, until about sun-down when, if the weather permitted, we had "dress parade" on the main parade ground. This was a more elaborate ceremony than guard mounting. It was always interesting to me and I liked to attend it. The post band turned out and all the armed soldiers on the island were present as well as our "Field Music Battalion." We made a fine show, and sometimes we had a few spectators who came from the city in row boats. Once in every two months we had muster and general inspection by the commanding officer of the post, who called the roll and looked over the arms, accoutrements, clothing and quarters. For this inspection we were obliged to appear on parade in full marching order, our knapsacks packed and bulging with our spare clothing. Muster was a preliminary to pay day, an event always welcomed.

On my second day on the island I was taken to the quartermaster's store house to draw the first installment of my yearly clothing allowance. There were issued to me, one blanket, one great coat, two fatigue jackets, two pairs of trousers, two pairs of white flannel shirts, two pairs of Canton flannel drawers, two pairs of woolen stockings, two pairs of shoes, one forage cap and one leather stock, also a knapsack, a haversack and a canteen.

The blanket was coarse and heavy; it weighed five pounds and measured seven by five and a half feet. It was grayish brown in color and had "U. S." in four inch black letters worked in the centre. The overcoat as well as the trousers and jacket, were of coarse sky-blue cloth. The overcoat was single breasted and had a cape reaching down to the elbows; there was a row of brass buttons on the breast and on the cape and some more on the coat tails. The jacket came to the hips, had a standing collar, an inside breast pocket, a row of brass buttons down the front and a few on the sleeves. The shoes were coarse looking with broad toes and heels and leather thongs, but they were good serviceable marching shoes. The trousers were plain without stripes and had two pockets. There were no waistcoats issued. The forage or fatigue cap was a heavy, clumsy looking affair, made of thick dark blue cloth. It had a large overhanging crown with a welt, a chin-strap with a brass button on each side and a leather visor.

The most objectionable part of the whole uniform was the leather stock or "dog collar," as we called it, intended to serve as a cravat and keep the soldier's chin elevated. It was a strip of stiff black shoe leather about two and one-half inches high and arranged to fasten at the back of the neck with a leather thong. It was torture to wear it in hot weather, but we found means to modify the annoyance by reducing the height of the stock and shaving down the thickness of the leather until it became soft and pliable.

As the soldiers' clothing was made up in men's sizes only, there were none to fit the boys. I believe there were about six different sizes in shoes and three or four in clothing. The smallest size in clothing, No. 1, was issued to me, and I was sent to the post tailor. He took my measure and altered the great coat, jackets and trousers. He also put some white braid on the collar and sleeves of one of my jackets. The cost of these alterations were deducted from my first pay due. It was moderate enough, for the tailor's price as well as those of the laundress and the sutler were fixed by the Post Council of Administration. With the shirts and drawers I was obliged to get along without alterations, voluminous though they were. The shoes were too large for me also, but the thick woolen socks helped to fill them. No dress coats were furnished to the boys while they were on the Island. We only got those after joining a regiment.

In about a week my clothes were ready. I arrayed myself in my new sky-blue uniform, experiencing a boy's pleasure in a new suit and some pride in what I considered my fine soldierly appearance. We were not allowed to keep any citizen's clothing, so I sold my clothes to a Hebrew "Old Clo' Man" who often visited the island for that purpose. He paid me a dollar for them, the possession of which made me quite popular with a few of the boys who showed me where we could buy pies and ginger-pop at the sutler's store.

On the third day after my arrival, I was ordered to commence attending school and to learn music. The school was in a room within the South Battery, which was much too small for the attendance. There were some pine desks and benches, a blackboard, desks and chairs for two teachers and some shelves. We were divided into several classes and were instructed in three R's by Sergeant Evans who taught the older boys and by Corporal Washburn who had charge of the younger ones. Each of the teachers had a rattan, for it required more than patience on their part to keep the unruly element quiet. I think both the sergeant and the corporal were very forbearing men. They were excused from all other duties and paraded at muster only, receiving a mere pittance of extra pay from the post fund.

Every month Sergeant Evans read to us the hundred and one Articles of War from the Army Regulations, wherein punishments were prescribed for all imaginable offenses, the ninety-ninth article covering everything else that might have been missed in the preceding articles so long as the offense was "to the prejudice of good order and military discipline." I noticed later that there were more charges and trials for "violation of the ninety-ninth article of war" than for any other. It seemed to fit nearly every case.

At eleven o'clock the two hour morning session of the school was over. The drummers who were nicknamed "sheepskin fiddlers," left the school room for an hour's practice, the fifers, called "straw blowers," by the drummers, had their instruments with them and remained in the school room. They got out their notes, and as soon as Sergeant Hanke and his assistant entered, commenced to practise, producing a terrific racket with their differing tunes. I was handed a "B" fife, the kind that was used at that time, and was shown how to hold it and place my fingers over the holes and my lips over the embouchure. I found it difficult to make a sound at first, but after a time I managed to produce some noise. I struggled with the gamut for a week or more and spent another in trying to play a bar or two of music correctly. After that I got along faster and commenced to learn some of the more simple calls and to understand the meaning of the notes in my music book. In about two months I had made sufficient progress to take my part in playing the reveille, retreat and tattoo. After that, I learned to play marches and other pieces. In the meantime, I had also made progress in drill and was considered sufficiently proficient at the end of three months to take part in parades and all other duties.

During the course of my musical instruction, I found the corporal instructor, whose name I do not recall, a rather impatient man very much given to scolding. Sergeant Hanke was more kindly, but he had a habit of taking a boy's fife out of his hands and playing part of the piece for him to show him how it should be done. As he was an inveterate tobacco-chewer this was very disagreeable. Wiping the fife on the sleeve of the jacket did not remove the strong odor. In my case I used soap and water as soon as I had the opportunity to do so.

I was obliged to submit to the customary "hazing," inflicted on new arrivals. I had to do various foolish stunts such as innocently asking Sergeant Moore for a pair of knapsack screws. He very promptly chased me out of his room. But the worst was what the boys named a "blanket court martial." This was performed in the quarters, a blanket was spread upon the floor, the victim was brought into the room blindfolded and placed standing upon the blanket by his guards. He was accused of a number of crimes such as stealing one of the heavy guns, swimming to Brooklyn with it and selling it for junk, and other ridiculous things.

Finally he was asked by the president of the court if he was guilty, and upon his reply "No!" the president said, "Then what are you standing there for?"

This was the signal for jerking away the blanket from under his feet, tumbling him to the floor. It was both rough and dangerous and I was sore after it.

I also had to have a few fights with some of the boys. These usually took place under the east wall of the Battery and were witnessed by a number of spectators. Such little affairs were not serious; the combatants usually had a rough and tumble scrap and the only damage I ever received was a bloody nose and a few scratches. Some of the older boys, however, occasionally had regular fist fights according to rules and had scouts out to give warning at the approach of any officer. Fighting was forbidden and the participants liable to be severely punished. After a time other "fresh fish" arrived and I ceased to be a novelty. I was then left at peace to pursue the regular course of events.

The greater part of the fifty or more music boys on the island at this time were from New York City like myself; the rest were from cities and small towns in adjoining states. There were half a dozen farmer's boys, mostly from Connecticut and the interior counties of New York State. A few of the boys were about my age, but most of them were from fifteen to eighteen or nineteen years old. None were enlisted without the consent of their parents or guardians whose inability to support them, no doubt, caused the greater part of them to join the army.

Some of them, however, seemed to have left good homes, or at least had prosperous looking visitors who brought them nice things to eat or gave them money. Poorly dressed women also appeared, mothers, who took their boys to some retired spot and had a cry over them. There was a very nice, genteel boy a year or two older than I, whose father owned a hotel on Broadway near Bleecker Street, in New York. I wondered why he left home to enlist. He and I became good friends and served in the same regiment later on, but he was always reticent on that point. By far the greater part of the boys were native born, but largely of foreign parentage, the Irish predominating.

With the exception of a dozen or so who were rather "hard cases" and boasted of it, and who formed a clique by themselves, the boys, I always thought, would compare quite favorably as regards morals and good behavior with an equal number of boys of even age at some private school. Discipline was of course stricter with us and punishment more severe. For minor offenses we got a few whacks over the shoulders with a rattan in the hands of one of the non-commissioned officers, confinement to quarters, or deprivation of passes to the city. The most frequent punishment of all was to "walk the ring," but this was inflicted only by order of the adjutant, who was the officer in command of the musicians. He could also confine an offender in a cell for twenty-four hours in the guard house without formal charges.

The ring was in front of the guard house under the observation of the sentinel of Post No. 1, who had orders to keep the culprits moving. They were required to walk around in a well beaten circular track of about thirty feet in diameter, sometimes two or three at one time. They had to attend to their duties and walk the ring during recreation time in the afternoon and from retreat to tattoo in the evening. This punishment might last anywhere from one day to a week or more at a stretch. Graver offenses were tried by a garrison court martial whose findings were submitted to a higher authority for revision or approval.

The punishments of a garrison court martial were limited to thirty days' confinement in the guard house, part of it, perhaps, solitary confinement on bread and water, or the forfeiture of a month's pay and allowances. Very serious offenses were tried before a general court martial which had power to sentence the prisoner to almost any kind of punishment, including death, according to "Articles of War." Their proceedings were reviewed, however, by the Judge Advocate at the War Department in Washington, and some cases required the decision of the President. There was also an intermediate court named a regimental court martial which had somewhat larger powers than a garrison court, but no such court convened at the island during my stay there, as there was no regimental headquarters, all the soldiers belonging to what was called the general service.

One day at a morning inspection for guard mounting, Sergeant Hanke noticed the end of a pipe stem protruding between the buttons of my jacket. I had carelessly thrust it into the inside breast pocket when the call to "fall in" sounded. He pulled it out and confiscated the pipe, remarking, "You will get a month on the ring for this." I was greatly alarmed at this threat of so severe a punishment and fully expected to receive orders to report to the sergeant of the guard after school that afternoon to be placed on the ring by him and commence my endless march. When the order was not given I thought sure it would some the next day, but it did not. It was a week before I felt safe and concluded that the sergeant had not reported me. Only on one occasion did I receive any punishment. I once threw a basin full of dirty water out of a window and inadvertently dashed it over Sergeant Moore, who was passing. He saw me and immediately got his rattan and gave me a good whipping.

Governor's Island in 1854 presented a very different appearance from what it does in 1914. It was much smaller. Its diameter was less than half a mile and there were but few buildings on it. More than a hundred acres have been added to it by filling in a part of the bay and a sea wall has been built around the entire island. Many buildings have been erected; trees, shrubbery and flowers have been planted and walks laid out; sewers have been put in; water, gas and electricity provided and the island generally improved and beautified.

Many of the venerable old buildings still remain, however, as they existed during my time. Castle Williams, at the southwest angle of the island, is a circular structure, pierced with three tiers of embrasures. At its portal can still be read the inscription cut in the stone, "Commenced 1807, finished 1811." It is built of brown stone, backed up with brick. The granite parapet on top was erected shortly after Civil War, replacing one of brown stone. As a work of defense it has long outlived its usefulness, but in 1854 there were still guns mounted in the first tier of casemates which were considered formidable, and others were mounted en barbette on the parapet. These guns were used sometimes in firing a salute to foreign warships in the harbor.

Northward from Castle Williams, near the northwest angle of the island, was the ordnance building, then came the guard house with its prison cells in the basement and the adjutant's office above them. The quartermasters' and commissary stores, the commanding officer's house and a few other houses for the married officers of the higher grade were all on the north side of the island. Next came the hospital on the east and near it, but somewhat to the west, a row of small two-story buildings partly used as the sutler's store and as quarters for some married soldiers and their families. At the southeast corner of the island was the South Battery, mounting a few guns. Some distance to the west was the chapel and next to it the graveyard, in which some officers and a number of soldiers were buried, most of whom had died of cholera and yellow fever which had often visited the island. Beyond the graveyard was the post garden, several acres in extent, in which all kinds of vegetables were raised. West of the garden was the parade ground, extending to the garrison, and from the commanding officers' house sloping gently to the shore line on the south.

Fort Jay, or Fort Columbus, as it was then called, was generally known as the "garrison." It is situated on the westerly part of the island on raised ground—a square-built, old style fortress with a dry moat, portcullis, draw bridge, and ramparts.

Guns are mounted en barbette on three of its sides. An artistic and elaborate piece of sculpture over the portal, representing the various arms of the service, cut in brown stone, is still in a fair state of preservation. Passing through the deep sallyport, the interior is found to be quite roomy, having a sodded parade ground with quarters surrounding it on four sides. The buildings in the south were used as quarters for the unmarried officers. On the east lived recruits, and on the west were the quarters of a company of soldiers, about seventy-five strong, who were officially called the Permanent Party. On the north was the post band on one side of the sallyport and the non-commissioned staff and some buglers on the other. There was a smaller gate on the south leading into the moat and a sunken way leading from there to the entrance to Castle Williams.

All of the buildings which I have described still exist except a few of the officers' cottages on the north side of the island, the sutler's row and the chapel which was destroyed by fire and lately replaced on another site by a much larger and finer building of cut stone, a gift of Trinity Church of New York. The post-garden has disappeared and so has the graveyard with its few monuments and many headstones. The remains were disinterred and reburied elsewhere, and the site is now covered with buildings.

Governor's Island was the principal recruiting depot in the east, and in 1854 Major John T. Sprague of the Eighth U. S. Infantry was in command. He was a West Point graduate, who had joined the army in 1837 and had been breveted as a Major during the Mexican War. Major Sprague was relieved and ordered elsewhere before my departure from the island. He was succeeded by Captain Mansfield Lovell, a dashing artillery officer, who later joined the confederate army and had something to do with the surrender of New Orleans. A captain or two, an ordnance officer and six or eight lieutenants from different branches of the service, were all detailed on detached service away from their regiments to serve here as instructors of recruits.

A very fine military band was connected with this post under the leadership of Bandmaster Bloomfield, who was a celebrated musician. There were two drummers in this band, brothers, named Jack and Pete Vigo, who were considered to be the best in the army. Later on both served in the band of the regiment which I joined, Pete Vigo, in the meantime, having married Bandmaster Bloomfield's daughter, who accompanied him to the frontiers.

The band played at guard mounting and dress parade, musters and general inspections. It also gave concerts on certain summer days in front of the commanding officers' quarters. Bandsmen had permission occasionally to play in New York City, which was lucrative for them. Indeed they were very much petted and pampered and enjoyed many privileges. They received extra pay and had especial fine uniforms and instruments, all of which had to be paid for out of the post fund.

The Permanent Party, also called Company "A," was a company of soldiers selected from the recruits for stature, physique and soldierly bearing. They were mostly tall men and, as I imagine, must have borne some resemblance to the grenadiers of Frederick the Great. They looked well on parade in their striking uniforms—dark blue coats with facings and sky-blue trousers, white cross and waist belts, epaulettes and black shakos with blue pompons and brass chin straps. Occasionally some were sent away to serve with a regiment at their own request or as a punishment. The Permanent Party did all of the guard duty that was required on the island, and guarded the prisoners who did the scavenging.

Other troops on the island were the recruits, generally several hundred of them, who were quartered in the garrison and in the upper casemates of Castle Williams. From time to time they were sent away in detachments of a hundred or more, generally accompanied by some of the drummers and fifers, to vacancies in regiments serving throughout the country. Officers were detailed to accompany these detachments to their destinations. The non-commissioned officers were generally selected from the most worthy and efficient of the recruits and promoted to lance sergeants and lance corporals, a rank with authority but without extra pay. Often a few re-enlisted old soldiers, rejoining regiments on the frontiers, went with these parties and helped to take charge of them.

The recruits were unarmed. Arms were furnished when they joined their regiments, unless it became necessary to march through a part of the Indian country to reach their destination. In that case they were armed and accompanied by an escort of experienced soldiers. These departures from the island were always occasions of considerable military ceremony. The recruits were escorted from the garrison to the wharf by the post band and the Permanent Party. And when they had embarked on the steamboat and the lines were cast off, the band would play, "The Girl I Left Behind Me," amid the parting cheers of the spectators.

The final complement that made up the garrison of Governors Island were the music boys, designated as Company "B," and stationed in the small South Battery. We were under special command of the Post-Adjutant, but never saw him there except on muster days. He troubled himself very little about us, leaving the care and management of the fifty or sixty boys to the two sergeants in charge. Sergeant Hanke, of whom I have spoken before, was a Dane who had been for many years in the United States service. He was of low stature, very corpulent, with a large round florid face, and was bald, except for a fringe of gray hair below the top of his ears. He had sharp twinkling eyes and a strong voice. He was married but had no children and lived in a couple of small rooms on the second floor of the quarters. His Irish wife was his counterpart in stature and corpulency. She generally wore a white cap and a red skirt. That she had a fine brogue we knew from overhearing her disputes with the sergeant. She had a loud voice and was more than a match for the sergeant, whose English failed him when he became excited. Sergeant Hanke, while a strict disciplinarian, was not an unkindly man. He often listened patiently to our complaints and forgave us for many minor transgressions when we were brought before him.

Sergeant Moore was an Irishman and married. He kept house with his wife and several children in some rooms on the lower floor of our quarters. He also had served a long time in the army. He was a tall thin man with iron gray hair, quick tempered and not so well liked by the boys as Sergeant Hanke. Both of these men remained in the service for more than sixty years and were finally retired and pensioned by the government. Sergeant Moore lived to be ninety-seven years old and Hanke nearly as long.

Corporal Butler, the assistant instructor, was a young man of medium size, with a fiery temper and a profusion of very red hair and mustache, the greasing, waxing and combing of which consumed much of his spare time. The other corporal, who was assistant fife instructor, and whose name, unless memory fails me, was Pfaefle, was a tall and very good looking young German of a more pleasant disposition. He spent much time in "primping" himself and the boys called him "the dude." I never learned what became of him in after years, but I did learn that Corporal Butler remained in the service all his life and died only recently at a military post at Sackett's Harbor, N. Y., at an advanced age. Sergeant Evans and Corporal Washburn, our school teachers, were both very fair men with no peculiarities. Later on I believe they became citizen clerks in the War Department at Washington.

With a couple of the older boys promoted to lance corporals, who had charge of some rooms, this completed the list of non-commissioned officers who had the immediate charge of the boys and were responsible to the post adjutant, who cared very little how things went.

It took but a short time for me to realize that the quantity of food we received was very scanty for growing boys. While we were not actually starved, we did not get enough to eat and often felt hungry. We had a limited amount of credit at the sutler's store, which was deducted from our pay. Much of this we consumed in buying crackers and cheese or an occasional piece of pie or cake to eke out our scanty food, the sameness of which often palled on us. In the summer months we were given a few vegetables once or twice a week from the post garden after the officers and their families had first received all they wanted. The poor recruits never got any, although they contributed their pro-rata share to the post fund, while the officers were not obliged to contribute anything.

Had we received the entire ration allowed us, it would have been sufficient and we could not have complained as to quantity. The soldier's daily ration at this time consisted of sixteen ounces of salt or fresh beef or twelve ounces of pork or bacon, eighteen ounces of soft bread or flour, or one pound of hard bread and the "small rations," as they were called, such as coffee, sugar, beans, peas, rice, salt, vinegar, dessicated vegetables, soap and candles, which were sufficient, when used collectively, for an entire company. The flour ration of eighteen ounces, when baked into bread, will produce about one-third more in weight of bread. Hence there was a saving of about one-third on flour which was sold to increase the post fund. But we boys never received eighteen ounces of bread per day, and all of our other rations were also reduced.

A post fund, according to army regulations, was created by a tax of ten cents per month to be paid by the sutler for every officer or soldier stationed there, also from the savings on the flour ration between eighteen ounces of flour and eighteen ounces of bread at the post bakery. No saving is supposed to be made on any other portion of the soldier's ration. The management of the fund was generally in the hands of three officers, one of whom acted as treasurer; they were called Post Council of Administration and had power to fix a tariff of prices for the sutler, laundresses, tailor, shoemaker, etc., and the expenditure of the fund for other purposes approved by the commanding officer.

At Governor's Island one of the largest expenses was the band whose members were paid extra (according to their ability) over and above their grade of soldier's pay. Their instruments, which the Government did not furnish, had to be purchased, as well as music and a showy uniform. Other expenses were the post bakery, the post garden and school for the boys. From all this the officers received the greater benefit and yet they were not required by army regulations to contribute to the fund.

When spring came, in pleasant weather I often sat on the west shore of the island, which faced Battery Park in New York, and watched the ferry boats and excursion steamers pass close by, crowded with people who were bent on enjoying themselves. This made me feel melancholy and homesick. Sometimes, when alone, tears would come to my eyes in spite of my efforts to restrain them. When the summer came, I felt less lonely and forsaken. We played ball and other games during our leisure hours and went in swimming very often on the south shore of the island where there was a good gravelly beach, interspersed with mossy rocks.

Early in June we received two months' pay. A private soldier's pay at this time was but seven dollars per month, but was raised by act of Congress to eleven dollars about six months after I entered the service. The officers' pay was raised also all along the line. The musician's pay was always one dollar more per month than that of a private, and I was, therefore, entitled to sixteen dollars for my two months' service; but after the sutler's, tailor's, and laundresses' bills were deducted, I had but a few dollars left.

Immediately after being paid the soldiers and some of the boys started gambling with cards and dice in secluded places all over the island, under trees, behind buildings and even in the grave yard. I was pressingly invited to join in some of the games but I refused as I had no inclination for playing. Gambling was forbidden and the gamblers punished if caught. I wished to get a pass to visit New York and did not care to take any chances. I applied for a pass and got permission to be absent from nine o'clock on a Saturday morning to Retreat at sundown on Sunday.

I put on my best uniform, polished my shoes and buttons, exhibited my pass to the guard on the dock and was rowed over to the Battery in New York, whence I had departed two and a half months before. I walked rapidly through Battery Park and up Broadway towards my home. I was anxious to see my mother from whom I had only heard by letter since my departure. I had not gone far when I was jeered at by boys and larger hoodlums and saluted with such questions as "Soger will ye work?" and their replies of "No! First I'd sell me shirt." I flushed with anger but could do nothing except to hasten my steps and get away from my tormentors, only to encounter others on my way home. Even respectable people looked me over as though I was a freak or a curiosity of some kind.

A soldier at that period was but little respected by civilians in the east. Only the people on the Western frontiers appreciated him and understood how much he did toward making the new country a safe place for them to acquire homes and develop the land. It required the lesson of the Civil War to teach the east the value of soldiers and sailors. The soldier particularly was looked upon as an individual too lazy to work for a living. He had not been much in evidence since the Mexican War. The entire U. S. Army contained less than twelve thousand men scattered over a large territory.

When my pass expired I caught the boat for Governor's Island, and reported for duty on time. I did not receive another leave of absence for about three months. The cholera broke out in New York and Brooklyn and soon made its appearance on Governor's Island, where it had been a frequent visitor as well as the yellow fever. Passes were suspended except in urgent cases, and communication with the city restricted as much as possible. A few of the boys were attacked but recovered. Some of the Permanent Party died of it, but the recruits suffered most. A considerable number of them died and were buried in the island grave yard. The funeral march was often heard and the report from the corporal's firing squad of eight, who fired three rounds over the grave, was the last farewell to the poor soldier, as no religious services were held.

I had formed a few friendships among the soldiers of the Permanent Party, particularly with a man named Lovell, a very tall, fine-looking soldier who later on became the drum-major of my regiment. Another of my friends was a man named Fisher, an estimable soldier. One evening Fisher sent for me from the hospital where he was sick with the cholera. I found the building crowded with cholera patients and others. Fisher was suffering intensely but was conscious. He expressed a wish, in the presence of the nurses, that in case of his death his trunk, keepsakes and money were to be given to me. I left him after a while and next morning learned that he had died during the night.

I got permission to attend his funeral, and the next day I went to the hospital to claim my inheritance, but the hospital steward, named Campbell, chased me away and for a long time I blamed him unjustly for depriving me of the little legacy, for his own benefit, as I supposed. He was an ill tempered man not liked by the boys. But later on I learned that he was within his rights in not allowing me to take anything. There is a great deal of military red tape in disposing of a soldier's effects and I dropped the matter. Steward Campbell was shortly after relieved by David Robinson, a kindly man, who at the present time is still on the island, retired and living in a cottage there.

The island, even when free from epidemics, was not a healthy place. There were no sewers, the water was supplied from cisterns and a few wells. There was no gas and on dark nights lanterns were carried. First sergeants of companies called the roll at tattoo by their aid. As the island had no sea wall and was directly in line of the tide currents of the East River, which it divided into two parts, much of the floating filth from the city was deposited on its shore. Dead cats, dogs and other small animals were washed on to the beach daily. Sometimes a horse and, on a few occasions, a human body. Fruit of all kinds, but all more or less decayed, great quantities of wood, all sorts of boxes and cases, in fact anything that could float, seemed to be cast upon the island's shore. A squad of prisoners under guard were busy all day long in "beach combing," gathering up this filth and burning it.

One day, when passing along the south shore, I noticed a curious looking object partly covered by rubbish. It was high and dry up on the beach, where it must have lain for some days exposed to the hot sun. It was very brown and very small, and I thought it was a dead monkey or perhaps a mummy of some kind. I called the attention of the prisoners' guard, who were close by, to the object. They uncovered it and declared it to be a new born infant. One of the prisoners carried it on a shovel to the grave yard, only a few steps away, where he dug a shallow hole in a corner of the fence and buried it.

Some parts of the shore were sandy, and at low tide I often saw some of the hungry recruits gathering soft clams and eating them after boiling them in a rusty can, picked up along the shore. They also ate much of the fruit cast up by the tide. All this no doubt contributed to the greater mortality among them during the prevalence of the cholera. Very few boys, I think, ever touched any of the fruit. We were strictly cautioned against it.

Changes made by boys being sent away to join regiments made it possible for me to move to a room on the second floor which was more cheerful and to have a more congenial bunkie, whose name was William J. Milligan. He was a New York boy, whose mother kept a millinery store on upper Broadway. We became fast friends and remained so as long as he lived. We were separated when he was sent to join the Sixth U. S. Infantry, as a fifer, and I did not meet him again until we both served in the same brigade in the Army of the Potomac, during the Civil War.

One day orders were given to prepare for a grand inspection

of all the soldiers on the island by General Winfield Scott, who was the Commander-in-Chief of the army. We were busy for some days cleaning up for the great inspection. Finally the day arrived, so did the general in his cocked hat, a gorgeous uniform and splendid sword. He was very tall, large and dignified. Despite his age he was erect and soldierly. He was accompanied by some of the officers of his staff, also in full uniform. As he debarked, a salute of thirteen guns thundered from Castle Williams. All the soldiers on the island, not on other duty, were drawn up on the parade ground and the band played "Hail to the Chief." For occasions of this sort we were required to appear fully equipped and with knapsacks packed.

There was always a rivalry among us as to who could pack his kit the neatest and show the fewest creases in the overcoat when rolled up and strapped on top of the knapsack. In this particular we never seemed to be able to equal the Permanent Party, whose overcoats were faultlessly rolled. The usual formula of a general inspection was carried through, as prescribed in the regulations, ending up with opening ranks, unslinging and opening knapsacks and displaying our kits. The General and his aides-de-camp, accompanied by the commanding officer and the adjutant, first inspected the band, then passed through the boys' opened ranks without any comments and on through the ranks of the Permanent Party, each of whom stood like a statue at the position "order arms." An officer of the General's staff, remarking the immaculate rolling of many of the overcoats, tapped one of them with the scabbard of his sword. It emitted a hollow sound. He asked the soldier what it was, and the man explained that it was a dummy made out of a piece of stove pipe covered with blue cloth. The old General noticed the incident but merely smiled as did some of the other officers. However, it proved to be the end of the dummy overcoats on parade.

One summer's day several French ships of war arrived in the harbor, opposite Governor's Island. They fired a national salute which it was necessary to reply to, gun for gun, according to custom. Unfortunately at that particular time there were no artillery soldiers on the island, but a sergeant of the Permanent Party was found who understood how to load and discharge guns. He was furnished with a detail of infantry men to assist him. Salutes were always fired from the first or ground tier of guns at Castle Williams, about a dozen in number. When not in use the embrasures for these guns were closed with wooden shutters which could be removed and taken inside while firing.

The Sergeant ordered the shutters to be detached from their fastenings and laid down flat in the openings. He then commenced firing, and at every discharge we saw the shutters being blown to splinters into the harbor, fortunately without damage to any one. When all the guns in the tier had been discharged the Sergeant and his inexperienced crew had to go back to reload and fire them over again. This caused a long gap in the completion of the salute, which should have been fired continuously, and no doubt astonished our French visitors.

A day or two later on a Saturday afternoon the French admiral, with some of his officers, accompanied by the post adjutant, came on an informal visit to the island. I was on the scrubbing squad that day when they passed through the sallyport of the South Battery, unannounced. I was the first boy whom they encountered, hatless, barefooted, in shirt sleeves, with my trousers rolled up to the knees and a broom in my hands. I was startled, but stood to attention and came to a salute, which was returned by the admiral. My few companions did the same. Most of the boys were out fishing, swimming and playing games. The distinguished party remained but a few minutes and did not enter the quarters. I think they were not favorably impressed by our sloppy appearance.

Sometimes recruits deserted the island by arranging to have a row boat appear on the shores at night or by swimming across the Buttermilk Channel to Brooklyn in the night time when the tide was right. If recaptured they were tried by a general court martial and sentenced to severe punishments. There were few desertions among the boys; but two of them who failed to return from leave of absence were caught after a time. They were tried and sentenced to receive twenty-five strokes with a rattan well applied to their "bare buttocks," so the sentence read, and to be confined in the guard house at hard labor for two months, also forfeit their pay for the same period.

We were turned out and formed in ranks on a spot near the graveyard to witness the punishment of the poor fellows. They were marched to the place under guard. The Adjutant read the sentence of the court martial. Then one of the boys was laid face down on a long bench and held by a member of the guard at his head and another at his feet. His clothes were removed sufficiently to expose his buttocks, and at the adjutant's command, a corporal commenced to apply the rattan, which left a red mark at every stroke and made the boy squirm and groan and finally cry out with pain before the adjutant cried "Halt" at the twenty-fifth blow. While the blows were not inflicted with anything like full force, yet they were cruel enough if only by their number.

The unfortunate second victim was obliged to witness his comrade's punishment and then endure the same himself. Both of the boys were about seventeen years of age and served out their enlistment. One of them I met during the Civil War as a lieutenant of a volunteer regiment. The trembling and sobbing boys were reconducted to the guard house, and we marched back to quarters after this distressing scene.

The summer passed away, the cholera, both in the city and on the island, was almost extinct. Leave of absence was again granted and I went to the city a few times during the fall and early winter. One morning I felt ill and reported at "doctor's call." I was taken before the surgeon, who examined me and ordered me to bed in the hospital, thinking, no doubt, that I was about to have an attack of fever. I did not expect this and hoped that I would simply be marked "sick in quarters" and excused from duty. I was put to bed in a ward that contained about eight beds occupied by soldiers with all sorts of ailments, some of them very disagreeable. Some of the boys who had been in the hospital had told me that tea and toast was served there to the sick. I hankered for some of it, as I had not tasted any for a long time. I got it twice a day and a little thin gruel, but nothing else. On the third day, I begged to be let go. I was disgusted with the hospital and its inmates. As no serious complications had developed, I was sent back to quarters and excused from duty for a few days.

As the winter approached we were obliged to give up many of our little outdoor diversions and confine ourselves more to our crowded quarters. As there was no place indoors for exercise or amusement, our condition became more melancholy and dejected. Our clothing we found insufficient to keep us warm. Many of us bought woolen knit jackets, which we wore instead of a vest and which gave us some protection against the fierce cold winds that blew across the island and chilled us to the marrow when we were on parade. When we began to have severe frosts, the bandsmen did not appear at guard mounting on the plea that their instruments would freeze. The fifes and drums furnished the only music. Often our fingers were so numb with the cold that we could hardly play a note. The drummers could manage to beat a march with gloves on their hands and suffered less.

One cold night late in November there was an alarm of fire which proved to be in the sutler's row near the hospital. It broke out in several places at once. There was some excitement in getting out the soldiers' wives and children who lived there, but none were injured. There were no fire extinguishing appliances on the island, save fire buckets. The soldiers formed lines to the nearest pump and cistern and passed the buckets along. But they could make no impression on the fire, and the row was a mass of ruins in little more than an hour. Long before a ferry boat brought some firemen and a hand engine from the city there was nothing left to save.

Two of the older boys were accused of setting the houses on fire. They were arrested and confined in the guard house on charges of arson and were still awaiting trial when I was ordered away shortly after.

The winter had set in early. It was very cold at times and there was snow on the ground. We felt generally depressed and miserable, when quite unexpectedly, one day in the early part of December, 1854, two other boys and myself received orders to prepare to depart to Carlisle Barracks, at Carlisle, Pa., there to be assigned to the Second U. S. Infantry. I do not know why I was selected to go. Quite a number of the boys had been on the island longer than I, and some were more proficient. But I felt glad. Surely any kind of a change would be for the better. The next day I and my companions, Peter Moritz and Edward Young, both a year or two older than I, received a pass to go to New York and say farewell to our parents or relatives, whom we were not likely to see again for years.

A trusty corporal was placed in charge of us. He had orders not to allow us to separate nor to lose sight of us and to return with us to the island before evening. In this way we were obliged to witness each other's leave taking in the presence of our conductor. There were tears and lamenting, and the corporal, who was kindly, but did not like his task, was importuned when about to leave one house for another to "let the poor boy stay just five minutes longer." When he acceded it generally extended to fifteen minutes or more. As none of us had any intention to desert this painful way of parting might have been spared us. There was no special need to hurry us away, and sufficient time could have been given to notify our relatives to come to the island and bid us farewell there. I always looked upon this as unnecessarily harsh treatment.

We all had some lunch in an eating house, made a few small purchases and in due time returned to the island, angry at the way we had been humiliated by the orders of either the commanding officer or the adjutant. Next morning we packed our kits and started for the boat landing shortly after noon, accompanied by some of the boys and another corporal who was to take us to Carlisle. We boarded the barge in which I had come to the island on the day of my enlistment nearly nine months before. Sergeant Brown, who soon after became a member of my company at Carlisle, was still cockswain. We pushed off amid the cheers of our comrades and passed over the East River to New York.

No one seemed to have any clear idea as to where Carlisle was or how long a time it would take to get there, so they loaded us with three days' rations of boiled salt beef and bread, which filled our haversacks to bursting. This, together with a canteen filled with cold coffee, made no inconsiderable load. We wore our overcoats, and our knapsacks were packed with a five-pound blanket, an extra jacket and trousers, underwear and stockings, an extra pair of shoes, clothes and shoe brushes and knick-knacks. A tin wash basin was strapped onto the back of the knapsack. All this made a load enough for a man to carry. We passed through Battery Park and staggered along West Street in the direction of the Jersey City Ferry, making occasional halts for a rest, when crowds would collect about us and ask us many questions. No doubt we three small boys looked ridiculous to them, overloaded as we were. I overheard a longshoreman remark that he'd "be damned before he'd make a pack horse of himself for Uncle Sam."

We reached the ferry, crossed the North River to Jersey City and were put on a car that had wooden seats without any cushions. It was the first time that I had ever been away from New York on a railroad train and I was much interested in watching the scenery all the way to Philadelphia, where we arrived about dusk and changed trains for Harrisburg. I opened my haversack, ate my frugal supper and went to sleep, tired out with the day's excitement. About midnight the corporal woke us up at Harrisburg to change cars for Carlisle, but we found that there would be no train to Carlisle until eight o'clock next morning. The station master kindly allowed us to stay in the waiting room of the depot for the remainder of the night. There was a good fire in the stove and some benches to lie on, so we passed the night quite comfortably. We all had a little money and got some hot coffee and rolls at the depot next morning before we left on the eight o'clock train for Carlisle. We arrived there in less than two hours, with our three days' rations almost intact. There was snow on the ground, through which we trudged laboriously towards the garrison about a mile away.

I was glad to leave Governor's Island. Its narrow limits impressed me as a place of confinement. The quarters were overcrowded, the food was bad and insufficient, the discipline very strict, and there was little time or opportunity for recreation. It was monotonous and depressing, and although later during my service I suffered much hardship and encountered many dangers, I never wished myself back on the island again. Among the many boys whom I knew on the island I saw but few again, outside of those in my own regiment. They were scattered all over the country, serving at distant posts and often changing. Probably but few are living now, and I know the whereabouts of only one, who served in the Seventh U. S. Infantry for many years and now resides in New York, where I see him occasionally and talk over old times.

PART II.

At Carlisle Barracks, Pa., in 1855.

AFTER a tramp through the snow with our heavy loads from the Carlisle depot, we reached the barracks tired out. The corporal reported our arrival at the adjutant's office, and we were assigned to companies. Moritz went as drummer to Company I, Young as fifer to Company A, and myself as fifer to Company D of the Second United States Infantry.

The regimental headquarters were there together with the field and staff, and the band, companies A, G and I had been recruited to their full strength, but Company D, to which I was assigned, had no real existence as yet. There were only two officers, a few sergeants and corporals, together with three or four privates, some of whom had served in the Mexican War, which was all that was left of Company D on its return from the Pacific coast, where the regiment had served for a number of years. All of these men were attached to other companies until such time as recruits would be received to fill up the ranks. I was ordered to duty temporarily with Company I.

The Second Regiment of the United States Infantry was one of the oldest in the service. It was organized by act of Congress on March 3, 1791, and was engaged with the Indians on Miami River, November 4, 1791. It had fought in other Indian Wars, principally against the Seminoles in Florida. It took part in the War of 1812, and participated in the engagements of the Mexican War from Vera Cruz to the City of Mexico. After the Mexican War, and at about the time of the discovery of gold in California, it was sent there, where its men built Benicia Barracks near San Francisco, Fort Yuma and other posts.

About 1850 it became known that the Government was enlisting many recruits at Governor's Island for service in California. The gold fever was at its height and hundreds of soldiers were deserting to the mines. Men who had served their terms scorned re-enlistment when they saw so many digging wealth from the hills or dipping it up from the mountain streams. For the same reason it was impossible to get recruits in gold-mad California.

But no such difficulty was experienced in the East. There were plenty of recruits, but the sudden increase in enlistments brought into the army some of the worst men that ever joined it. They put on the uniform solely for the purpose of getting free transportation to California at the Government's expense. I had the story from some of the survivors of the eventful trip made by these recruits from New York to San Francisco.

A steamship was chartered, loaded with army supplies and some hundreds of the recruits. They were under the command of Brevet Major George W. Patten, of the Second United States Infantry, with whom I served later on the frontiers. Major Patten had served in the Mexican War, where he had lost two fingers of his right hand, and was brevetted for gallantry. By the rank and file he was called "Three-fingered Jack," and was known as an easy going soul who hated any sort of trouble, of which he and the young and inexperienced lieutenants with him got plenty before they reached their destination.

Almost the first day at sea the bad element among the recruits began fighting with the sailors. They stole all the provisions they could lay their hands on. Fortunately they had no arms; these were packed in armchests, and stowed in the hold of the ship. Only some of the sergeants carried sidearms.

The first stop of the steamship was at Kingston, Jamaica, for coal. There the recruits overran the guards, got possession of a coal pile and had a pitched battle with a strong force of negro police, who were trying to keep them on the dock. They soon routed the police, swarmed all over the town and committed many depredations. It required several companies of white British troops to round them up, drive them back to the ship and keep them there while she was coaling.

All the way to San Francisco the unruly element made trouble. They laughed at the mild way in which the good old major disciplined some of them. I was told that when one of the ring-leaders was brought before him he asked his name and promised to make him a sergeant in his own regiment when they arrived in California, if he would only behave himself. After their arrival in San Francisco, most of these ruffians deserted as soon as opportunity offered. Many of them made their way to the gold diggings, and very few of them were ever recaptured.

In 1854 the Second United States Infantry had become greatly reduced in numbers from various casualties, and what remained of the regiment was ordered East. Some companies were consolidated, and the skeleton organizations of others filled up with recruits. A few were entirely re-enlisted. Companies A, D, G and I were at Carlisle, Pa., and the remaining six companies were at Forts Snelling, Ridgely and Ripely on the upper Mississippi and Minnesota Rivers, protecting the settlers from the Indians.

I found Carlisle barracks a very agreeable change from Governors Island. It had been built to serve as a dragoon barracks, and had quarters and stables enough for a regiment, but during my time, was used only for the Infantry. On July 1, 1864, a part of the Confederate Army, on their march to Gettysburg, fired some shells into the town of Carlisle and set fire to the barracks, but they succeeded in destroying only a part of the buildings. On a recent visit there I found some of the former officers' and soldiers' quarters still standing, also the commanding officer's house, the adjutant's office and guard house, all of which, together with a number of new buildings, are now used as a Government Indian school and have been for many years.

The soldiers' quarters were three-story buildings with a wide veranda at every floor, facing the parade ground. There company roll calls were held in bad weather. The rooms were large enough not to be crowded; but the bunks were the old-fashioned two-tier kind. Two men slept in each of the lower and upper bunks, and it was uncomfortable. The rooms were heated by stoves in which we burned wood. They were comfortably warm during the winter, which I found less severe in Southern Pennsylvania than in New York.

Our rations were much improved. We were able to add many extras from the company funds. We were in the midst of a fine farming region and could purchase all kinds of vegetables, and other products very cheap from the farmers who came to the barracks for that purpose. When spring came we took long walks. We were allowed to go anywhere within a mile limit without a pass, but generally went much further. Few depredations were committed, and many of the farmers were delightfully hospitable, often giving us milk, and other things, on our tramps about the country.

Carlisle, the county seat of Cumberland County, Pa., was then a town of about seven thousand inhabitants, having churches, schools, hotels, banks, stores, some saloons and many good private houses. There also was Dickinson College, a Methodist institution of renown, which is still flourishing. The town was easy of access for the soldiers, who often went there without the formality of a pass. It was but a mile away from the barracks, and considerably less for those who used a favorite route, crossing a small creek on a log, and cutting across the intervening fields.

Unfortunately for some of the soldiers, there was a distillery on the outskirts of the town quite near where the log crossed the stream, where newly made whiskey was sold for a shilling (twelve and a half cents) per quart, or eighteen cents for a canteen full. Shillings were still in circulation, and there was no high tax on spirits. This cheap and easy way to procure liquor was the means of sending many a soldier to the guard house.

Occasionally, during the winter, there was a theatrical performance in the town, which a limited number of soldiers received leave of absence to attend. Another favorite amusement was a dance at a tavern or roadhouse outside of the town where we had a chance to meet some of the farmers' daughters. I borrowed a gun sometimes, and got a few rabbits. I also had some sleigh rides. Indeed, our liberty contrasted so favorably with the narrow confines of Governor's Island that the mild winter passed very quickly.

In about a month after my arrival at Carlisle, the complement of recruits required for Company D was sent on from Governor's Island, and the company took up quarters by themselves in a new two-story building, with a messroom in the basement, on the easterly side of the barracks. The recruits were all young men, twenty to twenty-five years old, hailing from various parts of the country. A considerable portion were foreign-born, mostly Irish, although there were some Germans and a few other nationalities. Their previous occupations ranged all the way from a school teacher to farm laborer. Some were fairly well educated and others ignorant to the point of illiteracy. There were many mechanics of all sorts among them who had worked as journeymen at their trades. Also there were some runaway apprentices. We found those of a mechanical experience very useful later on at the frontiers.

As usual, they had enlisted for various reasons. Some had the "Wanderlust"; others had a taste for adventure and hoped to satisfy it in a soldier's life. Some had joined from sheer necessity, or inability to find any other occupation to support themselves. This last was a very common cause. There were also a few "ne'er-do-wells" who were of no use anywhere, and a detriment to the army. It took months to drill and discipline these men, and to make serviceable soldiers of them. But after a time their awkwardness disappeared. They carried themselves erect, and there was a marked improvement, except in a few who seemed too stupid to be taught and strained the drill sergeant's patience to the breaking point. Every company seemed to have a few members so awkward as to disarrange any well drilled company. Whenever possible these were detailed to some special duty, which kept them out of the ranks.

The men were left to choose their bunkies, and pair off as they pleased. I bunked with one of the sergeants of the company who had served in Mexico and in California. He was a middle aged man of exemplary character, who took a sort of fatherly interest in me. He taught me many things useful in a soldier's life.

I met with one great disappointment on joining Company D. I had hoped to have as a companion a drummer-boy of about my own age, with whom I could chum. This desire was strengthened by the knowledge that the fifer was considered to rank the drummer and in the absence of special instructions could order the drummer to play such tunes or marches as he chose. But I found myself associated with a man who was a dozen years my senior. He was serving his second enlistment, and had been transferred from some other regiment and sent to Carlisle. He was a married man without any children, and lived in another part of the garrison away from the company. His wife, a rather attractive and genteel young woman, was one of the four laundresses which the army regulations allowed to each company, and provided free with a soldier's daily ration, quarters, transportation, and medical attendance.

My drummer was a tall, haggard man with a sallow face. I was still a few inches short of having attained the height of five feet, and when my tall drummer and I marched at the head of the company we were called the "long and the short of it," which greatly annoyed me as I was very sensitive to ridicule. Another annoyance was the fact that he was not a very good drummer, and would not take the trouble to learn any new and fancy pieces, as we boys did. Whenever I had to play with him alone I was obliged to content myself with the old repertoire. Aside from these differences, we managed to get along well enough, as he was a sober and solemn man who kept very much to himself. But I always missed the companionship of a more youthful spirit.

The commander of my company at this time was Captain and Brevet Major Samuel P. Heintzelman, a native of Pennsylvania who during the Civil War commanded an army corps in the army of the Potomac, and became a major general. His grey hair and beard gave him a fatherly appearance, and he was well liked by the men. He was fond of bean soup, the kind that only soldiers can make. He frequently sent his servant to the Company kitchen for a quart of bean soup. Captain Heintzelman remained with us but a few months when he was promoted to Major of the First Regiment of Infantry. We regretted to lose him. The first lieutenant was Thomas W. Sweeney, a native of Ireland, who had lost an arm in the Mexican War. He retired from the service in 1870, with the rank of Brigadier General. He was a good soldier. The second lieutenant was John D. O'Connell, of Pennsylvania, a tall, fine-looking man, somewhat given to swearing when he got angry, but a fair and just man. I do not know what became of him after the war. We had three efficient officers who took good care of the company. Captain Heintzelman and Lieutenant O'Connell, were both West Point graduates. The commander of the post was John J. Abercrombie, lieutenant colonel of our regiment. He was also a West Pointer and had joined the army in 1822. He was a good tactician and a very proud and dignified officer.

In March, 1855, great changes took place. The U. S. Army, which then consisted of only eight regiments of infantry, two of dragoons, one of mounted rifles, four of artillery, of which but two companies in each regiment were batteries, and a few engineer and ordnance soldiers, was authorized by act of Congress on March 3, 1855, to be increased by the formation of two additional regiments of infantry, the Ninth and Tenth, and two of cavalry, the First and Second. The old names of "Dragoons" and "Mounted Rifles" were dropped, and those regiments were thereafter known as the Third, Fourth and Fifth Cavalry. General Scott's infantry tactics were abandoned for Colonel Hardee's.

The old smooth bore musket, which carried a ball and three buckshots at short range, was replaced by a long range rifle with a barrel of a dull finish and a sword bayonet. The old fashioned cross belts were done away with, and the cartridge boxes made smaller. The heavy shakos and clumsy fatigue caps were replaced by a lighter and neater uniform hat, and a Képi, after the French army style. The cut of the dress coat was altered and made to look smarter, and polished brass epaulets were worn. All this made a decided improvement in the appearance of the soldiers on parade.

The change in tactics made extra drilling necessary. The old had to be unlearned and the new acquired. After we had become proficient in the new drill, Colonel Abercrombie sometimes marched the four companies, with the band and field music ahead, through the town to the Dickinson College grounds which were on the side nearly opposite to the barracks. There he put us through a battalion drill. These drills and marches through the town took place on fine spring days, much to the delight of Carlisle's citizens, who turned out in great numbers to see the spectacle and to hear the band play.

I had a very easy time at Carlisle barracks. I attended the roll calls at reveille, retreat, tattoo and guard mounting; drilled and practiced for an hour each day except Saturdays, and served as orderly at the adjutant's office about once a week. I had a great deal of spare time which I spent in roving around the country. I also went to town quite often. There was no school so I bought some books and did some studying evenings with the assistance of some of the men in my company. I began to like "soldiering." I wore a fine, showy uniform dress coat of dark blue cloth with the standing collar, cuffs and breast faced with light blue cloth, which made it very conspicuous and distinguished the musicians from the non-commissioned officers and privates. The trousers were of light blue cloth, and the Képi (cap) of dark blue ornamented with a small brass bugle and the regimental number above a straight visor. I had a pair of brass epaulets, or "scales," as we called them, which, together with my coat buttons and cap ornaments, I kept highly polished. I also had a bright sword, for each musician, and the first or orderly sergeant of each infantry company carried a straight sword. The sword belt was made of black leather and had a brass clasp ornamented with an eagle and a wreath of white metal. My sword was rather long for me at this time, and it used to get between my legs at first when marching, and trip me up. It took some time to become accustomed to it.

My pay was twelve dollars per month, with everything found and I looked pityingly upon citizen boys of my age who had to slave for a couple of dollars per week.

I was approaching my fourteenth year, and outside of my military obligations felt that I was my own master. This, I suppose, made me think I was a man in spite of my youth. I fear that at this period I felt "a little cockey" or vain, and showed it. This feeling, however, I got rid of after I experienced real service in the frontiers. I bought some white shirts, "boiled shirts," as we soldiers called them, also neckties and "bear's grease" for my hair. With all this I arrayed myself gorgeously when I went to town. Sometimes I wore a red sash instead of my belt and sword which I was not allowed to carry into town. I began to correspond with some of the town girls, who admired the soldiers, and I made calls on some of them.

We music boys patronized a small ice cream and candy store kept by a widow and her daughter. There was a back room where we often met and were served with soft drinks and cake. Between pay days, when we had run out of money, the widow gave us credit.

The freedom I enjoyed here was a great contrast to my unhappy experience on Governor's Island, where I had but little liberty, was half starved and was badly treated in many ways. I look back with pleasure to my six months' stay at Carlisle, whose citizens were always friendly to the soldiers. There was but little of the rough element in that staid old Pennsylvania town, and I cannot recall that any serious difficulty or encounter ever took place between the citizens and soldiers during our stay there.

While at Carlisle barracks, I was obliged to take part in a disgraceful scene—the drumming out of two soldiers. They had been tried for desertion by a general court martial, found guilty and sentenced to be indelibly marked on the left hip with the letter D, four inches in height, to have their heads shaved, to be dishonorably discharged and drummed out of service. This sentence was executed one cold winter morning, directly after reveille. The companies who had just answered roll call were kept formed while all of the fifers and drummers marched to the guard house. There we formed ranks, the two prisoners in front, bare headed, closely followed by four privates and a corporal, their guns at a position of "Charge bayonets." The field music was behind, playing what is called "The Rogue's March." In this way the prisoners, whose closely shaved heads presented an absurd appearance, were marched around the four sides of the parade ground, past the companies standing in ranks, back to the guard house and through the gate adjoining. There we halted, their caps and small bundles containing their little belongings were handed to them, also a dishonorable discharge, then we watched them for a while as they hastened down the road towards the town. They did not enter it, however, but cut across the fields and soon disappeared from sight.

This spectacular exhibition of a brutal punishment seemed to me like a relic of barbarity. It was conceived in the virulent minds of some of the officers who tried the prisoners. The sentence was duly approved by a higher authority, although it was not in accordance with the punishments as prescribed in the army regulations. Young as I was, I felt ashamed and indignant at being compelled to be an actor in this disgraceful scene.

A company of soldiers, after they have served together for some months, become like a large family. My own company was a fair sample. We soon knew each other's good points, failings and weaknesses. It took but a short time for the company to separate itself into two parties; the larger of which contained the men who kept themselves clean, and took some pride in soldiering. The other contingent, happily small in numbers, were often slovenly, disorderly, and sometimes vicious. They were given to quarrelling, and occasional fighting. Though they banded together, they were not able to create much trouble while in the quarters, as they were so largely outnumbered. It became necessary sometimes to teach one of them a severe lesson, and I remember one case wherein a man of filthy habits was taken to the creek by his comrades, stripped and washed with soap and sand until his skin was raw.

As we had no way to lock up anything we owned we were particularly severe on petty thieves, taking the law into our own hands, by giving the guilty one a sound beating. This had a good effect. Of those we punished none ever complained of their treatment to the officers, knowing that they would receive small consolation from them. After a few rigorous punishments it was seldom that a soldier missed anything.

Tricks were played upon us boys once in a while. We played our calls at the flag staff in front of the commanding officer's house, where, when commencing to play, some fifer would nearly burst himself trying to blow his instrument. Upon investigation he would find it stuffed with paper or rags. Sometimes a drummer would find the drumhead greased or the snares loosened. The bandsmen also had their troubles. Their brass instruments were filled with water or stuffed with rags; these experiences soon taught us to examine our instruments before going to the parade ground.

Early in March, 1855, Major Edmund B. Alexander of the Eighth Infantry, arrived after having been promoted to colonel of the Tenth Infantry, one of the new regiments. As he ranked Lieutenant Colonel Abercrombie he took command of the post. The headquarters of the Tenth Infantry were established at Carlisle barracks. Officers and recruits for the new regiment began to arrive, and the post took on a more lively appearance as company after company of the new regiment was formed. We began to be somewhat crowded. The parade ground within the barracks proved to be too small for drilling all the companies at the same time, and some of them were obliged to exercise in adjoining fields.

The addition of four new regiments to the United States Army, and the necessary increase of more than one hundred and fifty officers brought joy to the hearts of many of the old officers, who had long waited for promotion. Advancement in time of peace is naturally very slow. Many grey haired first lieutenants became captains, some elderly captains became majors, and a few majors were promoted to colonels. The second lieutenants were supplied from West Point as far as possible. There was a very scanty promotion from the ranks, but quite a number of appointments from civil life—many of these through political influence more than for any merit the candidates possessed.

Before the raising of the four new regiments the number of officers in the army who had been appointed from civil life was very small. Most of them dated from the war with Mexico. These men had seen service and were experienced. We did not take kindly to the newly appointed lieutenants from civil life. Few of them knew anything of military work, and for some we had contempt. But we respected the young officers from the military academy, who understood their business.

The various promotions caused many transfers of officers to serve in higher grades in other regiments. My company lost Captain and Brevet Major Samuel P. Heintzelman, who left us, much to our regret, to become a Major of the First United States Infantry; William M. Gardner, a native of the State of Georgia, and a West Point man, became our next captain, having been promoted and transferred from another regiment. He was an ardent Southerner who most cordially hated the "Abolitionist"—a haughty, high-spirited, irritable man, more feared than liked by the soldiers. He was middle-aged and unmarried, slight and of medium size with a swarthy complexion. His delicate physique caused him to suffer much from the severe hardships endured while on the frontiers, but he bore them courageously and without a murmur.

He remained captain of Company D until his native state seceded from the Union, when he resigned his commission, and joined the Confederacy. There, I have been told, he became a brigadier general and lost a leg during the war. I remember Captain Gardner with the kindest of feelings, and I am grateful to him for special acts of kindness and indulgence. He never was harsh or hasty to me, and often he gave me good advice, which to my regret I did not always follow.

We had a mild winter at Carlisle, as I have said, and spring opened early. In May it was warm enough to bathe in the deep holes of the small creek, near the garrison, and we often enjoyed swimming in a river some miles away. There was a large cave in that vicinity into which we often went for the pleasure of shouting and hearing the echoes. The country was beautiful. There were large farms, with prosperous-looking houses. I never tired of wandering about on the good roads that stretched in all directions.

I found much amusement in watching the drilling of the raw recruits of the Tenth Infantry, for we of the Second considered ourselves trained soldiers now and laughed at their awkwardness as others had probably laughed at us.

A certain Irish sergeant had a most peculiar way of his own of elucidating the tactics to the recruits, and often lost his temper when things were done wrong. One day, after he had patiently explained and demonstrated to his squad that, when given the command, "Forward march," each man must step off with his left foot, about half of the squad advanced the right foot.

"Didn't I tell y'es the roight fut's not the roight fut?" he shouted. "The lift fut's the roight fut."

Sometimes it happened that some inattention of the instructor himself would cause amusement when drilling some of the larger squads in marching. At the command "By the right flank, right face, forward march," one-half of the squad misunderstanding the command, would face to the left, and march on until brought up against a fence or other obstruction. At the same time the other half marched with the instructor at their flank in the opposite direction, until he commanded, "Halt, front face," and discovered the missing half on the other side of the parade ground "marking time," and waiting for a command.

An old soldier of my company named Coffey was married and had several children. One of them was called "Kitty." She was a little freckled-faced four-year-old who had the most astonishing red hair that I ever saw. Kitty had a roving disposition, and wandered all over the garrison, and into the soldiers' quarters. Everyone played with her, and she was a general favorite. She loved the soldiers, and the only way we could make her go home was to say to her, "Kitty your hair's on fire, run home and tell your mother." Kitty would then scamper off crying.

She dearly loved to hear the band play, and often got in the way on the parade ground. One day at guard mounting, Lieutenant O'Connoll, of my company, who had a keen sense of humor, was acting as adjutant. He was about to march the guard in review, when he discovered Kitty directly in front of the band, gazing at them with admiration. He changed the customary words of command to "Column forward, guide right—Kitty Coffey get out of the way—March!" all in the same tone of voice.

I have seen Lieutenant O'Connoll, a big raw-boned, black-whiskered Pennsylvanian, whom we learned to like in spite of his very forcible language, fly into such a passion at drill that he would plunge his sword into the ground half way up to the hilt and hold up his hands in despair, vigorously berating the company for some false movement. Sometimes, however, he would laud them when they did their work well.

About the first of June, 1855, orders arrived for the immediate departure of the four companies of the Second Infantry stationed at Carlisle to Fort Pierre on the Missouri River in Nebraska Territory. We were to form a part of the Sioux Expedition, under Brigadier General William S. Harney, for the purpose of chastising one of the tribes of the Sioux nation, who nearly a year before had massacred Lieutenant John L. Grattan, and his escort of twenty-one soldiers, who had been sent out from Fort Laramie to hold a parley with them. As the Government had but a handful of soldiers at Laramie, vengeance had to be delayed until a sufficient number of troops from our small army could be gathered for the purpose.

General Harney had been made leader of the expedition because he was an old experienced Indian fighter, known and feared by many of the Indians. We made our preparations quickly, paid some farewell visits in the town and in a day or two were ready to start as soon as transportation could be provided.

I had some regrets at leaving Carlisle Barracks, where I had experienced none of the ennui of a soldier's life, but had thoroughly enjoyed myself. I think, however, that my regrets were more than counter-balanced by the prospect of new scenes far away from civilization in a country inhabited only by savages, and which at that time had been but imperfectly explored.

PART III.

JOURNEY FROM CARLISLE TO FORT PIERRE, NEBRASKA TERRITORY IN 1855.

COMPANIES A, D, G and I left Carlisle Barracks about the first week in June, 1855. We formed on the parade ground for the last time on a Saturday afternoon in full marching order, our haversacks filled with three days' rations of hard bread and boiled salt pork. At the command of Col. Abercrombie we started off in a quick step, the band playing alternately, "The Girl I Left Behind Me" and "The Bold Soldier Boy," both old-fashioned tunes that it was customary to play on such occasions. We marched past the guard house where the officer of the day and guard of the Tenth Infantry saluted us with a "Present arms."

We passed down the road to a point on the railroad track leading into the town where a special train awaited us on a siding. The train was made up of a few baggage cars, a passenger car with upholstered seats for the officers, and "emigrant cars" with bare wooden seats, for the enlisted men and the wives and children of the married soldiers. None of the officers' wives and children went with us; two years or more elapsed before they saw them again.

Lieut. Sweeney of my company was left behind, detailed for some special duty. Capt. Gardner and Lieut. O'Connell, both bachelors, were with the company. The last farewells were said, and amid tears and cheers from some of the soldiers of the Tenth Infantry and the citizens from the town, we started on our long journey.

I had a seat at a car window and was greatly interested in the constantly changing scenery. We had to go back to Harrisburgh to get to the main line to Pittsburgh. Traveling by railroad was slow at that time, particularly so in our case as we had to keep out of the way of passenger trains. We put in a bad night on the hard seats and in the morning were at Altoona, where hot coffee was brought into the cars and served to us from milk cans. Arrangements had been made to give us coffee two or three times per day while en route.

We made slow progress over the Allegheny Mountains, sometimes having an extra locomotive to push us along, and it was late Sunday afternoon when we reached Pittsburgh. We had to change trains here, and as we marched through the streets to another depot, a crowd of people followed us. There were four companies with a band and colors, probably more regular soldiers than they had ever seen at one time before. We were delayed a long time at the depot; but finally we started, and after another miserable night on the hard seats, we left the cars in the morning, crossed a river on a ferryboat and were in Toledo, Ohio. Stacking arms in one of the streets, we sat on the curb stones and ate our meager breakfast of hard bread and pork, together with hot coffee served in our quart tin cups.

A crowd of citizens watched us with interest. They asked many questions and made remarks, some not very complimentary to our appearance. We had been two nights on the dusty cars with no opportunity to wash ourselves or to clean our clothing. I remember overhearing a stylish young lady say to her dudish escort, "Oh! John, see how dirty they are and look at the big shoes they wear."

We waited for some hours and then left for Chicago on another train. Next morning, stiff and sore from our cramped seats, we were outside of Chicago on the Illinois prairies, going south towards Alton on the Mississippi. During this third night on the cars, as many as could find room lay down on their blankets in the passage-way, securing a few hours of fitful sleep at the risk of being stepped on.

Towns and villages were far apart in Illinois at that time.

We traveled many miles without seeing a tree or a bush. It was my first view of a prairie. Towards evening we arrived at Alton and detrained on the outskirts of the town. There we took shelter in some empty barns and other vacant buildings, on the floors of which we were glad to get a night's rest. Next morning we were greeted by a furious rain which continued for two days and nights. During all that time we were kept in the barns. Sentinels were posted to allow no one to go into the town; nevertheless, some of the men succeeded in obtaining whiskey.

On the morning of the third day the sun was shining bright and warm. We received orders to "fall in" and marched down to the wharf where four steamboats were awaiting us. One company went on board each boat, the headquarters, field and staff and the band going on the largest boat with one of the companies. The boats cast off at intervals of about a half an hour each and got under way. They carried no other passengers. My company embarked on the "Australia," which was the third boat in the line. The steamboats were of the usual style of light-draft river craft, built to carry freight and passengers. They were all equipped with high pressure engines which noisily ejected a great puff of steam through exhaust pipes on the top deck at every thrust of the piston. They were sidewheelers and each had two tall smoke-stacks.

On each side of the foredeck rested the butt end of a great spar, hanging forward at an angle and secured at the top with tackle. These long spars were used in working the boats off sand bars, I found out later.

Freight was carried on these boats in a very shallow hold and on deck behind the boilers, which were located well forward. Above the boiler deck was the cabin or passenger deck, containing the staterooms, and over that, the "Texas" or hurrican deck, on which was the pilot house in front, and back of that the officers' cabins. The crew was provided for on the boiler deck. The construction was very frail above the boiler deck. The boats shook and shivered when under way, and as everything was constructed of light joists and thin boards, the danger of fire was always present.

Our boats had been very heavily loaded at St. Louis, Mo., with a cargo of military and sutler's stores and material for portable wooden houses. The company was quartered in the forward staterooms on the cabin deck, two to each room. We found the rooms stripped of every article of bedding and furniture. Even the slats in the bunks had been taken out, and we had to lie on our blankets on the floor. For our morning ablutions we went to the lower deck and threw overboard a bucket at the end of a rope. In these pails of muddy Missouri River water we washed ourselves. The company cooks prepared our meals in a kitchen on the lower deck and we ate them wherever we could find room to squat down on the deck among the deckhands, who were all whites. While on board we got no fresh bread and only salt meats. The boat's crew, or "roust-a-bouts," had better food than we, plenty of it and a variety. They often guyed us about it, but we had the laugh on them when the boat landed at a wood pile and the burly mate chased them along with a club or rope's end while they loaded cord wood.

We drank from barrels in which the muddy river water had stood until the mud had settled. It became fairly clear, when undisturbed for about twelve hours, and was not unpalatable.

We had a citizen doctor on board, hired by the Government for the trip. There was no work for him just then, but when we got to Fort Leavenworth he was kept busy.

On leaving Alton we went down the Mississippi to its junction with the Missouri, the "Big Muddy," where we could see the distinctly marked line of the two rivers for miles before the waters seemed to blend. The water of the Mississippi was comparatively clear and seemed loath to mingle with that of its murky companion. The Missouri was high at this time, during the usual June rise. The current was strong, and our heavily laden boats made but slow progress. This, however, did away with the necessity for sounding and enabled us to run at night, at least as far as Fort Leavenworth or further.

Except for three daily roll calls I had nothing to do. The weather was fine. I watched the engines occasionally but spent most of the day sitting in the front of the cabin deck looking out upon the mighty river whose windings disclosed constant changes of scenery. I was enchanted with it, and it never became monotonous to me. Sometimes a steamer carrying many passengers passed us, for no railroads then connected any of the river towns, except one inland from St. Louis as far as Jefferson City, the capitol of Missouri. A few of the passenger boats were equipped with a calliope, or steam organ, and would play old plantation melodies on approaching or departing from a town. To hear "Suwanee River," "The Old Folks at Home" or "Susannah" reverberating from the hills on a calm summer's evening was charming.

There were not many towns on the Missouri in 1855; the principal ones that I remember were St. Charles, Hermann, Jefferson City, Booneville, Glasgow, Kansas City, Leavenworth and St. Joseph, which was then about the end of civilization and the white settlements. Smaller places, not yet even named, were starting up, and some of them are prosperous towns now. I had a good school atlas with me so that I could locate the direction of the river and its principal tributaries. It proved to be an interesting and useful companion, giving me general information about the country and the distances between various points.

All of the steamboats used cord wood for fuel. This was supplied from wood yards along the river as far north as the white settlements extended. They were generally located in the wilderness far away from any town, but were well known to the pilots, who, when running short of wood, would sound a warning whistle on nearing a wood yard, which would bring out of the woods to the river bank a bushy-whiskered, matted-haired individual in a red shirt, with one suspender holding up his corduroy pants, the bottoms of which were thrust into cowhide boots.

The pilot would run the boat close in to shore and slacken speed while the captain opened a parley with the man in the red shirt about the price of the wood per cord and haggle about it until a bargain was made. If the price was low a large quantity would be shipped, or on the contrary, only enough to reach the next yard. Occasionally it happened that the captain would not take any fuel at the price offered and would start away to take his chances at the next wood pile, if he was sure he had enough fuel to get there.

When it was decided to take in wood, the boat tied up to the trees. Two gang planks run out, and the captain, the chief engineer and the purser of the boat went on shore and inspected and measured the wood. If satisfactory, they gave the word to the mate, who had his crew ready, and with a shout started them off on a run. Each man rushed to the pile, grabbed as many sticks as he could carry and ran into the boat on one gangway and out on the other. The mate, in the meantime, shouted and swore at them on the run, sometimes giving a slow man an unfriendly rap over the shoulders, to hurry him along. This was kept up without a moment's rest until all the wood wanted was on board. The poor devils of deck hands and firemen were exhausted and dripping with perspiration when their hard task was over. When this scene was enacted at night time under the fitful blaze of pitch-pine burnt on shore in iron baskets, it had a weird, unearthly aspect.

We made fair progress, without delay or accident, until we were within a few miles of the village of Booneville, Mo. It was noon, the weather was beautiful and the boat was making her best speed. I was sitting on a barrel on the lower deck forward, and had just finished my dinner and was talking to some comrades, when suddenly a crashing shock threw me down to the deck some distance away. I could hear the timbers and upper wood work of the boat crunching and straining. I looked up and saw the two tall smoke stacks wabbling dangerously and straining at their guys. The two great spars at the bow of the boat were swinging to and fro, and threatened to fall to the deck.

Finding that I was not injured, I rushed to the upper deck and looked down upon the scene of confusion below. There were cries of "Snag! Snag!" that dreaded obstruction to river navigation that had wrecked so many steamboats. In a moment the forward lower deck was crowded with hurrying boat hands and shouting officers. A hatchway was uncovered and half a dozen men jumped down into the hold. Mattresses and blankets were dropped to them with which they tried to stop the leak. But the inrush of the water was so strong that their efforts were futile and in less than five minutes they scrambled hastily on deck.

In the meantime, the pilot tried to back away from the snag, but the boat seemed to be caught in a trap. Fortunately, some one now gave orders to draw the fires and to blow off steam to avoid an explosion of the boilers. The roar of escaping steam and steady shriek of the big whistle added to the excitement and confusion. The soldiers' wives and children ran about the cabin deck, screaming with terror. We soldiers were made to understand, despite the noise, that we were to take the life preservers from our staterooms and assemble on the hurricane deck. This was promptly done. There I noticed that we were seventy-five to a hundred yards from the east bank of the river, with no habitation nor any other boat in sight.

There were some life boats on this deck which our officers had ordered us to help the crew to launch when word came that this would not be necessary, as soundings had shown that there was no danger of the boat being entirely submerged. This quieted the frightened ones, and when the steam had about escaped from the boiler and the noise lessened, we were ordered to descend to the cabin deck again to pack our knapsacks, take our arms and reassemble on the upper deck. There we saw five or six miles down the river the steamboat, *Grey Cloud* with company A on board hastening to our assistance.

During all this time the boat had been sinking steadily, but not so rapidly as I expected. We could plainly hear the air pressure in the hold force off some of the hatchway covers and noticed a hissing sound when the water reached the still hot boilers. But there was no danger of explosion; the steam had been let off just in time. Occasionally the boat gave a sudden lurch and listed alarmingly to one side and when the water had entirely submerged the boiler deck and the boat began to sink more rapidly, we laid down our knapsacks and arms and began to put on the life preservers, as we feared the water would lift off the cabin deck and float us out into the river to drown, in spite of the assurance that the river at this point was too shallow for that to happen.

We watched the final struggles of the boat filled with the fear that she might break in two. Then with a huge straining and a terrifying tremor she settled on the bed of the river. Her bow was much higher than the stern, she had a strong list away from shore and the water was about three feet below the cabin deck.

I have no clear idea as to the time that elapsed between the striking of the snag and the grounding of the battered hull on the river bottom. But I know that the *Grey Cloud*, which we were anxiously watching, drew up alongside of our wreck about an hour after we had sighted her, and took us on board. No one was lost or injured. We saved the company books and papers and our own private property, except our dress coats and uniform hats, which had been packed away where we could not get at them. For these we were reimbursed later on.

The sun was still high when we cast off aboard the *Grey Cloud* and started up the river again. We took a couple of the *Australia's* officers with us and landed them at Booneville, a few miles away, to seek help. The captain and crew remained on board and were launching one of the life boats as we left. The last we saw of the wounded steamboat before a bend in the river hid her forever from our view, was her upper deck, with her paddle boxes and smoke stacks sticking out of the water. We learned later that she soon went to pieces and was a total wreck.

Snags, such as that which caused us so much trouble, are trees which have been washed away by freshets. They float down the river and the largest of them frequently become fixed with the heavy butt and great roots fast in the river's bed where they are held until one of the constant shiftings of the channel releases them. The branches of these trees in time drop off, leaving only the solid trunk, invisible at high water. It was such a one that sunk the *Australia.* We saw thousands of snags on the upper Missouri when the water was low. The pilots when descending the river pay but little attention to the smaller ones. They are pointed downstream and the boats often run directly over them without any injury as they readily bend under the impact.

The addition of my company crowded the *Grey Cloud.* We had to put up on the floor of the saloon for a few days until we reached Fort Leavenworth, where we disembarked and were to remain until another steamboat could be loaded and fitted out at St. Louis to take us up the river to Fort Pierre. The remainder of our little fleet had already passed on. The soldiers' wives and children of my company were left on board with Company A, fortunately for them. Their husbands, however, were ordered to disembark and serve with the company.

It was in the early forenoon that we marched up the steep hill from which Fort Leavenworth, Kansas, overlooked the river. We were assigned to quarters in an old two-story building close to some vacant cavalry stables on the western side of the fort, near some brush and woods. Fort Leavenworth was an old frontier post and its buildings were dilapidated. Its garrison at that time consisted of two companies of cavalry and a large number of unmounted recruits for one of the new cavalry regiments that was being formed there. The place was crowded and the cholera was raging. The hospital had long been overcrowded and one of the largest barrack buildings was also used as a hospital where the sick filled both of its large floors.

We had not been there many days before the dread disease made its appearance in my company and soon we had a dozen men sick of it. They were placed on straw beds on the floor of one of the old stables near our quarters, which had been hastily cleaned up for the purpose, although it was so infested with rats that they ran over the helpless sick even in the day time. There were no conveniences of any kind. The weather was intensely hot. The only drinking water to be had was brought from the Missouri River in barrels, into which each one dipped his tin cup. There was no ice, not even for the sick, and medical attendance was altogether inadequate.

After a day or two of illness one of our men died and was soon followed by another. During our short stay the company lost four members, as well as Brevet Second Lieutenant Samuel T. Sheppard, who died June 27, 1855. He was assigned to duty with us after our arrival. Lieutenant Sheppard was a fine young officer and had only lately been graduated from West Point. As there were no musicians at Fort Leavenworth except my drummer and myself and a few buglers of the cavalry companies, we two were ordered to attend all the funerals to play the "Dead March," and as my company was the only infantry present, they furnished the escort for the recruits who died in the hospitals. During our stay of about three weeks I cannot recall more than two or three days without a funeral, held usually in the morning, but often followed by another in the afternoon or evening. I frequently saw two or three coffins carried at one time in the two horse, covered delivery wagon which did duty as a hearse.

These funerals were simple affairs. A funeral escort of a corporal, eight privates and my drummer and myself appeared at one of the hospitals and waited until the coffin or coffins were loaded on the wagon. Sometimes we were kept waiting rather long, while the corpses were being placed in the coffins, and nailed up in the presence of the sick and dying. There was no dead houses or separate place for the bodies; they were left lying where they died on their straw beds on the floor, simply covered with a blanket until the time for the next funeral.

When the coffins were brought out the escort presented arms, and when they were loaded on the wagon, the corporal commanded, "Shoulder arms, right face, reverse arms, forward march." Then we marched off in slow time, playing the solemn "Dead March," which could be plainly heard by the unfortunate patients in the hospital. We continued the slow march and music, until a short distance outside of the fort, when we ceased playing, and marched at the "Route Step," until we entered the cemetery, which was more than a mile away. There we resumed the slow step and doleful music, until we arrived at the grave. The coffin was lowered without any further ceremony, except the firing of three rounds of blank cartridges by the escort, across the grave. We then marched back to the garrison, while the grave diggers filled in the earth on top of the coffin.

One morning, while waiting at the temporary hospital on our usual sad duty, I was seized by a strong desire to see with my own eyes the awful conditions in the building, of which I had heard much. I entered the hallway and passed through a wide open door into a large barrack room. On the two long sides of the room, lying on the floor upon bedsacks stuffed with straw, were about three dozen men in all stages of the terrible disease. Some were unconscious of their surroundings; their features had turned to a bluish black color. Flies in great numbers swarmed around them, and settled on their open lips and staring eyes. Others, in the earlier stages, feebly tried to free themselves from these pests. The doors and windows were all open, but the heat and stench were terrible. There was no furniture in the room, except a table for medicines, and a few chairs for the soldier-nurses.

Two rude oblong boxes rested on the floor near the door. They were of pine, and not even stained any color. Into these two almost nude bodies of men who had died during the night were being placed or packed—literally packed, for one of the bodies was that of a very large man for whom the coffin was too short. When his head and feet were in, his chest bulged up, which made it necessary for one of the attendants to sit on the cover while it was being nailed down. All this was done in plain view of the patients. What a sight for those who were conscious! What must have been the thoughts and feeling of the unfortunate sufferers?

I turned with horror and indignation from the room, sickened and shuddering at the sight I had seen. What should be said of the commander of the post, an officer of high rank? And what of the chief medical officer? They permitted this brutal and inhuman treatment of the sick to continue, while there was plenty of space and tents to shelter the stricken, to separate the convalescent from the sick and to remove the dead from their proximity?

I am aware that medical science, at that time, knew but little concerning either the prevention or cure of cholera, but at Fort Leavenworth absolutely nothing was done to prevent the disease from becoming epidemic. No orders, caution or instructions were ever given to us in regard to it, and it was left to each man to guard himself as his intelligence might dictate.

The afflicted of my company fared a little better than the poor recruits. They were not crowded, and our little fat citizen doctor did his duty conscientiously. After about two weeks no more new cases developed in my company, and those still under his care were convalescent.

There was a man in the company at this time, who claimed to know of an infallible preventative of cholera. Before enlisting he had worked in some of the Mississippi river towns, as far south as New Orleans, where cholera and yellow fever were prevalent. He claimed to have acquired his knowledge from an old negro doctor. He said all he needed was a gallon of whiskey, and he could furnish the rest of the required ingredients. He talked so much and so earnestly about this, that he finally persuaded another and myself to put up the money for the liquor, as he had none himself. He went down to

Leavenworth City, a few miles away, and bought a gallon demijohn of corn whiskey, which he secretly carried into the woods back of our quarters. Then he dug up some roots. These, with some bark, he cut up and put into the whiskey. After digging a hole among the bushes deep enough to hold the demijohn, he concealed it with brush-wood.

Every morning between reveille and breakfast, we sneaked away to the woods by divers routes. Careful to be unobserved we pulled out the demijohn and each took a drink of the mixture. It was vile and strong stuff. One of the ingredients, I think, was sassafras, but I do not know what else it contained, for we were never told. We did this regularly every morning during our stay. I do not know whether the stuff had any real merit, but none of our syndicate had any symptom of the disease, and we succeeded in keeping our cache a secret.

After we had been at Fort Leavenworth about three weeks, we received the heartening news one morning that the steamboat *Genoa* had arrived from St. Louis, and was ready to take us aboard. We embarked in the afternoon, and at once started up the river. It was on the third day of July, a date impressed on my memory by the joy of getting away from a pestilential place, and the fact that we hoisted the United States flag and fired a salute at noon next day, with the little one-pounder cannon on board of the boat.

The *Genoa* was almost a duplicate of the *Australia,* on which we had been sunk near Booneville. Our accommodations were about the same, except that the slats had been generously left in the berths, so that we did not have to lie on the floor. I had my first view of Indians a short distance above Leavenworth. They belonged to the Kickapoo tribe and did not impress me much. There were half a dozen of them loafing around a wood pile where we had stopped. They looked sad and lazy and begged for tobacco. They lived near the white settlements, and appeared to have degenerated by contact with the whites.

The June rise of the river was over, and the water was much lower; we could no longer run in the night, but tied up at the river bank as soon as darkness fell. In a few days we passed St. Joseph, Mo., which, save for a few small settlements a little further on, marked the end of civilization. Council Bluff, Omaha, Nebraska City, Sioux City, and others, had no existence as yet. St. Joseph was one of the starting points for emigrants, who went to Utah and overland to California. It was also the place of departure on the Missouri from the United States Mail Route and the Pony Express.

We had not yet seen the last of the cholera. A sergeant of my company was stricken, on the second day out from Leavenworth, and was immediately isolated on the lower deck of the boat. Fortunately, it proved to be a mild case, and under the doctor's care he recovered in a short time. This case was the last we had.

At this time I shared my cabin with Corporal Clifford of my company, who was my bunkie. We had been on the river but a few days, when one night while I was preparing to lie down in my bunk, after tattoo roll call, he told me he was going down to the lower deck and would be back directly. When he failed to return within a reasonable time, I reported his absence to the first sergeant. A thorough search of the boat and the shore revealed no trace of him. It was concluded that he had fallen overboard and drowned, though no outcry had been heard. Some months later we read in a newspaper of the finding of a soldier's body in the river, away down near Kansas City. The description seemed to fit Corporal Clifford. Everyone liked him and his loss was deeply felt.

The captain of the *Genoa* was named Throckmorton, an experienced Western riverman. He had his son with him, a lad about my age, with whom I spent a good deal of time. The boy had a shot gun, and once or twice he took me with him shooting birds and small game on shore, while the boat laid up for wood.

There were no wood yards beyond St. Joseph, and we encountered no more steamboats, except those which had taken Companies A, G and I to Fort Pierre, and were now returning laden with furs. When wood ran short, the boat made a landing at a suitable place, and all the firemen and deck hands went on shore to cut down trees and chop them up to cordwood size. A quantity of logs were also taken on board to be sawed and split on deck, while the boat was under way. This saved time, for the "wooding up" of the boat consumed many hours, and had to be repeated every few days. The wood was of poor quality, mostly cotton wood, and of course, very green for firing. Some of the soldiers voluntarily assisted at the wood chopping, tempted no doubt by the small pay per hour, and a drink of whiskey, which was also served to all the boat hands.

Navigation became more difficult as we slowly advanced up the tortuous stream which often seemed to double on itself. At times we were heading south instead of north, and appeared to be going down the river instead of up.

It was the mid-summer period of low water in the Missouri, and no improvement could be expected before the fall rains. There was no well defined channel, for the erratic river was constantly changing its course. Islands that had existed the previous year were washed away by the spring floods, or so changed in contour as to be unrecognizable. New islands were formed, and soon covered with a growth of willows and brush. Land was washed away from shores and added in other places. No reliable chart of the upper river existed. The pilot was guided only by his own judgment of the current, the appearance of the water, the visible sand bars, and the numerous snags that showed their branches above the water's level.

Appearances were sometimes deceptive and caused the pilot to run the boat up on the wrong side of a long island, only to find that the channel was too narrow to get through or too much obstructed by snags. He would then have to back out and run back for miles in order to try the other side of the island. Many times each day we heard the pilot's single toll of the bell on the forward deck. This was the signal to take soundings on the starboard side, and was usually followed by his ring to the engine room to slacken speed. A man would commence to "heave-the-lead" attached to a line, that had marks in various colors at intervals, to indicate the depth of water. He would cry out measurements, such as "No bottom, mark-twain, half-twain, quarterless-twain, six feet, five feet," then perhaps suddenly "Nine feet," or "Three feet," when we could feel the boat slide onto a sand bar, if the pilot had not reversed the engines in time. Soundings were sometimes taken in a row boat at some distance away.

We frequently ran onto sand bars lightly, and managed to get off by reversing the paddle-wheels, but often it took many hours or several days to float the boat again. When it was found that the steamer was hard and fast, the great spars carried forward were brought into use. The butt end of one of the spars was lowered over the side into the water well forward. It sunk firmly into the sandy bottom by its own weight. A double set of strong pulley blocks, attached to the top of the spar, were connected by a cable which wound around the drum of a powerful capstan on the forward deck. The capstan bars were manned by as many of the deck hands as could find room. Then they began turning, very slowly after the strain was on, going around in a circle and keeping up a kind of a chant, such as sailors often sing on ships when raising the anchor by hand. It was exhausting labor, but the soldiers often volunteered to help.

By this operation a part of the boat was practically lifted, and by placing the spar at the proper inclination, it was also sheered away from the bar at the same time. Progress seemed to be made by inches. Many times the spar had to be lifted and reset in a new position, and often a portion of the deck freight had to be shifted before the boat could be freed. During all this time the sand in the river kept on drifting against the boat and added to the difficulty. If the boat ran into a bar near the shore, where a cable could be fastened to trees, we could get off again with much less trouble, and without the use of the spars.

We proceeded in this laborious way, until we were fifty miles or more north of where Sioux City is now located. There a series of very bad turns in the river made Captain Throckmorton decide that the *Genoa* was too heavily laden to pass, and that at least one-half of her freight must be put on shore. A place deemed suitable was selected on the east bank of the river, and the unloading was commenced. The freight consisting of all manner of commissary, quartermaster and sutler's stores. It was put ashore on skids by the deck hands and piled up under tarpaulins.

The company went on shore, including the citizen doctor, and put up so-called "A" tents, which we found among the quartermaster's stores. Thus we established a camp, where extra ammunition and other necessaries were provided. A guard of a half a dozen men under a corporal remained on board, and the *Genoa* resumed her journey towards Fort Pierre, a few hundred miles away. But, when something more than half way there, and just below the upper "Big Bend," the captain unloaded another part of his freight and left it on shore without any guards.

Along the entire distance from St. Joseph to "Camp Gardner," our destination, which the soldiers named after our captain, we saw no indications of white settlements, except at the mouth of the Big Sioux River, a few miles north of the site where Sioux City was founded the following year. There, as we passed, we noticed some white men erecting a saw-mill. They ran down to the river bank and motioned to us to stop, but we kept on our course. We saw no Indians, for, according to their custom, they had departed in the spring to hunt buffalo and other game on the plains and would not return to the river until late in the fall.

We saw a few herds of buffalo grazing on the prairies some miles away from the river. But when they became aware of the steamer, they rushed away, and soon disappeared from sight.

We were greatly annoyed by mosquitoes at night. So persistent were these pests on a few occasions that men from the company were detailed to remain on shore all night and tend small fires whose smoke enveloped the boat.

One night there was an alarm of Indians. The sentinel on shore reported to the corporal of the guard that he had seen moving lights some distance away, that appeared to be signals. The company was quietly called under arms, and the lights on the boat extinguished. We remained on the alert until daylight, but nothing happened. It seemed to have been a false alarm.

While at Leavenworth, a married soldier had joined our company, and he and his wife went up the river with us. She was the only woman on board. A girl baby was born to her before we reached Camp Gardner, and it was named Genoa Harrison, after the steamer.

We had not been more than a week on the river, when I became very ill and had to take to my berth. I had not felt well for some days, and now had a throbbing headache and a high fever, being part of the time delirious. I was furnished with a mattress to lie on, and a man was detailed to wait on me. The doctor was very attentive, and managed to pull me through. When I got so that I began to eat a little, the doctor got Captain Throckmorton's permission to have my meals served from the cabin table. They were brought to me by the captain's colored boy, who served me cheerfully. He was a happy, grinning young darky, about my own age, and so black that the soldiers said charcoal would make a white mark on him. I had no money to reward him, but when we got to the end of our journey, I gave him one of my jackets and a soldier's cap, which made him very proud and happy. As for the doctor, I remember him most gratefully; but I never saw him nor heard of him again, after he left us. I was able to be up about a week before we got to Camp Gardner, and was convalescent, but still weak. I suppose now that I had typhoid fever, although the doctor did not tell me so at the time.

It was about a month after we had left Leavenworth that

we encamped, and in all that time we had accomplished less than five hundred miles. The camp was on a knoll close to a ravine, in which were some trees and bushes. The country round about was hilly, and without any woods. I think the captain chose the position as one of good defense against Indians, in case our rich booty of freight should tempt them to attack us. We never saw an Indian while there, but sentinels were posted in the day time, where they could overlook much of the country, and were withdrawn nearer to the camp at night.

It was August and the weather was intensely hot. To escape the sun we spent much time in the shady ravine. We also went swimming often, and fished for cat-fish in the Missouri. Rattlesnakes, which were numerous, were a cause for anxiety, but we escaped being stung by them and killed many.

It was at Camp Gardner that we first made use of some of the mechanical talent of my company. A couple of masons built a bake-oven, near the river bank, out of stones found there. It had a stone bed and was regularly arched on a wooden center made of barrel staves, and was provided with a smoke flue. The builders had no lime or cement, so they covered it all over, about a foot thick, with earth and sods. It worked well, and in a few days a practical baker of the company made such good use of it that we all had bread which tasted delicious after eating "hardtack" for a month. We had plenty of flour, but I do not know how he made yeast. Perhaps that was found in the shape of powders among the sutler's stores.

Tobacco had become very scarce among the men. Some of them smoked tea, coffee or dried leaves, until the captain, who, I think wanted some himself, authorized the first sergeant to search the sutler's stores in the freight pile Boxes of plug tobacco were found, and a plentiful supply was distributed, for which the sutler was reimbursed. Later on we learned to make use of the Indian's substitute for tobacco, when in want of it.

We had been without any fresh meat or vegetables, since we left Leavenworth, but at Camp Gardner we caught plenty of large catfish, of which our cooks made a very palatable chowder. It was an agreeable change of diet. In some of the ravines we found quantities of wild plums, smaller than the domestic fruit, and yellow, but fairly sweet and deliciously flavored. There were also plenty of wild grapes, but not yet ripe enough to eat. We had an easy time in camp, performing no duties except guard. A stone cutter among the soldiers wiled away part of his spare time carving deeply into the soft rock face of a cliff on the river's edge: "Camp Gardner, August, 1855. Here was caught a fifty-pound catfish by John O'Meara, Company D, Second U. S. Infantry," The man who caught this great fish was henceforth called "Catfish O'Meara."

After nearly three weeks, the *Genoa* returned from Fort Pierre. The freight was reloaded and Camp Gardner abandoned. The company's baker baked an extra supply of "soft bread," which we took with us when we resumed our slow, monotonous journey up the river.

Evenings, when the mosquitoes were not too numerous, we gathered at the bow of the boat and sang songs to the music of a mouth harmonica, which one of the soldiers played, or told stories and tried to be cheerful. But we were again overtaken by a calamity, about the third day after leaving camp.

The boat was tied up to get fuel one afternoon, and some of the soldiers took a swim in the river.

A sergeant named Schott, a strong, athletic young man and a good swimmer, took a dive from the shore into the river, at a point about two hundred feet ahead of the boat, and in plain view of many on deck. We saw one of his hands appear above the water twice, near the place he went in. But, as the minutes passed, his head did not appear, and we gave the alarm. By the time the place was reached, there was no longer any hope of rescue. Some hours were spent in grappling for the body unsuccessfully. The small cannon was brought on shore, and fired over the place where he was last seen, a half-dozen times; but it failed to raise the body, which was never recovered. This event cast a shadow of gloom over us. It was the second case of death by drowning since we had been on the *Genoa*.

The river was now at its lowest. The summer had been unusually dry, and when we got to the mouth of the L'Eau qui Court River, now called the Niabrara River, it was found to have formed a sand bar across the Missouri. This new barrier made a lot of trouble, although we had only half a load of freight. So, when Captain Throckmorton reached the place just below the Big Bend, on the way up, where he had left a part of his freight, consisting of a lot of barrels of salt pork, he decided that he could not make his way through the Bend. The freight was once more divided, and we went into camp on the east side of the river, while the boat steamed on to Fort Pierre again.

This camp was named "Camp O'Connell", after our lieutenant. It was in the woods, where we were sheltered from the hot sun, but we found the ground rather damp. We cleared away the underbrush and covered the floors of our tents with brushwood and leaves. When this did not keep out the moisture, we built bunks about a foot high. We did not build a bake oven this time, as we expected the boat to return in a week. We were now only about one hundred miles from the end of our journey. By this time we had become more indifferent about Indians, as we had encountered none at Camp Gardner, and wandered further from camp, in small squads, always taking our rifles and ammunition. A few men got permission to go hunting. One of them shot a small deer, but they had little success with rifles on small game and prairie hens.

One day some of the men discovered a large cornfield in the bottom land near the river. The stalks were tall enough to hide a man on horseback, but there were many weeds. The ears of corn seemed as large as a man's forearm, and were just about ripe enough to eat on the cob. Next day I was one of a party that brought a kettle from camp, and we boiled corn on the river bank. For a few days we had a daily feast of this delicious corn. Many of the ears were red or blue or mixed in color. We did not let the officers know about our find, fearing they would forbid us to take any of it. We learned later that this corn belonged to some of the Yankton tribe, whose squaws had planted it in the spring before the Indians started on their summer buffalo hunt. No care was taken of it, but it grew to immense size in the rich soil, despite the weeds. On their return, late in the fall, the Yanktons gathered it.

In about a week the *Genoa* returned, and once more we re-embarked. In taking down our tents, it was found that some snakes had lodged in the brush and leaves under some of the low bunks, and it made some of the occupants turn pale on learning that they had peacefully slept so close to the dangerous reptiles. As the boat now carried only about one quarter of the amount of freight she had started with, we made better progress, and were only delayed by frequent soundings. I think we reached Fort Pierre on the morning of the fourth day from Camp O'Connell, about the middle of September, 1855, just fifty-one years since the Lewis and Clark expedition had passed that way on its long journey across the continent.

As I look back over this long, weary and unfortunate journey, I realize that it took about three and a half months to go from Carlisle, Pa., to Fort Pierre, Nebraska Territory. Of this time, we were more than seven weeks on the Missouri River, and it had cost the company seven lives—one officer and four privates, by cholera, and two non-commissioned officers, by drowning—a rather mournful remembrance for this early period of my service.

PART IV.

FORT PIERRE AND THE SIOUX INDIANS, 1855-1856.

FORT Pierre, situated on the west bank of the Missouri River, about fifteen hundred miles above St. Louis, Mo., was an old trading post belonging to the American Fur Co., which also had another post or two higher up the river and one on the Yellowstone River. Fort Pierre was the headquarters. It was a stockade structure, built of split logs firmly set in the ground and twenty feet or more in height. There were sheltered and protected turrets at the corners on top, which afforded a look-out over a large area of flat country. The fort set back a short distance from the bank and had a large gate on the river side. There were also one or two smaller gates. The stockade enclosed a square space, containing several well built log houses for the traders, trappers, hunters and others. There were also storehouses and a central vacant space of considerable size within the barrier. The fort was built in 1832 by Pierre Chouteau, Jr., and recently sold to the Government.

The stockade was built on high bottom land, well placed for defense against the Indians. The prospect was uninterrupted for miles up or down the river, and to the west the land was level and bare for some miles to the foot-hills. To the east was the Missouri with a large island opposite the fort and hilly land on the other side of the river. To the north, on the bank of the river, less than half a mile away, there was an Indian settlement of about twenty-five lodges. It was there that the Indians who came to trade usually camped. The surroundings were bleak and dreary to the extreme. One saw nothing but prairie or a few stunted bushes in some shallow ravines near the river. Wood for fuel had to be hauled a long distance.

We found here the three companies that had preceded us, also companies "B" and "C" of my regiment who had marched across the country from Fort Ridgely, Minnesota Territory. They were the first soldiers that had ever been stationed in that part of the country. They brought a herd of beef cattle and mules in charge of herders, who had managed to get them there during the summer season with small loss.

During the six weeks or more that these five companies had preceded us, they had been very busy setting up the portable houses that had been brought up on the steamers. These houses were placed a short distance behind the stockade, around three sides of a large parallelogram, forming the parade ground—officers' houses on one side, company quarters opposite and other houses on one end. The necessary store houses were erected on the river front. The company houses were intended to hold half a company each without crowding. We moved into two of them on our arrival and had a little less than thirty men in each house. They were single-story affairs with but one room and of the flimsiest wood construction. The sills and floor beams were entirely too light for the live weight to be carried, the upright studding was about three by two inches, grooved on two sides to receive panels made of three-quarter inch boards, which was all the protection there was against the intense winter cold of that latitude. There was no interior finish of any kind. The roof was of thin boards covered with tarred paper and had a low pitch from a ridge to the sides. The houses were set on wooden posts about two feet above the ground.

Each house was furnished with two sheet iron stoves for burning wood, and had stove pipes passing through the roof. The officers' houses were the same, except that they were smaller and were divided into two rooms by a thin board partition. These houses were very easily set up. There was but little work on them except driving nails. They had been previously painted a dark red color, both inside and out. Whoever designed these cardboard houses—for they proved to be but little better—had but a small conception of the requirements of that climate. The winters were long, with deep snow and frequent blizzards. The architect of these shelters was indirectly the cause of much suffering. We built log huts for company kitchens, but we had no mess-rooms.

On the day before the steamboat *Genoa* left on her return trip to St. Louis, partly loaded with furs, a paymaster, who returned on her paid us for four months. We did not see a paymaster again until the following May or June. A sutler had established a store, with a miscellaneous stock of goods such as soldiers needed, also goods for trading with the Indians. But the prices were so high that we could not afford to buy much. This was due to the high cost of steamboat transportation, which amounted to about fifty dollars per ton from St. Louis.

About two weeks after our arrival at Fort Pierre, a courier from Brigadier General William S. Harney, commander of the Sioux expedition, arrived from Ash Hollow with an order for four companies of the Second Infantry to be sent to him as re-enforcements.

It appeared that General Harney had fought a battle with the Brulé and Ogalalla tribes of the Sioux, on September 3rd, 1855, at Ash Hollow on the Blue Water creek. This is a tributary of the Platte River, about two hundred and fifty miles south-west of Fort Pierre.

These were the Indians who had massacred Lieutenant Grattan and twenty-one soldiers more than a year before, and for whose punishment the Government had organized the Sioux expedition.

General Harney had started out from Fort Laramie with six small companies of infantry and two of cavalry. After a march of nearly one hundred and fifty miles, he skillfully approached the Indians' camp, without the presence of his troops being suspected.

The Indians had been buffalo hunting during the summer, acquiring many skins, and much dried buffalo meat. About seventy lodges had encamped on the Blue Water in a sheltered valley, where they probably expected to pass the coming winter.

The troops surprised the camp at day break, and attacked it simultaneously from two sides. The Indians, unable to make any organized resistance, fled in the direction where their ponies were herded, but were pursued by the cavalry. Many were killed, among them a number of squaws, for in the confusion it was difficult to distinguish them from the warriors.

The chief, Little Thunderer, made his escape. The soldiers lost few in this action, but the punishment to the Indians was very severe; and it had its effect, for as long as we remained among the Sioux, only small skirmishes took place.

The loss of all their lodges, provisions, arms, furs and other property, which the general caused to be burned, was a severe blow to them. They were also deprived of many of their ponies. After the battle, the troops were encamped in a stronger position nearby. There they awaited re-enforcements from Fort Pierre, where they intended to winter, as the general deemed it imprudent to march his small force to the fort, across the enemy's country, fearing that other tribes to the north and east might form a coalition with the vanquished Indians.

My company was one of the four ordered to join General Harney, at Ash Hollow; but I and a few more of the young boys were not taken along. We were left at Fort Pierre with the two companies retained there. The march proved to be very severe. Part of the route was across the "Mauvaises Terres" (Bad Lands), where there was no vegetation. It was a desert, where wood and water had to be carried in the waggons from one camp to another.

Many curious specimens of fossil remains, picked up in the Bad Lands, were brought by the soldiers to Fort Pierre. There were petrified fish, lizards, frogs, etc. But nearly all were imperfect, and more or less broken.

After a short rest, the united troops under General Harney, twelve companies in all—quite a little army for those days—took up their march for Fort Pierre, and arrived there early in November, without any molestation from the Indians.

I have often regretted since that I was not allowed to go on this march. I wanted to see that part of the country, through which but few white men had ever traveled before.

General Harney's additional troops went into camp near our quarters. The weather was getting cold; winter was approaching; firewood was scarce, and had to be hauled a long distance. There was but a small supply of forage for the cavalry horses, and scarcely any grass in the vicinity of the fort. That had been eaten up by the mules and Indian ponies. Water also had to be carted quite a distance from the river. In view of these conditions, and as there were not enough portable houses to shelter them, it was decided to put the six companies of the Sixth Infantry, and the two companies of cavalry into cantonment. They were accordingly sent about six miles up the river, where they built log houses in the woods on the east bank of the Missouri and remained there until the following spring.

General Harney took quarters in one of the buildings in the stockade. Whenever it was my turn as orderly at the adjutant's office, one of my duties was to bring the general, in a sealed envelope, the "countersign," or watchword for the night. When I approached him, saluted, and said: "General. the countersign," he would reply in his gruff, stentorian voice, "Lay it on the table." I was always glad to hustle out of his presence.

The general was very tall and powerfully built. He wore a long white beard, and his white hair was also long. In spite of his age, he was erect—a remarkably commanding figure. Many of the Indians knew and feared him. Among them he was known as the "Great White Chief."

General Harney had been in the Seminole, and other Indian wars. He was colonel of the Second Dragoons, in the war with Mexico, and was promoted to Brevet Brigadier General.

During the absence of my company on the march to Ash Hollow and return, I had but little to do and spent much of my time in wandering about the environs of Fort Pierre. With others I crossed the river in a canoe, and on the opposite side we found great quantities of wild grapes, which were fairly good to eat, though somewhat tart. We squeezed the juice out of them, and with the addition of sugar and water, made a very palatable drink.

There were some prairie-dog villages on the plain west of the fort, and it was interesting to watch these alert and nimble animals, no larger than a squirrel, running about and having sentinels posted on some higher point near their underground dwellings. These sentries sat upon their haunches, and watched carefully in all directions. Whenever we got within a certain distance of them, they gave a shrill, sharp bark, which started all the others running for the various holes. No matter how quiet we kept, or how long we remained, they did not come out again until we were a long distance away.

I became acquainted with some of the employees of the American Fur Company, who were mostly French-Canadians, with a few half-breed Indians among them. Some of them were married to squaws and lived at the Indian camp close by. From these men, who were mostly hunters, trappers or guides, I heard many interesting stories of their hazardous lives and their experiences among the Indians, whose language most of them spoke. They were often useful as interpreters.

To me, the most interesting people at Fort Pierre were the Indians, among whom I passed the greater part of my leisure time. This intimate association with the savages continued all through my service on the frontiers, a period of about five years in Nebraska and Minnesota Territories.

I have read the beautiful stories of Fennimore Cooper and other writers of Indian romances. I have also read some of the stories of explorers and the able and interesting works of men who lived among the North American Indians and studied them. But I do not intend to quote from any of them. I shall simply relate here what I learned about the Indians from persons living in close contact with them during my time and the impressions they made on my youthful mind, as I can remember them now, after a period of fifty years since I left the Indian country to take part in the Civil War, in 1861.

Nebraska Territory in 1855, extended from Minnesota Territory, on the east, to the Rocky mountains, on the west; and from Kansas Territory, on the south, to the British possessions, on the north. It has since been partitioned into North and South Dakota, Nebraska, Wyoming and Montana. The greater part of this immense territory was claimed and inhabited by the Sioux Indians, a name given to them by the French-Canadians, who also gave French names to some of the tribes composing the Sioux, such as the Gross Ventres, Brules, etc. These Frenchmen also named the rivers, streams and mountains, many of which have since been re-named.

The Indians called themselve Dakotas, and did not recognize the name of Sioux. They were divided into a number of tribes, each ruled by a chief. The following are the names of some of the tribes, with the most of whom we came in contact: Poncas, Yanktons, Yanktonnas, Uncapapas, Blackfeet, Rikarees, Minnikanye, Ogallalas, Brules. Certain tribes were sub-divided into bands, such as the "Two-Kettle-Band," and "Smutty-Bear-Band," both of whom were Yanktons.

Lieutenant Gouverneur K. Warren, of the Topographical Engineers, U. S. A., who made surveys in the Dakota country in 1855, 1856 and 1857, and to whom we furnished an escort, estimated the Dakota Indians at about three thousand lodges, which would represent a population of twenty-four thousand, of which five thousand were warriors.

During a decade, their numbers had decreased from wars with the Chippewa Indians and other tribes in the north, while in the south, near the white settlements, the mortality from the small-pox had been very great among Poncas and Yanktons. I noticed that many of them were pock-marked, and some had become blind in one eye from the disease, which their medicine-men could neither cure nor prevent from becoming epidemic.

It was obvious that the more northern tribes of the Dakotas, who had seen but a few whites, were superior to those of the south, near the settlements, whose contact with the whites had degraded them. The Indians who inhabited the more northern and western parts of Nebraska were fine specimens of their race, for they still lived in their aboriginal way. Game was yet abundant. They were proud and warlike and possessed many ponies. Their tepees were larger, finer and more decorated. They were rich in furs of all kinds, which they bartered with the traders for guns, powder, lead, beads, calico, knives, tomahawks, etc. Many of them had guns, but most of these were old flint-locks. Bows and arrows were by no means abandoned and they continued to manufacture and use them. They also had many dogs, which closely resembled wolves, except in color. These dogs, some of them very large, they used in many ways, often as beasts of burden—and as a choice article of food on festive occasions.

The distinctive features of the Dakotas were their broad faces with high cheek bones; their high, broad, receding foreheads and coarse, coal-black hair, slightly wavy like a horse's mane. The men, or bucks, as we called them, wore no beards. The very little hair that grew on their faces, they carefully removed. I often saw them engaged in plucking out hairs from their faces with tweezers and the aid of a small mirror. Some of them even plucked the hair from their eyebrows. The men were generally tall, or looked so because of their erect bearing. Sinewy and slender as a rule, quick and active, they seemed better looking than the women. They wore buckskin leggings and buckskin shirts in winter, fringed and ornamented, moccasins, elaborately beaded, and colored blankets or soft buffalo robes. They wore no head covering, simply a few eagle feathers. Hats or war bonnets were only worn on special occasions. They were fond of wearing large brass rings in their ears, the weight of which pulled the lobes so far down as to be grotesque. Many wore armlets and wristlets of heavy brass wire, wound around many times, and a necklace of bears' claws.

The complexion of the Dakotas ranged all the way from a pale saffron to a deep copper color. When they were decked out in their full paraphernalia, with their faces and upper parts of their bodies painted in various colors, knives and tomahawks thrust into their belts, and bows and quivers slung over their shoulders, they presented a formidable and picturesque appearance.

I saw but a small proportion of very old bucks or squaws among them. Possibly they had a way of getting rid of them when they became old and helpless. Neither were children very numerous, although they practised polygamy. I suppose many of these died in infancy.

Of the many Indian chiefs whom I saw at Fort Pierre, I can only recall the names of two, Struck-by-the-Ree and Smutty-Bear, who were there frequently and in whose tepees I smoked the pipe. Both were well along in years.

Of the squaws but few could be called handsome and it would be flattery to say that many were even good looking. While they were generally lithe and graceful in their youth, laborious work and severe hardships aged them early. They inclined to stoutness more than the males, and many of the elder ones had backs that were bent from carrying heavy burdens.

The squaws planted corn, dug up edible roots, gathered and dried fruit, skinned the game which the men killed, cut up and dried the buffalo meat, tanned the skins, made moccasins and garments, did the cooking, fetched water and carried fire wood or buffalo chips for long distances on their backs. They put up and took down the teepees, loaded the ponies, and did all kinds of other work, frequently with a papoose or two fastened to their backs.

The males did little more than hunt and fish, make bows

and arrows, and carve pipes and stems. The young Indians herded and took care of the ponies and some few horses which had probably been stolen from the settlers. Sometimes they helped the squaws in setting up the large, heavy teepees. This is about all I ever saw them do, save for playing polo with a ball and crooked stick, while mounted on their fleet and active ponies, very much the same as the game is played among the whites to-day.

The squaws' clothing closely resembled that of the bucks. They wore buckskin mocassins, leggings and a skirt, but they were very fond of gay colored calico garments, which they wore in the summer time. The material for these they obtain from traders or soldiers. We often bought calico of the sutler and traded it with the squaws for moccasins or furs. We could always make a better bargain if the calico had glaring colors and fantastic figures. The squaws also wore a blanket or robe, and when they covered up their heads with that, leaving only their broad faces exposed, they looked so much like the young bucks that it was difficult to distinguish the sexes by sight. This was the cause of some ridiculous mistakes by the soldiers.

Observance of ceremonies and duties toward the dead was also the performance of squaws. When an Indian died the squaws sewed up the body in several wraps of buffalo hide together with his personal belongings—his gun, his bow and arrows, his knife, tomahawk, pipe and, in fact, all his minor property. Some ears of corn and other food were always placed inside the shroud to provision him for the journey to the spirit land.

The Dakotas did not bury their dead. They either secured them in the branches of trees or on a rude, strong scaffold made of forked sticks and poles, set atop some hill, where it was plainly visible for miles around. Among the Ponca tribe, however, I saw bodies placed on the ground on top of a knoll with a pediment-shaped structure of split logs over them. They were encased in stones and sods to secure them, but many had fallen into decay and were partly open to the ravages of wolves and other animals.

Sometimes on marches through the country we had a few Indian guides who took some of their squaws with them. Whenever the squaws sighted an Indian burial place they rode towards it, dismounted, and set up a mournful howl. Then they deposited some ears of corn or some pemican at the foot of the tree or scaffold.

On a hill within sight of Fort Pierre, there was a large, high scaffold, on which some dozens of Indians' bodies were lashed with strips of buffalo skins. I visited the place one day with some companions. We found that a recent storm had demolished a part of the old structure, and nearly a dozen of the bodies had fallen to the ground. In many cases the dry, brittle wrappings of skins had been broken open by the fall, exposing the contents to plain view.

It seemed to me most singular that the bodies had not putrified, but appeared to have simply shriveled up in that pure, dry atmosphere. It was as if they had been mumified by nature. There appeared to be no flesh, but a parchment like skin clung to the bones, and the raven black hair adhered to the skull.

The bodies were all fully dressed and had on all their ornaments. I noticed one among them that wore a British officer's red uniform coat with epaulets and gilded buttons. I regret to say that some of the soldiers committed the sacrilege of appropriating some of the articles inclosed with the bodies, such as knives, tomahawks, flints and steel, and made practical use of them.

A group of squaws sometimes visited the fort with cunning looking little papooses' heads peeping out over their shoulders followed by small children who were afraid of the soldiers. They meandered around until they found the huts where the soldiers' wives and families lived. There they would squat on the ground and spend hours watching the white women at their domestic work. By way of diversion they occasionally placed one of their children between their knees, and set to work picking small insects out of the child's hair. They had a very original and effective way of disposing of the captive. They held him between the thumb and finger, placed him between the front teeth and bit him to death.

The squaws wore their black, coarse hair in two long braids. The parting in the center was generally made conspicuous with vermillion paint. The color of their cheeks was heightened by the same material, with perhaps a yellow ring around the eyes. If in mourning, a simple, irregular patch of white paint on the forehead seemed to be all that was needed. They greased their hair liberally with buffalo fat which, when rancid, emitted an unpleasant odor.

It was interesting to watch the arrival of a band of Indians at a military post. This happened often at Fort Pierre except in winter. Sometimes they came with a grievance against white settlers or hunters, or with a complaint against a neighboring tribe who were violating a treaty. But often they visited us simply out of curiosity. They came in large and small parties, sometimes several hundred or more, including squaws and children.

I often watched the long line coming down the hills or across the prairie, the men riding in advance two by two on their unshod ponies. After them came squaws riding straddle and leading pack horses. Next came a line of ponies in single file, with a number of long lodge poles lashed to their sides. One end of the poles dragged on the ground behind, making what is called an Indian trail. On these poles, behind the pony, there was fastened a network on which were piled the teepees, furs, cooking utensils, and other articles used by the Indians. The ponies were led by boys or girls mounted or on foot. Frontiersmen called these conveyances "travoys." Bringing up the rear were a number of large dogs dragging smaller travoys in which children rode. Old squaws or invalids rode as best they could on top of the baggage on the larger travoys.

When a suitable camping place near the post was reached, there was a halt and a closing up of the long column. The bucks had a short parley with the squaws. Then they dismounted and sat down on the grass in groups and commenced smoking their pipes, while the squaws unpacked the ponies, and began to put up the teepees in line and at regular intervals. Some of the larger teepees, with their long poles, were heavy to raise and required the assistance of the younger bucks. When the ponies were all unpacked and unsaddled, they were driven off to water and graze on the prairie. The tired dogs lay down, and went to sleep. The squaws continued at their tasks. Some in search of fire-wood, others went off with kettles for water or were busy within the teepees. When the teepees were ready, the Indians entered them and after a time emerged, if the sun was not too low, dressed—or rather undressed—in full war paint. They were naked from the waist up. Some wore feathered bonnets; others had eagle feathers in their hair. But the faces of all were grotesquely painted in colors that suited their fancy. Some were hideous.

They also painted part of their bodies, particularly the ribs. When this was done alternately in white and black it made them look like living skeletons. They were unarmed, except for a knife or tomahawk carried in their waist belts. A few squaws, their faces also painted, and each with a small drum like a tambourine, joined them.

By this time an interpreter had appeared. They donned their robes or blankets, and without any regular formation, started for the parade ground. In front of the commanding officer's house they came to a halt. The commandant with other officers was ready to receive them. A lot of the soldiers not on duty and citizen employees soon formed a group of spectators. The Indians threw off their robes and blankets and formed a circle. The squaws stationed outside of the circle commenced a monosyllabic chant in a low voice at first, but gradually rising. This was responded to by the bucks in a like manner, while the squaws beat a tom-tom on their drums. Then they began to dance around the circle, slowly at first, with heads and bodies thrust forward, backs curved, feet moving stiffly up and down, elbows against the sides, forearms extended straight forward and fists doubled. In this way the dance went on for five or ten minutes, increasing in speed until it ended in a furious beating of the drums and an ear piercing yell or war-whoop.

After this interesting ceremony had been repeated once or twice, the Indians advanced in a body towards the officers, headed by their chief, who commenced a "talk," which was interpreted to the commanding officer, and was frequently assented to by a grunt from the other Indians. When the chief had concluded, his place would be taken by another, a real orator perhaps, whose language was fluent and gestures dramatic.

The complaints of the Indians were often about settlers encroaching on their lands, or about a party of white hunters who had caused the buffaloes to migrate to other parts. If they had no particular grievance, they would tell that they were good Indians and loved the whites, especially the soldiers. Then they would ask for food. When the Indians had finished the commanding officer's reply was interpreted to them, and received with grunts of satisfaction or dissent. Sometimes another talk was held on the following day, but they all ended by an order on the commissary for several days' rations for every member of the party. Sometimes the Indians prolonged their stay and induced the commanding officer to grant them a second issue of rations. By the time they reached the commissary store house, a number of the squaws were on hand ready to receive the rations which consisted of bacon, flour or hard bread (biscuits) in barrels, rice, beans, ground coffee and sugar. No salt, pepper, vinegar, candles or soap was issued to them. They had no use or desire for these—particularly the soap.

To watch the distribution of the rations, which were given to them in bulk and in the original packages so far as possible, was very amusing. At first everything received was carried to a clear place some distance from the store house. The barrels were carried as well as the boxes, for the Indians did not understand about rolling them until some of the soldiers showed them how to do it. The squaws, who represented families, spread blankets or robes on the grass into which to receive their share. Some of the Indians opened the barrels and boxes awkwardly with tomahawks and knives and commenced the division under the supervision of the chief, with a lot of jabbering from the squaws. They seemed to get along fairly well with articles that could be counted, such as sides of bacon or biscuits; but coffee, sugar, rice, etc., they divided in small cupfulls for each individual, until the supply was exhausted. The squaws then shouldered the bundles and followed the bucks back to their camp with happy expressions.

I have also seen one of our beef cattle issued to a large party. The Indians would drive the frightened animal near to their camp and kill him by shooting. Then the squaws skinned him and cut him up, utilizing many parts of the carcass that a white man would throw away.

On the night when rations had been issued there was a feast in camp. They gorged themselves, beat their drums, and sang long after we soldiers had to retire after tattoo.

I distinctly remember my first visit to the Indian camp at Fort Pierre, accompanied by some other soldiers. There were about two dozen lodges. Half of them were visitors. The others remained there permanently, and lived on what they got from the soldiers and fur company employees. The latter were a rather lazy lot and did but little hunting, so long as they could get enough to eat around the fort. The first salute we received was from a pack of wolfish-looking dogs of all sizes which barked furiously but did not attempt to bite and were easily shooed away.

We walked all through the camp and noted that there were large, fine-looking teepees, decorated with Indian paintings of animals, etc., on the exterior. These had an air of opulence about them that seemed to indicate the owner to be the possessor of many squaws and ponies. There were also many more teepees that were less pretentious and a few small, old and tattered ones that showed the poverty of the owner. It was much like other villages the world over. The palace and the hovel were in close proximity. Back of the teepees squaws were cooking something in kettles hung on a pole, supported over the fire by two forked sticks. They always cooked outside until the weather got cold. Some children played and ran around just as white children do.

The teepees were of tanned buffalo hides, closely sewed together with a strong thread made from the sinews of the same animal. They were conical in shape and were upheld by a number of long, slender but very strong poles, placed in a circle on the bottom at regular intervals and meeting on top where they were interlocked. There was an opening above for the smoke to escape. The entrance was through a slit on the side, high enough for a man to pass through nearly upright and spread apart on the bottom to make the passage easier. Over this opening a piece of tanned hide was usually hung to keep out the weather. These teepees could be kept warm and comfortable in the coldest of weather, and were far more durable than the best canvas tents.

We entered one of the best lodges without the formality of knocking against the side of the opening and saying "How-kota," as we had not yet learned Indian etiquette. The interior appeared dark at first after the bright sunlight; but we distinguished the inmates to consist of several Indians, some squaws and a few children. They all squatted onto robes spread around the sides of the lodge, which formed their bedding. We were apparently received in a friendly manner, and by words and signs were invited to sit down among them. We squatted like our hosts with our legs crossed. The Indians did not appear to have been doing anything but conversing. Some of the squaws, however, were sewing beads on mossacins.

The smaller children shrunk back and stared at us. Presently one of the bucks produced a long wooden stemmed pipe of polished red stone, which he filled with kinnikinic, the Indians' substitute for tobacco, from a buckskin pouch and lit the pipe with a piece of punk ignited from a flint and steel. He took five or six whiffs of the pipe very deliberately, and swallowed all the smoke. Then he handed the pipe to a soldier on his left. As he did this he began to exhale all the smoke he had in him slowly through his nostrils. The soldier imitated the Indian in taking a half a dozen whiffs, but he did not swallow the smoke. In this way the "Pipe of Peace" passed around the circle from Indian to soldier, and soldier to Indian, myself included. We understood enough not to offend against the Indian custom of passing the pipe from mouth to mouth by wiping the mouth piece. After the smoke there was an attempt at talk of which neither party understood anything. The young squaws watched us closely and giggled occasionally. I tried to make one of them understand that I wanted a pair of moccasins. She brought out a bundle of them, and showed me some handsome ones. But we failed to make a bargain. I had to make a few visits with an experienced person before I learned to trade with them.

The kinnikinic that the Indians smoked was the bark of a red willow that grew along the streams. They first removed the outside red bark, then carefully scraped off the greenish second bark with a knife without cutting into the wood. These shavings were dried in the sun or before a fire. When crisp they were rubbed into small particles between the hands. The Indians were fond of mixing a little tobacco, cut up small, with the bark, but I never saw them smoke pure tobacco, as they could not inhale its smoke. The bark of the red willow, when mixed with tobacco, made an agreeable, fragrant smoke. The soldiers often used it.

Before we left the teepee we gave the Indians a generous piece of plug tobacco which seemed to please them very much and caused them to say, "Was-te-da," which means "good."

We entered several other lodges on this, our first visit, and had more smokes. But I learned later that the smoking ceremony only took place on the first visit, and not on subsequent calls, unless we brought with us a stranger who had not visited the lodge before. We were received in a friendly way in most of the lodges, yet once in a while we heard an ominous growl from within and thought it best to keep out.

While many of the older Indians were very austere and dignified in their intercourse with soldiers, the younger ones were inclined to be droll, particularly the younger squaws, with whom, on account of my youth I suppose, I seemed to become a welcome visitor. I went to the Indian camp almost daily, sometimes with a companion but more often without one.

Many of the soldiers became as much interested in the Indians as I was. We began to imitate them. We wore moccasins when not on duty. We sometimes built a council fire back of our quarters, around which we squatted after dark wrapped in blankets like Indians. We smoked the "pipe of peace," and we had "talks." There were some good mimics among us, who could deliver a speech to the rest of the "warriors," which neither the orator nor anyone else understood. We painted our faces and imitated war dances with their accompanying drum beats and chant, not forgetting to yell furiously at the end. We called each other by the most ridiculous "Indian" names. Mine was, "Why-a-so," but that was a real name given to me by some of the young Indians and squaws. It meant "musician."

We got up imitation war parties and scalped our helpless prisoners or burned them at the stake. In fact, we were like a lot of boys, and got plenty of fun out of it while the novelty lasted.

I soon became interested in the Dakota language and tried to learn all I could. I got a memorandum book and pencil. When in a teepee I asked the names of various objects to which I pointed. When these were given to me, I wrote them in my book in phonetic spelling. When I read them off to the Indians on my next visit they were much interested and laughed when I mispronounced a word. In this way I picked up quite a vocabulary, but when it came to pronouns, adjectives and verbs, my progress was slow. This was partly due to the various meanings of the same word. Numbers were easy for the Dakotas could not count above ten. After that it was so many tens and units. They generally kept a tally for any considerable number that was to be remembered by making notches on a stick. I never attained any considerable proficiency in the language, but I learned enough to ask simple questions and make my wants known. I could understand the meaning of much of what they said after I became a little familiar with the many signs used when talking. Some of the Indians evinced a desire to learn English and easily acquired some nouns. But beyond that they could only imitate sounds without understanding their meanings. This was taken advantage of by some wags among the soldiers, who taught them to utter the most ridiculous phrases. This never failed to provoke a laugh, which seemed to please the Indians.

About the first thing I remarked in the Dakota language, was that the vowels a, e, i, o, and u, had the long Italian sound in pronunciation, and that the greater part of the words, whether nouns, pronouns, verbs, or adjectives, ended in a vowel, which was always accented, and of which the following are examples:

Buffalo	Ta-tai-ka
Horse	Shun-ka-ka
Dog	Shun-ka
Blanket	Shin-na-hota
Water	Mi-ni
Whiskey	Mi-ni-wa-ka
Silver Money	Kash-pa-pi
Bread or Crackers	Ak-yu-a-pe
Woman	Wee-a
Plenty	O-ta
Missouri River	Mi-ni-tan-ka
Mississippi River	Mi-ni-so-ta
I, thou, he	Mi-a, Ni-a, Ee-a
Ride	Ga-ki-a
Far	Te-ha
Large	Tan-ka

Many signs were used by the Indians in their conversation, as for instance, the phrase "Mi-a, ga-ki-a, te-ha, shun-ka-ka," meaning "I am going to ride far," had to be accompanied by the sign of straddling the first finger of the left hand with the first two fingers of the right, to indicate riding on horseback. Each tribe also had a sign by which the members could make themselves known. That of the Dakotas was the drawing of the open right hand across the throat from left to right.

Another peculiarity of the language was the total absence of the consonant "R." I cannot recall a single word that had any sound resembling that letter in it.

Early in November ice began to form on the edge of the river in places where the current was not strong. The nights were cold, and we found our blankets insufficient for comfort. Buffalo robes and other furs were still fairly plentiful, and could be had from traders or Indians at a very moderate price. Many of the soldiers bought them to keep warm. I got a fine large one in trade for about three dollars, also a deer skin for two dollars. Old and worn robes could be had much cheaper.

The Indians who lived near the fort permanently soon learned the value of money and how to spend it at the sutler's store. They liked the bright silver dollars, for one of which the squaws would sell us a pair of nice moccasins ornamented with beads. A plainer pair could be had for half a dollar.

The army at the present time is very wisely supplied with clothing suitable to the climate the soldiers are serving in. In my time, however, the kind and quantity of clothing was the same, whether you were stationed in Florida or Nebraska. Any additional clothing we needed in that cold climate we were obliged to provide and pay for ourselves.

By the latter part of November, the Missouri river was entirely frozen over with ice thick enough for wagons to cross. We had snow, but no great quantity as yet. The thin walls of our pasteboard houses were covered on the inside with a hoar-frost, which stayed there and grew thicker. We dug deep trenches around the houses and banked up the earth against them to make the floors warmer. One day we had a furious wind storm, accompanied by drifting snow. The roofs of some of the more exposed houses were carried off and the sides blown in, fortunately without serious damage to the inmates. Other houses were only saved by the passing of ropes over the roofs and putting braces against the sides. This was the beginning of a period of suffering, which lasted until the following spring and was the worst we had in the Dakota country. After the storm it was realized that the frail houses, the scarcity of fire wood and the bleak location, made Fort Pierre an unsuitable place to winter troops. Therefore, one company was ordered to a well wooded island below the fort, while three companies, of which mine was one, were sent to build log huts in the woods on the opposite side of the river, about five miles above and within a mile of where the companies of the Sixth Infantry and the two cavalry companies were located. Two other companies, the headquarters and the band, remained at Fort Pierre. They improved the houses they occupied with the debris from the houses that the storm had destroyed. We put up tents near the river bank. A place about a half mile back on higher ground was selected for the cantonment, where it was not likely to be overflowed by the rise of the river in the spring. We cleared it of underbrush and cut down the trees, mostly cottonwoods. There we commenced to erect log huts.

We had been furnished with a lot of axes, large saws, crow bars, picks and shovels by the quartermaster's department. Every man not required for any other duty was put to work on the huts. We worked with a will, for we suffered severely from the constantly increasing cold in our tents, which we could not heat. They were not "Sibley" tents, and we had no iron stoves. The ground was frozen hard and the snow was deep. Evenings, when our work was done and if the wind was not too strong, we built large fires in the company streets in front of the tents. Before these we warmed ourselves before turning in for the night. Soon nearly every man's blue trousers were scorched brown on the backs from standing too close to the fires. Our clothing was insufficient. We had to wear two shirts at one time and two pairs of trousers and stockings.

Although I was not required to work on the log huts, I did so voluntarily to keep from freezing. I could not stay in the tent without being covered up with my bedding, and I did not wish to stand or sit around a fire all day, to be scorched on one side and frozen on the other, while my eyes smarted with the smoke.

We built two log cabins for each company in the roughest way, leaving the bark on the logs, notching them at the angles, and roughly cutting off the projections at the corners. We sawed out an opening for one door and one window, and built a wide fire place at one end opposite the end that was pierced by the single window. We had great difficulty finding stone enough to build the fire places, which were about six feet high and had wooden chimneys plastered with mud. These chimneys gave us much trouble by constantly getting on fire.

The roofs we formed of split logs, laid with the split side down on a pitch, and reaching from one wall to the other in a single span. On this we put a thick layer of brush and shrub, covered with about twelve inches of earth pounded down hard. The cracks between the logs were chinked with wood and daubed with mud. We had to build fires to take the frost out of the ground before we could dig for our mud. When we mixed it with warm water to the proper consistency for daubing, it froze so quickly that we could not make the walls and roof tight enough to keep the cold wind out.

The huts had a dirt floor. We constructed rude two-story bunks of split logs along both sides, with a passage only six feet between them. There was a little more space around the fire place. There was no lumber of any kind for doors and no sashes for windows, so we hung a piece of an old canvas wagon cover over the door-holes, both inside and out. The window opening we covered with a piece of white muslin bought at the sutler's store. We built smaller single-room huts for the officers and the married soldiers whose wives had been left at Fort Pierre until the huts were ready for them. We also built a kitchen for each company, with a bread oven in it, some store houses, a small hospital and a guard house. We did not build any messrooms. Each soldier had to go to the kitchen for his rations and eat them in his quarters.

I think it was about the middle of December, when we broke up our camp at the river and moved into the log huts at "Cantonment Miller," as it was officially named. The change was for the better, but the huts proved to be very uncomfortable. The stationary bunks took up so much of the room that we were uncomfortably crowded and the place was dark. When we started a fire the ground began to thaw out for some distance in front of the fireplace and turn to soft mud, but the earth remained frozen hard at the other end of the room. The fire had little effect on the cold air of the room in severe weather, except in its immediate vicinity. We burned green cottonwood, a very poor material for heating. While the logs burned on one end the sap ran out at the other. We got some ash and a little cedar wood, which was better, although we had to go long distances for it. Details of men went out and dragged in on home-made sleds the better kind of wood needed for cooking and baking. Cottonwood was plentiful all around us.

In January and February the thermometer sometimes dropped to forty degree below zero, but when we made an unusually large fire the chimney caught fire. We had to keep pails of water ready to extinguish the blaze. On very cold nights the men took hourly turns to keep up the fire and to watch the chimney. The snow was deep and drifted through the chinks of our log huts. We often found large patches of snow covering our bedding in the morning.

At supper-time every evening we got a loaf of bread which the company baker had made that day. We put it into our haversacks, which were hung against the wall of the hut. The next morning it was frozen as hard as stone. We had to knock off chunks with an axe and thaw them at the fire before we could bite into them. Some of the men took their haversacks to bed with them to keep their bread from freezing.

Three soldiers at Fort Pierre attempted to desert to the settlements. They perished before they had gone a hundred miles, and their skeletons were found the following summer by a scouting party.

We hauled our water from the Missouri half a mile away. The ice was more than three feet thick and the hole we had cut through it to get at the water froze over every night and had to be re-opened in the morning.

By this time we had accumulated plenty of furs. My bunkie, Sergeant McMillan, and I possessed three buffalo robes, two deer skins and some wolf skins. With these and four blankets, we had a warm bed on the coldest nights. I had the company tailor make a sort of a cloak for me from a buffalo skin, beaver skin mittens and a cap with ear-laps. A squaw made a pair of buffalo skin boots for me with the hair inside and large enough to wear over my shoes. Most of the soldiers made their own fur clothing, such as caps, mittens, coats and boots, and produced some curious looking objects. One of them made for himself a complete outfit of boots, pantaloons, jacket and cap of buffalo skin with the hair outside. He presented a weird picture when dressed in them and was given the name of "Standing Buffalo."

We were permitted to wear anything we pleased on or off duty, except at inspection or muster. These, however, took place in the company quarters during the severest cold. To expose ourselves, even for ten minutes on parade out of doors, without furs, would have resulted in frost-bitten ears and noses. The officers clothed themselves about the same as the soldiers. There was a herd of beef cattle on our side of the river and when the snow became too deep for them to find any more prairie grass, and as there was neither forage nor hay for them, they were driven into the woods to feed on the bark of young trees. They began to die off rapidly from starvation and exposure after the change.

The French-Canadian chief cattle-herder, who reported to the commissary officer each day, would say in his peculiar English, "M'sieu! One catt ees died! Two catt ees died!" as the case might be. The carcasses were left where they died, and were quickly devoured by the wolves. The wolves often came around our quarters at night, attracted by the offal from the kitchens. They howled hideously. We caught one occasionally by an ingenious trap. After many of the cattle died, the remainder were slaughtered. The meat was allowed to freeze and was piled up in the store houses. There was scarcely any trace of fat remaining. It was not nutritious. When boiled it showed greenish-yellow streaks running through it that made it repulsive. I could not eat any of it. When I needed a change from pork or bacon, I got some pemican from the Indians. Pemican is buffalo meat cut in thin slices, without any fat, and dried in the sun without salting. It was nutritious, but hard to chew. It could be pounded into a kind of meal, and when mixed with pork-fat and fried in a pan, it was an acceptable dish. This and a piece of game, when I could get it, made an agreeable change in diet.

The cavalry companies lost more than one-third of their horses during the long, severe winter. The shelter for the horses was built of brushwood and there was no forage. The men removed the snow where long dry grass was to be found, and stripped the bark from young trees to feed the horses. Some of the horses lost their ears or tails from frostbites. The mules stood the hardship better than the horses. Mortality was not so great among them, but they also lost some ears and tails.

About mid-winter, scurvy made its appearance. We had been fed on a salt meat diet for nearly eight months and, with the exception of a few wild fruits, had had no vegetables. Those who were attacked became pale and listless. After awhile their gums began to bleed and their teeth loosened. Their joints swelled and the flesh became soft. If a finger was pressed hard into the fleshy part of the arm, it left a dent that remained for hours. We did not suffer so much from scurvy at Cantonment Miller as did the soldiers at Fort Pierre. The few serious cases we had we sent to the hospital there. Little could be done for them, except to give them lime-juice, which was among the medical stores. With great trouble some potatoes were obtained during the winter from the "States," as we called it. These were given to the sick, raw, scraped fine and mixed with vinegar and improved their condition very much. However, a few men died of the diesase in the hospital at Fort Pierre. In the early spring, when the snow melted, we dug up roots that grew in the woods, a few inches below the ground as we saw the squaws do. The roots resembled a thin sweet potato in shape and were white in color. They could be eaten raw or boiled and were quite mealy and palatable. Not knowing the proper name for these roots we called them artichokes. The sick improved rapidly upon eating them, and as spring progressed, they all recovered.

An Indian camp of about twenty lodges, belonging to the Yonktonna tribe of the Dakotas, had located within easy distance of Cantonment Miller and remained there until the following spring. We soon had a well beaten path through the deep snow leading to the camp. There I had the best opportunity during my entire service to observe the Indians closely in their domestic relations. I became known to some of them myself and made progress in the study of their language. For a period of more than five months, I went to the camp very often in the day time and sometimes in the evening. I often remained for hours in one or two of some half a dozen lodges which I had selected as my favorites, after having made the round of the entire camp. The lodges had fires in them and were warmer and more comfortable than our huts and never ceased to interest me. The Indians seemed to have plenty to eat and lived quite comfortably. They had stores of pemican, corn, roots, dried fruits and buffalo tallow, which had been melted and put into bladders for preservation. They also had some game when the bucks went hunting.

I was invited to eat with them and did so a few times when they had cooked meat of some sort; but I excused myself when I saw any mysterious dish. I brought them some coffee and sugar once in a while and showed the squaws how to make coffee, of which they became very fond. When any of them visited the cantonment, which happened almost daily, I often gave those that I knew, part of my ration of bread for the papooses, or a piece of tobacco for the bucks. This, in a measure, repaid their hospitality. A singular thing which I noticed was that many of their children, from about three to five years of age, had abnormally developed paunches, which made them look ridiculous when they toddled almost naked about the teepee.

When the children attained their fifth or sixth year they became slender and graceful. I was told that an almost constant meat diet was supposed to be the cause of their curious development.

One day I saw a little toddler step into his father's dish of food. The man, without a word of scolding, took off the child's moccasin, scraped it clean with his horn spoon, then dug a hole in the dirt floor beside his dish, buried and covered up the scrapings and continued his meal, undisturbed by the incident.

Both parents showed affection for their children, and in my presence, at least, I never saw the Indians act with brutality toward their squaws or children. The children had dolls and played much as white children do. The older boys often practised shooting at a mark with a bow and arrow. They were very shy with the soldiers and so were the wolfish looking dogs. It was almost impossible to win the confidence of either. Nevertheless, a soldier of company I got the consent of the parents to take an Indian boy to our quarters and keep him there. He made a suit of soldier's clothes for him and slept with him all the winter. "Paddy," as we called him, became quite a pet in the company and was learning English with a comical Irish accent, acquired from his tutor, when his mother came and took him away in the spring. At the same time the rest of the Indians went away, and we never saw or heard of him again.

The Indians played games among themselves, and the soldiers tried to teach them the use of cards, but they were unable to learn or understand the simplest of such games. We, therefore, invented a special game for them, in which the greatest number of spots on a card took the trick, for they could count up to ten at least. They admired the Jacks more than the Kings. They were the big chiefs and the Kings next. Any card could beat the Queen, which was the "Wee-a" or squaw. They took great interest in this game. I could do a few simple tricks with cards, which mystified and amused them. Some of them had a considerable sense of humor and often laughed heartily.

I was shown some Indian scalps, which had long black hair dangling from them. The skin was soft, and looked and felt as though it had been tanned. To me it seemed very thick. I do not know if they had any white scalps. If so, they never showed us any.

Sometimes one of the Indians produced a buckskin bag ornamented with beads, wherein he kept his most cherished treasures, and drew therefrom a written paper, which some white trader or hunter had given to him. This he would proudly hand to us for examination. These papers were very much of the same tone as this model: "O-kee-ha (red heart) is a good and trustworthy Indian, and I recommend him to anyone who wants a safe guide and a good hunter." One of the Indians had several such papers, one of which he would always show last. This had evidently been written by some wag or, perhaps, a truthful man, and ran something like this: "Beware of this Indian, Big Crow, he is a thief and a liar, and will murder you if he gets a chance. Take warning!" As this paper never failed to provoke a laugh, he no doubt set a greater value on it than on all the others he owned.

When the weather was bad I sometimes watched the bucks making arrows and pipes, while the squaws were industriously employed on moccasins or some article of clothing. The making of arrows was quite a delicate operation, with the few tools they had. The stem of the arrow had to be true, straight and balanced properly. The feathers must be carefully glued on and the head firmly affixed with sinew, thread and gum. Metal arrow heads were made by laboriously grinding pieces of hoopiron, or the like, which they had picked up somewhere, to the required size and shape. Other heads were made of chipped flint. War arrow heads were made with sharp barbs to prevent them from being easily extracted.

Some of the pipes they manufactured were plain, and others handsomely inlaid with lead. They were made of a dense, fine grained but soft working stone of a beautiful red color. To obtain this stone they made long and weary journeys to the Pipe Mountain, which was somewhere in the northern part of Minnesota Territory. There, it is said, they prayed to the Great Spirit before removing any of the stone which they esteemed so highly. The pipes were carefully bored and finished with a high polish, which took many hours of patient labor. The long pipe stems were made of some tough, flexible wood, the same that they made their bows of. They were round or flat in shape, sometimes twisted, and the wood polished and ornamented. The hole through the stem was made slowly and carefully with a piece of wire heated red hot. The mouth piece was neatly tapered and rounded. These pipes were a valuable article of trade. A fine pipe was worth a pony in trade with the Indians in remote parts of the country. I bought one and paid a good price for it. I had great difficulty to persuade an Indian to sell me a piece of the stone to make a pipe for myself.

I have at times witnessed the entire performance of an Indian feast. A squaw selected a fat-looking dog, and tied him fast in some secluded place for several days, giving him nothing to eat, and only water to drink. She then fed him with a mixture of pemican and dried fruits made into a moist soft paste, and let him eat all he could of it. This, I suppose, was to serve as a stuffing or forcemeat, for she killed him by knocking him on the head with a tomahawk, before digestion commenced. His hind legs were then tied together, and he was hung by a cord head down from a pole supported on two forked sticks over a low fire. With a firebrand the squaw burnt off every hair on his body close to the skin, and rubbed him with buffalo fat. The squaw would sit for many hours turning and basting the carcass with melted fat. The dog was thus roasted whole, for he had not been disemboweled. In the evening the family were joined by relatives and friends whom they had invited. The teepee was well crowded when the feast commenced. The dog was cut up, and all gorged themselves to their full capacity. The most desired morsels seemed to be the bowels and other soft parts. When the eating was over, the squaws beat the drums, chanted songs, and all made merry until long after we soldiers were in bed. I looked in at some of these feasts and was invited to partake. Although it was considered an honor, I declined. A few of the soldiers did eat some roasted dog, and declared it tasted good. The Indians preferred it to the finest venison.

There was a young soldier in my company, who became so infatuated with the Indian life that he spent every spare minute in their camp. He made great progress in learning their language, and never missed a dog feast. He was a black haired, dark-complexioned man, who tried to make himself look as much like an Indian as possible by plucking out all the hair that grew on his face. In the spring, when the Indians broke camp and departed, he was missed a day or two later. We learned that he had joined the tribe, but no effort was then made to recapture him.

During the long, cold winter we got a mail from the "States" about once in three weeks. It went to Fort Pierre and was sent to us from there.

There was no sutler at Cantonment Miller. When we

wanted anything from the store, we had to go five miles to Fort Pierre for it or have it brought by a comrade who made the trip.

One calm sunny morning—we had a few such days—when the thermometer was but a few degrees below zero, another boy and I got a pass to go to the fort. Not anticipating any change in the weather, we did not dress ourselves quite so warmly as we should have done, for zero was considered a comfortable temperature if the wind was not blowing, and we discarded some of our heaviest furs when the temperature was at that point or higher. We two boys crossed the Missouri on the ice and walked down to the fort on the opposite side, which was less hilly than the east bank. We made a few purchases at the sutler's store, visited our friends and had dinner with them. It became much colder early in the afternoon, and the wind began to blow. We were admonished to return early, which we did; but by the time we had come about half way the wind was blowing a gale and the cold was increasing. We tried to cross the river and gain the woods on the other side, but the bare ice was as slippery as glass. The fierce wind knocked us over, and blew us like corks along on the ice. With great exertion we crawled on shore and got into a ravine where we were partly sheltered from the wind. Here we kept in motion. There was no wood to make a fire and to sit down meant freezing to death. We had our mittens and our fur caps protected our ears, but our noses and cheeks turned white with frost, and we rubbed them with snow several times. I think we both feared that we would perish in that ravine, when suddenly, as daylight began to fade, the wind died down and we were able to proceed. We arrived at our quarters half frozen, and it took some days to recover.

There was an officer at Cantonment Miller named James Curtis who was the First Lieutenant of Company B. He singled me out from among the boys and was most kind to me.

While stationed at Fort Pierre I had bought a flute from a member of the band, and took lessons from him. As I understood something about music and played on the fife, I made rapid progress on the flute and had become a fair player when Lieutenant Curtis asked me to come to his lonely cabin and play duets with him. He was an excellent player, and had a lot of music books, also works on history, science, etc. In fact, he owned quite a little library, for he was a great student and did not spend his time drinking whiskey and playing cards like some of the other officers did. He loaned me books to read and gave me lessons to study, which I recited to him and he corrected my exercises. After these lessons we played music until tattoo. This went on for there or four nights a week, while we were at the cantonment. I learned more during that time than during all my previous schooling.

Lieutenant Curtis was a graduate of West Point. Very much to my regret he resigned his commission in the spring to enter civil life. He rejoined the army in 1861, and served in the West during the Civil War. I never met him again, and do not know whether he is still living, but I remember him as a man who befriended me when I was a boy, and I shall always entertain the most profound feeling of gratitude toward him.

A contrast to Lieut. Curtis was the officer who commanded the company which wintered on the island below Fort Pierre. He was always more or less under the influence of liquor and abused the men in his command. In one of his drunken fits he shot a private of his company, wounding him so severely the man died a few days after. A pretense of an investigation was made. It was called an accident and hushed up, though the man was deliberately shot while lying in his tent after he had had some words with the officer. Two years later his slayer died wretchedly of delirium tremens at another military post.

In the early part of April we were startled one night by loud reports like the firing of a heavy cannon. This was caused by the cracking of the thick ice, which began to break up and move in a day or two and afforded an interesting spectacle. Some time later the river began to rise until it overflowed its banks, and was miles wide in the low lands. Then there came drift wood in enormous quantities. For several days at a time the river would be covered with it from shore to shore at the narrower places. It seemed as though a man could walk across on the floating logs. The high water continued for a long time. It fell very slowly and some time in May it seemed stationary for a while as the snows melted much further north. We were cut off from all communication with Fort Pierre for a time, until boats could cross the river after the flood subsided.

The Indians began to make preparations for departure. The squaws were busy dressing such skins as they had not tanned before cold weather. This they did by stretching them on an upright framework made of poles lashed together. Then they scraped them thin with a steel scraper and treated them wtih a preparation that made them soft and pliable.

About the first week in May, when their ponies had attained a fair condition, they struck their tents one day and disappeared over the hills.

We received orders to abandon Cantonment Miller and return to Fort Pierre, where all of General Harney's troops were to be assembled for a great treaty that was soon to be made there with the Indians. We crossed the river in a Mackinaw boat belonging to the American Fur Company. These were large, flat-bottomed boats with tapering prows and square sterns. They were used by the company to carry furs from its more northern posts on the Missouri and Yellowstone rivers.

We went into camp after we crossed the river as it was too late to march to Fort Pierre that day, and had just finished putting up our tents, when a tremendous wind storm struck us. It blew down the tents and scattered them as well as every other movable article over the prairie. It was all over in a short time, but we slept without tents that night. Next day after picking up all of the articles we could find, and loading them on wagons, we marched to Fort Pierre and went into permanent camp close to the stockade. Within a few days all of the troops had assembled, and encamped there.

In March General Harney had sent messages to all the tribes

of the Dakotas, to assemble at Fort Pierre on May twentieth for a council treaty.

The Indians had some way of noting the date, probably by tally on a stick of wood. I think that representatives from all the Dakotas were present on that day, except the Brules and the Ogallalas, who had been so severely punished the previous September.

The Indians began to arrive about ten days before the appointed time, and soon the great plain about Fort Pierre was dotted with nearly a thousand teepees.

Each of the tribes had a large representation of men, women and some children. It was estimated that seven thousand were present, of whom one-third were warriors. It was a grand spectacle, such an assemblage of Indians had not been seen for many years. Among them were proud and magnificent savages who had traveled long distances to be present.

As soon as the arriving Indians became numerous, we were forbidden to visit their camp. Neither were the Indians allowed within the sentinel lines of ours. At night the sentry posts were doubled and extra ammunition was issued. We practically slept on our arms while the council lasted, for their warriors outnumbered us at least three to one. Our garrison and camp were open to an attack from all sides, and the temper of so great a body of Indians was very uncertain.

On the appointed day the council commenced. At first only a few hundred of the chiefs and other head men of the tribes were present. The council was held outside of the stockade, the Indians sitting on the grass in a semi-circle facing the General. With the commandant were some other officers, clerks and interpreters, a few orderlies and a small guard of soldiers. These were all on a slightly raised platform, the officers being seated in front. The dignified, white-haired general was in the center and his imposing figure towered above all the others.

We could only view the council from a distance, as sentinels kept us beyond a certain boundary. But we could observe the dramatic gestures of the Indian orators and hear the grunts of approval. What the great talk was all about we did not know.

The council went on in this way for three to four days. On the fourth or fifth day the meeting commenced earlier, and nearly all the warriors, to the number of several thousand, were present. They were painted, and their lustrous dark skins glistened in the bright sunlight when they had cast off their robes and blankets. It was a sight long to be remembered, and the like of it was probably never seen in after years. On this day a treaty of peace was concluded. The Indians buried the hatchet, as it was customary to say. The Sioux War was over, and during our stay in their country we had no more serious trouble with them. It was only after the withdrawal of the regular soldiers to take part in the Civil War that they became unruly again, and committed atrocities among the settlers of Minnesota in 1862.

On the night of the day when the treaty had been concluded there seemed to be a great "pow-wow" in the Indian camp. We could hear the tom-toms, and the voices of the bucks and squaws until early morning. On the following afternoon we were treated to a remarkable sight. Two thousand Indians marched to the stockade, where General Harney had his headquarters, and saluted his appearance by blowing on reed musical instruments made from willows which grew abundantly along the river. At the same time a large number of squaws beat on drums. The curious noise could be heard for miles around.

While the council was on, the first steamboat of the season or "wa-ta-pe-ta-choo-choo," as the Indians called it, arrived. It was the *Genoa,* which had brought my company up the river the previous summer. With her arrived a paymaster and Lieutenant Gouverneur K. Warren, who later commanded the Fifth Army Corps in the Civil War. He was to make surveys in the Dakota country and was accompanied by some scientists. My regiment furnished him with an escort, who traveled with him until fall. He returned the following season and continued his surveys.

Many of the Indians present had never seen a steamboat. Hundreds of them and their squaws lined the river bank, when the *Genoa* was sighted. They noted the puffs of steam ejected by her engines, and declared that the wa-ta-pe-ta was puffing, out of breath, and tired out after her long journey.

The Indians had brought great quantities of furs with them, and trading with the American Fur Company and the sutler was brisk. The *Genoa* on her return trip could carry only a part of the vast quantity of furs the company had accumulated. Some of the Indians departed a few days after the treaty was made. Others lingered for a while, but in about two weeks nearly all had disappeared. When their numbers had materially diminished, restrictions against visiting their camps were withdrawn, and I had interesting experiences in observing the customs and manners of some far away tribes, whom I was not likely ever to see again.

About the first of June orders were issued to abandon Fort Pierre, as it was most unsuitable for a military post. The troops who had come from Fort Laramie in the fall returned there, and of my regiment four companies and the band took up their march to a point on the Missouri, a few hundred miles below Fort Pierre, where they built a post called Fort Randall. The other two companies, B and D, marched to a place on the Missouri, midway between Forts Pierre and Randall, to establish Fort Lookout.

The remaining portable houses at Fort Pierre were taken down and with other materials were put on rafts and floated down the river to be re-used in building quarters at the two new posts.

Our experience since we arrived at Fort Pierre had been very trying through the incompetency or carelessness of some one in authority. We were ill prepared for the rigors of so severe a climate as to clothing, food, quarters and medical stores. Men died from exposure and from scurvy, and many animals succumbed to starvation. Officers and soldiers suffered alike. The miserable huts in which we lived during the winter were unfit for stables. We almost froze in them, and when the spring came, the mud roofs leaked like sieves.

I look back upon the winter passed at Fort Pierre as one of great suffering and hardship, by far the worst that I went through during my service.

PART V.

Establishing Fort Lookout, 1856-1857.

COMPANIES B and D left Fort Pierre the first week in June, 1856, on their way to the site upon which Fort Lookout was to be built. Captain Nathaniel Lyon of Company B, being the ranking officer, was in command. Captain Gardner of my company and three lieutenants were the only other officers present. The details of this march, although a short one, will serve, except as to special incidents, as a description of all other marches that we made on the prairies.

We ascended the hills west of Fort Pierre to gain the higher tableland in order to avoid the many ravines and small creeks that flowed into the Missouri river, which we did not sight again until we reached our destination. The order of march for large or small columns of troops was as follows: First came the guides, either Indians, half-breeds or hunters, riding on ponies some distance in advance and sometimes going ahead for miles to search for a suitable point to ford a stream or locate a camp. When no guides were present the desired direction was kept by means of a compass, for there were no roads, nothing but an occasional trail, made by Indian travoys which the weather soon obliterated. At times there was not a hill, tree nor bush in sight. Only flat or rolling prairie land met the eye all day long, and it was easy to lose direction on a cloudy day without a compass. Officers in command of troops marching through an unknown country were obliged to keep a journal and draw rough maps of the route, showing the water courses, springs, hills, woods, camping places and all points worthy of notice, also the approximate distances between them. These journals and maps were afterwards forwarded to the War Department, to serve for future information.

After the guides, our small column was led by Captains Lyon and Gardner and one of the lieutenants, another lieutenant was in the rear of the column, and the acting quartermaster was with the wagon train. All of the officers were mounted, some at their own expense on ponies they had bought from the Indians, as in an infantry regiment the regulations only allowed horses and forage for the colonel, major, surgeon, adjutant and quartermaster, or for officers temporarily acting as such. For a year or more we had no medical officer, only a hospital steward. There was but little sickness, and we got along very well without a doctor. Following the leading officers, came the musicians, and we boys were rather proud to be able to set the pace for the entire column. Behind us marched the soldiers by fours at a route step carrying their arms "at will." The company in advance to-day was the rear company to-morrow. Following the soldiers was the wagon train and behind that marched the camp guard, bringing up the rear. We never carried any knapsacks on this kind of marches on the frontiers. We always had wagons enough to carry the tents, knapsacks, provisions and forage. Each soldier carried his arms and accoutrements, his canteen and his haversack, which contained only enough provisions for a noon-day meal. The musicians carried only a sword, canteen and haversack.

The speed at which we marched was generally about three miles per hour, or less, if the route was hilly or the marching difficult. About every five miles we halted for a rest of fifteen or twenty minutes with a somewhat longer rest in the middle of the day. The distance we marched each day averaged less than twenty miles, but it was irregular, for camping places had to be selected with an eye to obtaining wood and water. Some days we marched only about fifteen miles while on others we had to make more than twenty-five. On a few occasions we camped on the prairie, where there was neither wood nor water. We brought a scant supply with us in our wagons from the previous camp. Buffalo chips (dung) were sometimes used instead of wood and made a sufficiently hot fire to cook with.

The army wagons had canvas covers and looked something like the "Prairie Schooners" used by the emigrants in crossing the plains. There was a seat and a locker across the front and a detachable feed-box across the rear. They were provided with strong brakes. A team of six mules was hitched to each wagon, the pair in front were called "leaders," and were the smallest mules in the team, next came the "swings," a little larger and last the "wheelers," which were the largest and strongest mules of the lot. One of the wheel mules had a saddle on him on which the driver was mounted, who, with only a single line and the aid of a long whip, drove the team.

The drivers were generally citizen employes of the Quartermaster's Department, if they could be had, or soldiers who volunteered for the job. These were detailed on "extra duty," as it was called. Twenty-five cents per day from the quartermaster was added to their regular monthly pay, for which they were obliged to sign a roll. One of them wrote Thomas O'Brien, M. D., and when asked to explain the meaning of the two letters after his name, said they stood for mule driver. It was hard work driving mule teams where there were no roads. Steep hills and deep declivities, streams and water courses, soon made most of the drivers experts in profanity. They had names for all their mules, and we often heard one of them urging his team through a bad place with such words of encouragement as these: "Now, Mary Jane! pull like a good girl; pull, girl!" or "You, there, Pete! you black-hearted ———, I'll cut the hide off you, if you don't pull!"

On marches, reveille was sounded at day-break or even earlier if there was a long day's march ahead. Immediately after roll call we had our breakfast of salt pork or bacon, hard-tack and black coffee, which the company cooks had already prepared at their camp fire. Then the "General" was beaten by one of the drummers. This was the signal to "strike tents" and pack the wagons. Soon after sunrise we formed ranks and marched off. This was the time when we felt fresh after a good night's rest. There was talking, laughing and joking in the ranks. Sometimes a song was started and many joined in the chorus.

After about two hours of marching this exhilaration gradually died down and when the sun got high and began to scorch us—for it could be as hot in the summer on the plains as it was cold in winter—the voices were stilled. We trudged on noiselessly save for the rattling of the tin cups and canteens or the sharp rebuke of one soldier to another, who had perhaps jostled him, which was always annoying to a weary man.

The officers also enjoyed the cool of the morning. After the column had marched a while, I was often called by one of them to ride his horse, while he marched four or five miles. I would very much have preferred this ride at the end of the march when I would have enjoyed the rest. But I was always a good marcher and sometimes, when I felt like falling out, my pride kept me up until we reached camp.

The first day's march revealed the presence of a flat-footed man in the command who could not march more than a few miles, after which he had to ride in one of the wagons. He was discharged as soon as transportation to the settlement could be had. Sick or exhausted soldiers were permitted to ride in the wagons.

So fiercely did the rays of the sun beat down on the hot prarie, that during our brief periods of rest, we often crawled under the wagons, grateful for their slight shade even for a short time. If we came to a stream that could be forded we took off our shoes and stockings and sometimes our trousers, and waded across. If the current was strong we grasped each other to avoid being swept off our feet. On the opposite side we generally halted long enough to refill our canteens and rest.

At times we had to cross a river too deep for fording. Then the crossing meant several days of hard labor. It was accomplished by taking the wagons apart and making boats out of their bodies. This was done by enveloping the wagon bodies in several thicknesses of the canvas wagon covers. When the crude boats would float, some men swam across pulling a stout rope after them. They secured it on the other side to guide the boats in crossing. In this way we established ferries capable of taking all the men and freight to the other side. The horses and mules were forced to swim over. A few minor accidents occurred, but in the main the crossing was successfully although slowly made, as these canvas pontoon boats could carry but little at each trip.

On a few occasions we saw a herd of buffalo while on the march, but never got near them. We seldom met any Indians on the routes we traveled.

When we had a short day's march, we got into camp before noontime if the route had been favorable, but if we had to march twenty-five miles or more, it was the middle of the afternoon or much later before we finally halted. The first thing we did was to stack arms and lie down in the shade, if there was any. Tired out, we went to sleep while waiting for the wagons to come up. At the end of the day's march they were often some miles behind. They could not always make the short cuts that we could. When the wagons arrived we unpacked them and erected our tents. Practice made us experts at this. The cooks started a fire and prepared a meal, while the teamsters parked the wagons, unhitched the tired mules, watered and fed them, and then picketed them on the prairie to graze and rest.

The officers had wall-tents for their use, with a tent fly over them, which made them quite comfortable and cool when the sides were turned up. The soldiers had "Sibley" tents at that time, which were better than the small "A" tents previously used. These tents were the invention of Col. Henry W. Sibley of the United States Army. They were patterned after the Indian teepee, but differed from them in that but one tent pole was required. This fitted into the socket of a wrought iron tripod in the centre of the tent and upheld the shelter. A hood on top could be opened to emit the smoke from a sheet iron stove in cold weather. These tents, conical in shape, were large enough to shelter a dozen men without crowding.

When the tents had all been set up in "streets," we fished or went in bathing if the water was suitable. Fish were generally plentiful and were a welcome addition to our rations. At times we washed our clothing in the streams, for the laundresses did not perform that work on a march and were never with the troops except when changing stations. On these occasions they and their children rode in the wagons.

Our canteens were made of tin covered with felt, and held about three pints. An old soldier taught me to fill my canteen with water in the evening, saturating the felt covering thoroughly. By hanging it up exposed to the air during the night, the water would be kept cool until morning. Next day I was careful to keep the canteen on my shady side while marching. In this way I had a cool drink for a much longer time. Sentinels were posted about the camp and the wagons at night. We had an early tattoo and slept soundly until daybreak next morning. Rainy days added much to our discomfort while marching and made it necessary to make camp on soaked ground while our clothing was drenched.

We had half a dozen dogs with us on the march to Lookout, for dogs love soldiers. In the cool part of the morning they ran all over the prairie chasing birds or prairie dogs, and tired themselves out before the march was half done. When we halted for a rest they went to sleep, and it was difficult to make them go on again, except one wise dog who always trotted at the head of the column with the musicians and never wasted his energy in running around the prairie. At times these dogs became a nuisance. They sometimes got to a small pond or water-hole ahead of us, and by swimming around in it roiled the water until it was unfit to drink.

Our last day's march was long and hard, but we cheered up when in the middle of the hot afternoon we sighted the Missouri River about five miles away. It was hundreds of feet below us, for we were up on a high range of hills, which the wagons were able to descend only by making long detours.

We encamped on a shady spot near the river bank and remained there for two days while Captain Lyon and another officer explored the region for the most suitable place for the new post. Captain Lyon finally selected a spot three miles below our camp and thirty miles south of the Big Bend of the Missouri River. We moved there at once and encamped until our quarters were completed in the fall.

The site for Fort Lookout was well chosen. The river channel was on that side and the banks high enough not to be overflowed. The wooded bottom land extended two hundred yards back from the river, then ascended fifty feet above the water in an easy grade to a plateau. Two small water courses in ravines at right angles to the river and about half-a-mile apart drained the plateau on which the post was to be built. About a mile west of the river the land became rugged and hilly. There were plenty of woods in sight along the river bank as far as we could see.

Captain Nathaniel Lyon of Company B, Second United States Infantry, the commanding officer under whose direction Fort Lookout was to be built, was a native of Connecticut. He was of average size with sandy hair and beard. His voice had a distinct nasal twang. He was a graduate of West Point and had served in the Mexican War and in Florida. He was a strict disciplinarian, conscientious, patriotic and as strong an "Abolitionist" as Captain Gardner of my company was a "Pro-Slavery" advocate. Nevertheless the two captains seemed to get along very well on duty, but outside of that did not associate much. Captain Gardner usually had his tent put up at some distance from Captain Lyon's, who kept very much to himself and seemed to pass his time in reading and writing.

Captain Lyon was of a most peculiar temperament. While he preserved a fatherly attitude toward his company and saw to their comfort, he was very exacting. The least infringement of rules, which other officers would not notice, he would punish. He seldom put any of his men in the guardhouse, except for some serious offense; but punished them by making them do menial duties or by having them march in front of the company quarters where he could observe them, carrying a log or a heavily loaded knapsack or with a barrel over their shoulders, the head sticking out of the top. He had punishments to fit every grade of offense, most of which were of his own invention. However, he seldom court-martialed any of his men, though some of them would have preferred that to the humiliating punishments they received. When the war broke out, Captain Lyon was in command of the arsenal at St. Louis, Mo., which he saved to the Government. He broke up the rebel "Camp Jackson" under General Frost, defeated the troops under Governor Jackson at Booneville and fought the battle of Wilson's Creek, Mo., against superior numbers under Generals McCulloch and Price. He was killed in that battle on August tenth, 1861, while he was in command of the Union troops with the rank of brigadier-general. General Lyon did much to save the State of Missouri to the Union and in his early death, the Government lost a loyal and efficient officer. One of the last requests that General Lyon made just before his death was that "First Sergt. Griffin of his old company which was present at the battle should receive a commission as Lieutenant,"—which was granted.

As soon as our camp was permanently established at the top of the slope leading towards the river, we prepared to erect the necessary buildings. Gangs of men were sent into the woods to cut trees, trim them and haul in the logs.

Others were set to work making bricks for the chimneys

and bake ovens out of some suitable clay and sand that had been discovered near the river bank. The bricks were made in moulds and burnt in the usual way. They answered their purpose very well. Every man not required for guard duty was set to work either as a mechanic or a laborer at "extra duty". Carpenters, framers, masons and all other mechanics received forty cents per day and the laborers twenty-five cents per day, extra pay for ten hours' work. The mechanics remained at their work, but the laborers took turns at guard duties. I was put on extra duty myself for a while as a time-keeper and messenger and was rated and paid as a laborer.

Presently the raft which had been made up at Fort Pierre arrived and was unloaded and taken apart. About the first of July a steamboat came in with a full cargo for Fort Lookout, consisting of military stores and some building materials, such as doors, sashes, hardware, shingles, lime, etc. She also landed three citizen employes, a master-mechanic to take charge of construction and two carpenters. There were in addition some goods for the sutler, who came to establish himself. A cow and some hogs were put ashore consigned to Captain Lyon. To put this cargo in a suitable place on shore and protect it from the elements until store houses could be built, occupied some time. A small herd of beef cattle also arrived, having been driven up from the settlements.

One of the first things the master-mechanic did was to erect a whip-saw for getting out flooring and roofing boards. This saw was worked by two men, one above and the other below the elevated log. It was slow, laborious work. He next made a plan for quarters for three companies, for another company was to join us later in the season. He directed the carpenters and framers to hew the logs square and cut them into suitable lengths to form the walls of the houses, which were built large enough to hold a company apiece comfortably. They had the luxury of doors, windows and brick chimneys, a wooden floor and a shingled roof, but no ceiling. Log houses were built for the married soldiers, for company kitchens, a hospital, a bakery, the adjutant's office, the guard house and storehouses, but they were put up to be warm and comfortable and had brick fire places, doors and windows, wood floors and shingled roofs, the same as the quarters. For the officers the portable houses rafted down from Fort Pierre were re-erected, but made much stronger. The exterior walls were double with a filled space between them, which made them warmer. Chimneys and fireplaces were built. We built no company mess-rooms, leaving that to be done next year as we already had undertaken all we could possibly accomplish before cold weather.

Captain Lyon was quite busy for a time in outlining the post and locating the various buildings. He seemed very anxious about getting the post lined exact and true to the cardinal points, which he found a difficult task in the absence of proper instruments. He had a factotum named Charley Breen who was his valet, cook, hostler and assistant surveyor. When the captain went out on several nights to observe the north star for hours, he always took Charley who carried a lantern. Next day the lines were changed again. We had many a laugh with Charley about hunting for the north star with a lantern.

Captain Lyon laid out Fort Lookout in generous dimensions. Perhaps he had orders to do so. He occupied ground enough for about two regiments, the parade ground was large enough to manoevure a brigade of troops. The plan was a parallelogram in shape except at the west end where the officers' houses formed a semicircle. The east end near the river was square and there were located the guard house and store houses.

On the long sides were the company quarters, two on the south and one on the north side. They looked very lonely in that vast space. It was much more than a quarter mile from the guard house on the east to the officers' quarters in the west, and nearly half that across the parade ground between the company quarters from north to south. These great distances proved to be very inconvenient in winter, when the snow was deep and much time had to be consumed in relieving the widely scattered sentinels.

Uninterrupted progress was made all through the summer. We had no trouble with the Indians, in fact none came near us until fall, when they began to appear and dance for rations. The only soldiers who were absent from the fort were a small escort under a non-commissioned officer with Lieutenant Warren and his party who were surveying and mapping some of the Dakota country. They approached within a few hundred miles of the place where the National Yellowstone Park is now located, but did not seem to have ever heard of that wonderful region. It appeared to be unknown at that time. We never heard hunters or trappers speak of it, and if the Indians knew of it, they kept their knowledge to themselves.

A comet was visible for many weeks during the summer, larger and more brilliant and with a longer tail than any I have seen since. Unfortunately we had no opportunity to learn in what way the Indians regarded this phenomenon.

In the month of August, Company K arrived from Fort Ripley after a strenuous march. They crossed the Missouri at Fort Pierre in Mackinaw boats and from there came down the west bank to Fort Lookout. This company was much harassed by the Chippawa Indians, while marching through their country, though no direct attack was made. One soldier was stabbed to death by an Indian at a spring near one of their camps, where he had gone alone to fill his canteen. A sad accident occurred on this march. One sentinel shot another dead, mistaking him for an Indian because of his wearing a blanket on a cool night while on post.

Company K brought two Indian guides and their squaws with them; also an interpreter and his squaw. This interpreter proved to be the young man from my company who had deserted from Cantonment Miller about sixteen months before to join the Indians. Why he took the risk to come back in our direction I cannot imagine, unless he was misinformed at Fort Pierre in regard to the whereabouts of his old company. He was much changed, but was recognized in spite of his Indian make-up. He was arrested and put in the guard house, which at this time was a tent from which he escaped easily on the second night, and we never heard of him again.

Brevet Major George W. Patten, whom I have previously described, was in command of Company K. He wrote an able article about the march from Fort Ripley, which was published in Harper's Magazine. As Major Patten ranked Captain Lyon, he took command of Fort Lookout on his arrival, but Captain Lyon continued to superintend the building of the post.

During the summer Capt. Lyon got an idea that some other drink besides the Missouri river water would be good for the men, and he started in to make what he intended to be spruce beer. He put us boys to work gathering cactus plants, wild hops, sprigs of spruce and a few other plants of his own selection. Then he made us mash the cactus to a pulp and boil the entire mixture in camp kettles, adding water, some molasses and vinegar. We then strained it and put it into barrels. Under the Captain's supervision it took us a week to make three or four barrels, for, according to his habit, he fussed and spent as much of his time over it as he would have given to an important matter. When this hodge-podge was brewed it was offered to the soldiers. One drink was enough to satisfy most of them. If they took any more they were likely to be unfit for duty next day, but not from any intoxicating qualities of the mixture. When it began to ferment it threw off such a sickening odor and tasted so vile that no one would drink it. Cactus was plentiful in the vicinity. Some of it bore delicious and succulent prickly-pears. Wild plums and grapes were also plentiful.

One night we were startled by the sound of a shot that came from the direction of Post No. 3, a short distance from camp. There were cries of "Corporal of the guard, Post No. 3!" and for a few moments there was great excitement.

It turned out that the sentinel on that post had shot off the little finger of his left hand. He explained that he was carrying his rifle across the back of his neck, with the left hand over the muzzle and the right on the lock "when the durned thing went off."

We suspected that he did it on purpose, hoping to get his discharge from the army for physical disability. If so, he was not liberal enough with his self mutilation, for the sacrifice of his little finger did not procure his discharge.

Near the end of summer another steamboat on the way to Fort Pierre stopped and unloaded some more stores, including a quantity of potatoes, onions and turnips to prevent a reoccurrence of scurvy. This steamer also brought a second lieutenant to join one of our companies. He was one of the appointees from civil life—the only one at the post. He hailed from one of the southern states and, for a soldier, was the most ungainly, awkward and unmilitary figure that I ever saw. He was a young man, so excessively tall that he stooped over and so thin that he barely cast a shadow. He had a glass eye that had a roving disposition. It gave him a very droll appearance. He was quite ignorant of military matters and at his first appearance on parade as officer of the day appeared wearing his sash over the wrong shoulder. Major Patten appointed him Post Adjutant shortly after his arrival, in derision, I think.

At guard mounting he had to be coached by the acting sergeant major, or the officer of the day. When it came to that part of the ceremony where the adjutant turns "About face" and reports to the officer of the day "Sir, the guard is formed!" he nearly fell over himself with his sword scabbard between his legs. He never learned to make an "About face" gracefully. It was very difficult to repress our laughter. With all this, he was arrogant, domineering and conceited, and was thoroughly detested by his company.

When on duty as officer of the day he visited the sentinels on post, demanded their orders and received the customary reply: "To take charge of this post and all Government property in view, to salute all officers according to rank, to allow no one to pass or repass at night without the countersign, in case of fire to give an alarm," etc., etc.

Then he would torment the soldier with such absurd questions as: "What would you do if you saw a steamboat coming down over the hills, or a thousand Indians mounted on buffaloes charging out of the woods?"

One of the sentinels answered him, "I would call for the corporal of the guard to notify you immediately."

Whoever was responsible for his obtaining a commission in the Army had much to answer for. He resigned after a few years and disappeared from our sight and knowledge.

In October we were able to occupy our new quarters which appeared palatial to us in comparison with the wretched hovels in which we lived the previous winter. We had worked hard to accomplish this. About this time a singular affliction came upon nearly one-half of the garrison, which we called moon-blindness. Every evening after twilight they began to lose their vision, and when it became dark they could only distinguish a bright light if very close to them. They had to be led around like blind men. In the morning they could see as well as ever. This lasted about a fortnight, and made it hard for the unafflicted who had to do double guard duty. No one seemed to know the cause of this blindness. Some had an idea that the comet was responsible for it. I was one of the fortunate who escaped this affliction.

Small parties of Indians began to visit us; and about a dozen lodges established themselves in a permanent camp for the winter, but at an inconvenient distance from the fort. It was necessary to cross a deep ravine or make a long detour to get there.

An English sportsman, Sir St. George Gore, stopped for a day to visit the officers. He had been hunting along the upper Missouri and Yellowstone River for two years and was now on his way home. He had come with a crew on a large Mackinaw boat, loaded with furs and other hunting trophies.

Immense quantities of wild ducks and geese were now flying south. We managed to kill quite a number with our military rifles, loaded with shot which we made ourselves by pouring a ladle full of melted lead from an elevated position slowly into a pail of water placed on the ground. This produced shot of various sizes which we assorted, using the smaller shot for blackbirds which were abundant. This homemade shot was all egg-shaped instead of globular. It seemed to be effective enough when fired into large flocks.

As soon as steady frost appeared all of our beef cattle were killed and dressed. Profiting by our sad experience of the last winter this was done while they were still in good condition and the meat placed in a store house for use during the winter. Soon there was a deep fall of snow which remained and increased throughout the winter. A space was kept cleared of snow on the vast parade ground with paths leading to it from the officers' and company quarters, for the purpose of holding the daily guard mounting. Spaces were cleared around the quarters and the snow piled up until the buildings were half hidden. I think the winter was fully as cold as the previous one; but we had an abundant quantity of seasoned firewood, which we burnt in stoves and were comfortably warm, except on days when there was a high wind. When the thermometer fell to twenty degrees below zero, orders were issued to call in all the sentinels, except Post No. 1 in front of the guard house, and No. 2, at the store houses close by, and even these posts were relieved every half hour. Our food was more abundant and much better than at Cantonment Miller the previous winter. There was no re-appearance of scurvy and we had plenty of warm clothing.

Captain Lyon, who had imported some hogs, presented them to his company to be killed as a Christmas treat of fresh pork. The captain sometimes visited the pen and gave directions for their care. A sow had a litter of pigs in the fall, and fearing that she might kill them, he directed his first sergeant to have her watched for a few days. The Sergeant detailed some men for this purpose, among them a young German, who, considering this a very unmilitary duty, refused to serve, saying "To h—— mit der piggins, I'm no swiney doctor!"

There was very little sickness during the winter, but a number of cases of frost bites, none of them very serious. One death occurred during the midwinter in our little hospital, that of Sergeant Fiske of my company who was a veteran of the Mexican War, and had suffered for a long time from a malady to which soldiers long in the service are liable. Sergeant Fiske was an inveterate card player and smoker. On the evening of the night on which he died he sat cross legged on his bed and played his favorite game with some of the other hospital inmates. When he was placed in his coffin, some of his comrades slipped in a pack of cards and his pipe to be buried with him, Indian fashion. With great labor a grave was dug through the deeply frozen ground. On the top of a hill near the fort, we buried Sergeant Fiske with military honors, Lieutenant George H. Paige reading the burial service. A board was put up to mark the lonely grave; but in that bleak spot it probably remained only a short time before the weather obliterated all signs of it.

During this winter I saw but little of the Indians. There were only a small number in camp near the fort, and no others arrived. During the long winter evenings we played games or read the few books, magazines and occasional newspapers that we could procure. A mail from the "States" arrived but twice a month, and life at the post was monotonous.

At Christmas and on New Years' day an extra dinner was served for all the soldiers, with a dessert of pie made with dried apples by the company's baker. Whiskey punch was also provided. There was no chance for the soldiers to procure whiskey at Fort Lookout unless one of the officers gave them a drink of it, which happened rarely. This drove some of them who had a craving for it, to use essence of Jamaica ginger and bay-rum which they could buy at the sutler's store. They sometimes made a punch of it by adding sugar and hot water. The sutler had some imported ale and porter, which he was allowed to sell to soldiers; but as the price was seventy-five cents a pint bottle, very little of it was consumed.

In April, when the snow had melted, we began to drill again for the first time since leaving Carlisle Barracks. We had lived more like pioneers than soldiers. Early in May orders were received to abandon Fort Lookout, where we had worked so hard to build quarters, and to proceed to Fort Randall, where the regimental headquarters and four companies had gone when Fort Pierre was abandoned a year ago. We went into camp and began to tear down the company quarters for they were built of hewn timber, which it was desirable to save. We also took down the officers' houses. All this material was hauled down to the river bank to be made into a raft, and floated down to Fort Randall. We left all of the log cabins and the brick chimneys standing but removed the doors and sashes. Early in June a steamboat which had discharged her cargo at Fort Randall arrived at Fort Lookout and took on board the three companies and all of the commissary and quartermaster stores and other moveable property. The wagons and mules were sent overland in charge of an officer and escort.

When the steamboat started down the river, I went up on the hurricane deck to have a final look at what remained of Fort Lookout. I saw some Indians prowling around the abandoned log cabins. Brick chimneys alone marked the places where our quarters and the officers' houses had been. I could also make out the white board which marked the lonely grave of Sergt. Fiske on the hill.

We were soon out of sight, and arrived at Fort Randall in a few days.

PART VI.

SERVICE AT FORT RANDALL, CAMPAIGNING IN KANSAS AND
EXPIRATION OF MY ENLISTMENT.
1857-1859.

WE arrived at Fort Randall in June, 1857. It was located on the west bank of the Missouri river, about a hundred and twenty-five miles north of the Big Sioux river as the crow flies; but more than two hundred miles by following the tortuous water course. At Fort Randall an unusually sharp turn to the east, and another to the south, gave the fort a river front on two sides, east and north, with the protection of high banks sloping to a wide strip of bottom land along the shore. That the location was desirable is proved by the fact that it has been used as a military post up to the present time, and is now in the midst of a large reservation.

The four companies that went there when Fort Pierre was abandoned a year before, had also worked hard and put up substantial log houses, rough, but comfortable, around a parade ground of reasonable size. Our three companies went into camp and waited for the arrival of the raft from Fort Lookout, which came in about a week. Then the re-erection of our quarters and officers' houses commenced. The cabins for the married soldiers were all placed on the bottom land called "The Hollow". There also were the cabins of all the citizen commissary and quartermaster's employees, married and single, and near by was a considerable camp of Ponca Indians.

There were about a dozen of citizen mechanics at the fort who did the greater part of the work in re-erecting the quarters. They had the help of only a small detail of soldiers. The buildings were improved by ceilings, and a mess-room was built—something we had not had for two years.

A large post garden had been planted early in the spring by the companies there, and during the summer and fall we had an abundance of vegetables. I had never seen potatoes, onions, and tomatoes, attain such an astonishing size as they did in that rich virgin soil. A few soldiers detailed as gardeners lived beside the garden in tents about a mile west of the fort.

We drilled and performed guard duty and moved into our new quarters after the middle of August. I did not have much to do and spent a great part of my spare time swimming, fishing and visiting the Indian camp. One day, I swam acorss the Missouri with some companions, but we were so exhausted we had to come back in a canoe.

There was a singular hot spring or pit on the opposite side of the river. It could not be closely approached because of the dangerous quick-sand about it. There was no overflow, and the pit seemed to be bottomless. We threw long sticks into it from a distance. They went down but never came up. The spring emitted steam in winter, but it was overflowed by the river in the spring and disappeared.

Major Hannibal Day was in command at Fort Randall. There was a band and we did regular garrison duty, including Sunday dress parades and skirmish drills. Once in a while, an escort was furnished to accompany some wagons to Sioux City and back—a place which was then beginning to build up—or a company occasionally made a short march to settle a small Indian difficulty. Our duties were varied and the summer passed quickly.

The sutler had built a roomy store at Fort Randall, with lumber brought from St. Louis. It was stocked with goods for both soldiers and Indians, and the prices were lower than at Fort Pierre. He kept ale on draught which, with some restrictions, he was allowed to sell to the soldiers by the glass.

Whiskey began to be smuggled from Sioux City and was sold to the soldiers. This made more cases for the guard-house.

An enterprising soldier's wife fixed up a small still in her quarters at the "Hollow" and made a little corn whiskey which she sold to soldiers secretly, but she was informed on after a while and her distilling plant was destroyed. As a punishment, she was deprived of her ration allowance. Every company had some men who were slaves to the liquor habit. There was one in my company who, whenever he saw an intoxicated man, could not refrain from exclaiming, "I wish I had half of your sickness!"

A second lieutenant, a man of middle age, joined my regiment. He was appointed from civil life, but there was a rumor that he had served as an officer in the navy. If so, the navy was to be congratulated on its loss, for we soon discovered that he was one of those steady drinkers who, without being intoxicated, are almost constantly under the influence of liquor in a minor degree. He was saturated with it and exhaled it. Whenever any severe duty was to be performed he managed to get excused on the plea of sickness, and was away on leave as often as he could get it. Unfortunately, he remained with my regiment until after the beginning of the Civil War. By that time he was unfit for field duty. He was on the sick list most of the time, and never was present at any battle. We got rid of him in 1862, when he was retired as a captain.

All of the officers' families, from whom they had been separated for two years, joined them at Fort Randall. It was quite a novelty to see white ladies again and to see their children playing on the parade ground.

Captain Gardner was married here to the sister of a lieutenant of another company. He went home to Georgia on leave, and when he returned brought back with him a negro and his wife, both of whom were slaves. The woman cooked and the man did chores.

A partial alteration was made at this time in the army uniform. The tight fitting jacket was replaced by a loose fitting blouse of dark blue cloth, which was an agreeable change. The light blue trousers were replaced by trousers of dark blue cloth, but in less than two years were changed back to the light blue, which the army has adhered to ever since. There was an absurd change from the old uniform hat to a strange and unmilitary design. The new creation was made of stiff black felt with a broad brim and a high crown. The brim was looped up on the right side and fastened with a brass eagle, otherwise it would have interfered when the soldier had his gun at "shoulder-arms." On the front was a brass bugle with the regimental number in the centre of it, and a brass letter of the company above it. Around the hat was a worsted cord with tassels of light blue for the infantry. A single black feather or plume was fastened on the left side of the hat, which few of the soldiers knew how, or cared to keep curled neatly. In damp weather it looked like a drenched rooster's tail-feathers. The officers had similar hats of finer material with more generous plumes.

A substantial new guard-house of hewn logs with a large room for prisoners and a few dark cells had been built during the summer. It was at the head of the road leading down to the river, and chance made me the first inmate of one of the cells. Some soldiers who had deserted were recaptured and tried by a general court-martial, which sentenced them to receive thirty-nine lashes on their bare backs, laid on with a rawhide. They were also to be confined at hard labor for four months, lose all pay and allowances and be dishonorably discharged. On the autumn day on which the first part of the sentence was executed we were paraded, and formed three sides of a square, the guard-house and prison forming the fourth side. It was the first time that I had ever seen corporal punishment with a rawhide inflicted on a man while in the army, and was also the only time, as flogging for desertion was abolished forever by Act of Congress a few years later. The three prisoners were present under guard.

The officer of the day read the sentence, and called out the name of one of the deserters, who was led to the centre of the square, where a triangle formed of strong joists had been set up. Here he was divested of his jacket and shirt, his wrists were bound with cords. His arms were pulled up over his head and tied to the top, while his feet were spread apart and secured to the bottom of the triangle. It had always been the custom in the army for flogging to be administered by one of the musicians. Why they were selected to do it, I never learned. When all was ready the officer of the day called one of the older boys from the ranks. He was handed a rawhide and told by the officer to strike the prisoner hard from the shoulders to the loins.

At first the blows were moderate, but increased under the officer's threats until each blow left a dark red mark and then began to cut the skin until blood flowed. The poor wretch squirmed and groaned piteously, the more so when some ill directed blow struck him around the side. When the thirty-ninth blow had been struck, the officer who had kept count cried, "Halt". The victim was untied by the guards and, unable to stand on his feet, was dragged towards the guard-house.

The second prisoner was then led forward and prepared to receive his punishment. The officer of the day turned about to select another musician to strike the blows. His glance rested on me for an instant but he passed me by and called out another by name, for which I felt very thankful. The brutal scene was repeated in all of its revolting details.

When the last prisoner was ready the officer of the day called out my name; but I stood still and shook my head. He then peremptorily called me a second time, to which I replied, "I refuse." He ordered me to be placed in charge of the guard, and called on my drummer to execute the sentence which my refusal to act had delayed for a few minutes.

Charges of disobedience of orders were preferred against me, and in about a week I was tried by court-martial. I could only plead guilty, and in another week my sentence was promulgated. I was to be confined in the guard-house for thirty days, ten of them in solitary confinement on a diet of bread and water, the remainder at hard labor, and to forfeit one month's pay. My captain tried to have my sentence commuted, but it was so glaring a refusal to obey orders without any extenuating circumstances that he was unsuccessful.

I commenced to serve the first part of my ten days at hard labor by going out with the prison gang under guard at seven o'clock each mornign, chopping wood at the officers' quarters or sweeping the roads and keeping the parade ground clear until six o'clock in the evening with an interval of an hour for dinner. All of the prisoners "soldiered", and shirked their work as much as they could. None of us worked hard.

My second term of ten days was to be in one of the new cells on bread and water. But all of the sergeants in charge of the guard were friendly to me, and let me out of my cell into the guard room for hours at a time after dark. Some took the risk of letting me out in the day time after the officer of the day had made his customary rounds. As for bread and water, I never had any of that. Everyone seemed anxious to smuggle in something nice for me to eat, and I had to give away much of it to other prisoners. There was more than one boy could consume. Hot coffee was also supplied to me when it was brought in with the meals for the other prisoners. Friends furnished me with plenty of candles and books.

When my ten days of solitary confinement expired, I commenced the last term of ten days at hard labor the same as before. During those terms I had to sleep on the floor in the large prison room with the other prisoners. I would have preferred to sleep in the cell alone.

But there was enough that was amusing going on at the post to make the memory of my punishment soon lose its sting. For example, there was one man in my company, an old soldier of the Mexican War, who would sometimes take a drink too much. This always made him maudlin and melancholy. At such times he always spoke of the "beautiful senoritas," as he called them. Tears would come into his eyes when he told us the charmers called him "Senor Patrucio Martino". Then he would say with a sob, "Look at me! What am I now? Nothing but plain Paddy Martin," and burst into a flood of tears.

The winter was much milder than the two preceding ones. There were some bitterly cold days during January and February, yet we were quite comfortable. We had plenty to eat and a variety. The general health of all the soldiers was exceedingly good. We got up amusements to pass the time. There were some negro employees in the Quartermaster's Department who could sing plantation songs for us. One of them, a coal black negro who had been on the frontiers for a number of years with the Fur Company, was married to a squaw and had several children who were curious specimens of the human race, combining the most prominent features of the Indian and the negro. Both the father and the mother seemed very proud of them, however.

The Indian camp, of easy access to the garrison, always proved interesting. Its population was sometimes increased by visitors from the large Ponca Village, and from a Yankton village not far away. I spent much of my time with the Indians, as I had done two winters previous at Cantonment Miller.

In April, after the breaking up of the ice on the Missouri and the melting of the snow, flocks of wild ducks and geese made their appearance. For a time they came in incredible numbers and we managed to get all we wanted of them.

A man of my company named Jack Lynch, who had a habit of prowling about the country alone, showed us a spoonful of gold dust that he said he had found during his wanderings, but did not tell us where. About this time there were articles in the papers about the discovery of gold in the Black Hills, some hundreds of miles to the west of us; and we saw no good reason why gold should not exist in the bleak hills about Fort Randall. Our man brought in more samples of gold. He was watched and was discovered washing gold in a ravine, through which a small water course ran down from the hills a mile or more south of the fort.

Then excitement ran high. Crowds of soldiers went prospecting and washing gold. Places were discovered where it was more plentiful. In fact, too plentiful, for some of the more industrious quickly accumulated a considerable quantity of it. I had about a pint of it myself. Games of poker were played in the quarters evenings, at which the stakes were gold dust measured out in thimblefuls. Others hoarded their wealth and guarded it jealously. Hope of riches within our grasp warmed our hearts and cheered us.

The excitement had reached a high pitch, when, about a week after our "gold digging" started, some one thought of submitting a sample of the gold dust to the hospital steward, who had the necessary acids for a test. He promptly declared the stuff to be pyrites or "fools' gold". Some of the men were bitterly disappointed, others laughed. The discoverer and a few more, however, clung to their "gold dust". They believed that it was valuable until they got a report from St. Louis—where they had sent a sample to be assayed—which confirmed the hospital steward's opinion. After a while some of the soldiers began to think that Jack Lynch might have been playing a huge joke on us. He was a peculiar man in many ways, and was the possessor of a pair of eyes that did not match, one of them being light blue and the other dark gray.

During the early spring of 1858, we read much in the newspapers about the Mountain Meadow massacre in Utah in 1857, by Indians instigated by the Mormons. A large party of emigrants had been annihilated, except a few small children, and Col. Albert Sidney Johnson was gathering troops at Fort Bridger, Utah, to punish the Mormons. We also read about trouble on the border line between Missouri and Kansas Territory. Kansas desired to become a "free state," while the Missourians, together with some adherents in the territory, wanted it to become a "slave state." This led to many atrocities on the border line, where people were being driven off their farms and murdered by a gang called the "Border Ruffians."

Soon a rumor spread that some of the companies at Fort Randall would be withdrawn to serve either in Kansas or Utah, and presently an order arrived to send two companies to report at Fort Leavenworth, as soon as transportation by steamboat could be had. For this service my own company and Captain Lyon's Company B were selected. We were ordered to prepare ourselves in light marching order, leaving behind us all of our full dress uniforms, and other articles not required on a campaign. We also left behind us the alcoholic second lieutenant, who managed to be excused from going and remained at Fort Randall on duty with some other company. The officers' and soldiers' wives and children also remained. Captain Gardner and Lieutenant O'Connoll of my company and Captain Lyon and a lieutenant of Company B were the only officers to go.

We waited impatiently for a steamboat to arrive. She did not appear until near the middle of May, and with her came a paymaster who gave us eight months' pay before our departure. When the boat was unloaded and all was ready, we formed on the parade ground and, escorted by the band, marched to the boat. Among those who watched our departure were a number of Indians and squaws from the camp.

The river was still high and the current swift. The boat was but lightly loaded, so we did not strand on any sand bars and made good progress, running at night on the latter half of our trip. We still had to tie up now and then and cut wood to feed the boilers, but occasionally there was a pile of cord-wood for sale.

The great changes that had taken place since we had ascended the river three years before, were surprising to me. Then St. Joseph, Mo., marked the limit of the white settlements. Less than a hundred miles from Fort Randall by river, we made the first landing at Niabrana, where the river of the same name, flows into the Missouri. There was a small cluster of houses, and a somewhat pretentious hotel, a three-story frame building which some enterprising citizen had erected. Next we stopped at Sioux City, which had become a considerable village near the river bank of one and two story frame buildings, with a general store and a small church. Then came Council Bluffs, Omaha; Nebraska City; Atchison and some smaller places. All of them had sprung up within three years, and were busy and rapidly growing. We stopped at all these palces to take on passengers or a little freight.

Such comfort as the staterooms afforded was not for the soldiers. They were set apart for the use of the passengers and our officers, while we were very uncomfortably limited to the lower or boiler deck. We had to sleep anywhere we could find room to lie down, on piles of freight or on the bare deck. The weather was raw at first, and we had cold rains. With half a dozen others I slept under the boilers several times after the fires were banked and the boat laid up for the night. The rear of the boilers was elevated on iron supports three feet or more above the deck. It formed a warm and sheltered place when the cold wind blew fore and aft through the open deck from stem to stern. After the boat began to run at night, the place became too hot for us and we had to sleep elsewhere.

There were no docks or wharves at any of the landings. When the boat approached a town she sounded her whistle and rang a bell, which brought many of the inhabitants to the river bank. In making a landing while going down stream, the pilot slowed down, approached the shore at an acute angle and pressed "her nozzle ag'in the bank." There he held the boat, until the force of the current swung her around and the bow pointed up stream. The impact of the boat always dislodged a large quantity of soft earth from the river bank,

TEN YEARS IN THE RANKS U. S. ARMY

which fell into the water and left a big dent in the shore line. Every steamboat on its way down stream deprived the town of some of its real estate, if it made a landing.

In ten or twelve days, we reached Fort Leavenworth and went into quarters. I found the place very much improved. It had been cleaned up, the old buildings had been renovated and some new ones added. There was no cholera or other infectious sickness there then. It was a very busy place at that time. Soldiers were arriving and departing frequently, on their long march via Forts Kearney and Laramie to Fort Bridger, near Salt Lake City, where Col. Johnson was assembling a little army to punish the Mormons. At Leavenworth post I saw Robert E. Lee, who was then the colonel of one of the cavalry regiments and soon to become the Commander-in-Chief of the Confederate Army.

A few days after our arrival at the fort some comrades and myself obtained a twenty-four hour pass to go to Leavenworth City, only a few miles down the river. It had grown to a thriving town with many stores, hotels and saloons, on the business streets; churches, dwellings and shacks on others. All were built of wood and very few were more than two stories high.

We were in luck—a circus had come to town and was parading through the streets when we arrived. There was a steam organ on a decorated truck followed by a band and the mounted circus performers which drew a great crowd. Of course, we were on hand at the afternoon performance in the tent and thought it was great. In the evening we went to a theater in a barn-like building in the heart of the town, where we sat on wooden benches which were all on a level. There was no gallery. Three or four disreputable looking musicians, playing on wheezy instruments, made up the orchestra. The stage and the auditorium were lighted with candles. The floor of the stage creaked when the performers walked over it, and the scenery threatened to topple over. I distinctly remember that the piece played by the ambitious actors was "The Lady of Lyons," which they probably murdered. However, the audience that crowded the place applauded and seemed to enjoy it, and so did we. We slept at a hotel that night on a real bed for the first time in years, and next morning walked back to the fort.

A few days later we received orders to start for Utah. Each man bought a gray felt hat at the sutler's store, as we had seen other detachments do. These we wore on the march instead of the fatigue cap, which was a poor protection against the fierce rays of the sun on the prairies. Our first objective point was Fort Kearney on the Platte River, about two hundred and fifty miles away. But we had marched only about a week when we were recalled and retraced our steps to Fort Leavenworth. I felt disappointed, I had hoped to see the Grat Salt Lake and the Mormons. The long weary march did not intimidate me. On our return to the fort, we learned that fresh trouble had broken out on the Kansas border, and we were to go to Fort Scott in the south-eastern part of Kansas, a few miles from the Missouri border, to protect the settlers. In a few days our little command was ready to start. It included Companies B and D and a section of a battery of artillery consisting of two of the old style brass six pounders with their caissons, and necessary complement of artillerists commanded by First Lieutenant Beekman Du Barry, Third Artillery, who attained high rank later in the Army of the Potomac. Second Lieutenant J. B. Shinn was his assistant. The surgeon who accompanied us was Samuel W. Crawford, who later commanded the division of Pennsylvania Reserves at the battle of Gettysburg as a brigadier general. Captain Nathaniel Lyon, being the ranking officer, commanded the detachment. Captain Lyon, the firm abolitionist, and Captain Gardner, the ardent pro-slavery advocate, were there together, on a mission to keep the peace between rival factions, the free-soilers and the partisans of slavery. Whatever their feelings may have been, but they did not exhibit them. They were polite to each other but not cordial.

Our first day's march ended at a creek which was almost dry when we crossed it. That night there was a cloud-burst which drenched us, and next morning the dry creek had become a raging torrent many yards wide. We witnessed the drowning of a man and a horse, who attempted to swim over to our side, and to whom we could give no aid.

A few nights later we were encamped on low bottom land at the Kansas River, when after midnight a terrific rain storm flooded our camp with several inches of water. I sat until daylight in my tent on an inverted quart tin cup. My bare feet were in the water and I held my knapsack and clothing on my knees to keep them dry.

We crossed the Kansas river on a private ferry, which consisted of a flat-boat or scow large enough to carry a wagon with a team of horses. A cable was stretched across the stream high above the water. An ingenious arrangement of pulleys was attached to this cable and to the boat, so that it was guided from shore to shore while the current furnished the motive power. No steering was required and no labor, except to shove the boat off to take the current. It was easy work, but very slow. It took all day to pass the soldiers and wagons over the river. The artillery crossed on the following day.

We encamped one day near a small village called Shawneetown. In the evening many of the soldiers strolled to the village, where there was a hotel with a bar-room, in which a few citizens were drinking with some of the soldiers. It was becoming dark, and the saddled horses belonging to the citizens were hitched to posts on the street. This gave a joker of my company an opportunity to play a trick on one of the civilians. He pulled a hair out of a horse's tail, and tied it firmly around the animal's hind leg between the hoof and the fetlock, concealing the hair by carefully covering it with the hair on the horse's leg. Then he awaited developments.

After a while the civilians came out, mounted their horses, and started off. We leisurely followed them, as their road led in the direction of our camp. Soon one of the men noticed that his horse was going lame. It raised one of his hind feet higher than the others, and brought it down with a jerk, as though it were trying to kick off something which annoyed it. The rider dismounted and examined the horse's hoof but found nothing wrong. Then his two companions dismounted and examined it. As we passed we heard them say that the only thing to be done was to go back to the village and have the shoe taken off. This they did and I hope discovered the harmless trick that had been played on them.

After leaving Shawneetown, we directed our march close to the border line. Sometimes we were in Missouri, sometimes in Kansas. This continued all the way down to Fort Scott. We halted for a day's rest at a small village called West Point in Missouri, where we could overlook a valley and see some Indian mounds. By this time we had been joined by half a dozen dogs, who had left their owners and followed us. They seemed to love the soldiers, who petted and fed them. We had quite a pack before the summer was over. Our marches were easy. There was no hurry; it was desired to let the people know that there were troops for their protection near the border line.

The country was sparsely settled. When we had reached the border we began to see abandoned farms, and burned farm houses and cabins. Those of the settlers who remained were outspoken sympathizers with slavery. On some of the abandoned farms the gardens and fields had been planted in the spring and were now overgrown with weeds. The horses and cattle had been taken away too, but there were pigs in the woods and chickens and ducks running loose without any owners. Every day was a feast with us on that short march. We lived on fresh pork, chickens and all kinds of vegetables, disdaining of the government rations, except the hard bread.

We reached Fort Scott in the evening during a heavy thunder storm, soaked to the skin. We put up for the night in one of the old barrack buildings, and next morning established a camp just outside of the little town. Fort Scott was an old frontier post, built on the same plan as all the others, which had been abandoned and sold by the Government. Citizens now lived in the frame buildings, formerly occupied by officers and soldiers. One of the old barrack buildings had been converted into a hotel, and the parade ground, with its well in the centre, was now the pubilc square. On it faced the court house, in one of the old buildings, with the old guard-house serving for the prison.

The town of Fort Scott on the Marmiton river was the county seat of Bourbon County, Kansas. Some scattering houses had been erected outside of the old fort, but the entire population probably did not exceed two hundred at that time.

There appeared to be very little money in circulation. The farmers had none, and could only trade for their produce at the stores. They came to our camp, and sold us two chickens for twenty-five cents, eggs at five cents per dozen, two quarts of milk for five cents, and other produce in proportion, and seemed to be pleased to get real money. Two guileless farmer lads drove into camp one day with sixty pounds of choice butter. They said that "Ma" had told them that they must bring home six dollars for it. They had no scale, but a soldier loaned them one of our quart tin cups, which he said would hold just a pound, if filled and well heaped up. When they had sold all of their butter at ten cents per cup, they found to their chagrin that they had a little less than four dollars to take home to "Ma."

There were some abandoned farms around Fort Scott, but they were quite a distance from camp. Some of the soldiers, when they wanted green corn or potatoes, found it easier to get them from nearby farms when the farmer was not looking. One day a farmer complained to Captain Lyon about losing a calf and said he thought he could identify the soldier whom he suspected of taking it. We were paraded, but when he looked us over he said he could not pick out his man because we all looked alike. Some of the men who had dined on the calf made friends with the farmer, and took him to the hotel in town. There they filled him with whiskey and started him home feeling so happy that he invited them all to visit him at his farm.

One day three comrades and myself were enjoying a savory stew of chicken, young pork, potatoes and onions. We had it in an army mess pan which we had placed on the ground in our tent, and we were squatted around the pan, each dipping into it with his spoon in soldier fashion.

We had just started when one of the men began to sputter and kick.

"What in h—— is the matter with you," exclaimed one of the others. "Why don't you blow on it, if it is too hot?"

Instead of acting on this suggestion the man rolled over on his back, his mouth frothing and his eyes distended. He kicked over the pan and scattered our luscious dinner over the tent floor.

We sent for the doctor, who after a long time brought him back to consciousness. The man had had a fit. He had subsequent attacks and was soon after discharged from the service.

I suppose it was this incident that inspired a big red-haired Indiana "hoosier" in my company to try to get a discharge in the same way. One night he disturbed us by groaning and gnashing his teeth. We found that he was frothing soap-suds at the mouth, and was such a bad actor that it needed only a glance to show that he was shamming. The orderly sergeant threw a bucket of water over him and he had no more "fits."

A lot of pigs belonging to the towns' people ran around loose, and rooted about the camp until they became a nuisance. One day a soldier who craved some fresh pork, not daring to shoot a pig near the camp, baited a large fish hook with a piece of meat and when some of the pigs appeared in the company street he threw the hook just outside of his tent. Soon one of them took the bait, and only had time to let out one little squeal before the "fisherman" had him in the tent smothered in blankets. Roast pork was on the bill of fare for the mess next day.

We had easy duty while at Fort Scott and plenty to eat. We drilled for an hour during the cool part of the morning, for it was very hot there in midsummer. After that those who were not on guard or on some detail had the remainder of the day at their own disposal. I spent the greater part of my time on the shady banks of the Marmiton river, which was a fine lively stream of clear water with rocky embankments that showed out-croppings of soft coal. There were plenty of fine fish in the river, which we caught and often cooked on the bank, atlhough our camp was but a few hundred yards away. I went in swimming several times each day, and enjoyed it immensely. At the stream we also washed our clothes and sat under a tree while they dried hung on bushes in the hot sun.

One afternoon, while many of us were at the river, we heard the "Long Roll" beaten in the camp. We rushed back and got under arms. On a hill a mile from camp we saw two dozen mounted men who were examining our camp and prancing around in a defiant manner. They all seemed to carry guns and opened fire on us when they saw us forming ranks. All of their shots fell short, and when Captain Barry sent a shell over their heads, they soon scattered. Pursuit was out of the question, as they were well mounted and we were on foot. This was the only time during our stay in Kansas that we saw any of the Border Ruffians. They were careful to keep out of our reach. The little incident caused some excitement among the inhabitants of the town who were glad to have the soldiers there to protect them from a raid.

I think we had been a month at Fort Scott, when we broke camp one morning and commenced our march to Lawrence on the Kansas River by way of Ossawatomy, Kansas. This was the place where John Brown had a sharp fight with the Missouri raiders in 1856, and earned the name of "Old Ossawatomy Brown." We were told that he was in Kansas at that time earnestly working for the Free Soilers, but I don't think we met him. We made a leisurely march. I rode Dr. Crawford's horse for five or six miles every day. He seemed to enjoy marching in the cool part of the morning, as also did some of the other officers. At night we often camped at some small settlement or near a farm house. We found the natives ill-informed. They seldom saw a newspaper, and knew but little as to the cause of all the trouble in Kansas.

Some had never seen any soldiers before. One good old lady marveled at the "big pistols on wheels," when she saw the artillery. Money was almost a curiosity in some of the "way-back" places through which we passed, and they sold us their produce at ridiculously low prices to get a few coins.

We stayed but a few days at Lawrence and then marched south again by a different road, back to Fort Scott. Our empty wagons were sent from Lawrence to Fort Leavenworth, with a small escort for supplies, and rejoined us later at Fort Scott. On our re-arrival there, Captain Lyon encamped us about a mile from town, but as long as we were close to the Marmiton River we cared little for the town.

About the first week in September, we received orders to return to Fort Leavenworth, which we did by the same route along the border line, by which we had come down. We had done a considerable amount of marching since we had left Fort Leavenworth, three months before. Our clothing was nearly worn out, and some of the men would soon be barefooted, for we had left there in very light marching order, not expecting to remain away so long. Clothing and shoes were issued to us on our arrival at the fort.

I look back upon the summer I passed in Kansas, as an excursion when compared with the hardship of marching on the prairies. We always found a stream, a spring or a farmer's well within easy distance, which obviated the necessity of making distressingly long marches on account of the scarcity of water. We also fared well in the matter of food.

We remained but a few days at Fort Leavenworth before

a steamboat arrived which was to take us up the Missouri River to Fort Randall again. This boat was much smaller than the others we had traveled on. She was what is called a "stern-wheeler." Her paddle-wheels, on the stern instead of on the sides, made her shake more than the other type of boat. She carried no other passengers, and we had the use of the unfurnished cabins on the saloon deck in the rear next to the paddle-wheels. This boat was of very light draft and not heavily loaded, so we seldom ran on sand bars and made steady progress. We were tormented by mosquitoes when the boat was tied up at night, and had to make smokes on the shore.

I became ill with chills and fever soon after we started and remained so until we arrived at Fort Randall. Dr. Crawford dosed me so liberally with quinine, that I could scarcely hear anything at times.

We made the trip from Leavenworth to Randall in a little less than four weeks, and arrived there in the middle of October. We occupied our old quarters, and resumed the usual duties. There were but five companies at the post then, two others having been sent away during the summer to Fort Laramie. We arrived in time to take part in the fall duck shooting, and Sergeant McVeagh of my company and I got a two-day pass to go hunting at a lake on the other side of the Missouri River, about ten miles away, where wild ducks and geese abounded. We borrowed shot guns from some of the citizen employes, and carried blankets and some provisions with us, intending to camp at the lake for one night.

We hunted during the afternoon with fair success, and as evening approached made our way toward one end of the lake where we saw woods in which we intended to camp for the night. But on approaching closer we noticed smoke issuing from the tops of several Indian teepees among the trees. We quickly decided that it would be safer to trust to the Indians' hospitality than to camp alone, as they had no doubt discovered our presence. A furious barking of dogs announced our arrival, and we entered the largest of three lodges. We sat down, and after the customary smoke we made the savages understand that we were hungry, and wanted to sleep in their camp for the night. The Indian assented by pointing to a heap of skins on one side of the tent, and making the sign indicating sleep.

We found that these Indians belong to the Oo-he-non-pas (Two Kettle Band) of the Yankton tribe, and the inmates of the teepee consisted of an Indian with his two squaws, two girls about my age, two children five or six years old, and a wrinkled gray-haired squaw bent with age.

We gave the squaws all the ducks we had shot. They prepared some of them for supper, also some venison which they had. The sergeant and I made coffee for the whole family, and shared our bread with them. After supper we gave the Indian some tobacco, and we smoked our own pipes.

We talked with all of them as much as our limited knowledge of their language permitted and found out they had been far away hunting, and were going to winter with their tribes. They had been at the fort and knew the soldiers. Some visitors from the other two lodges dropped in. The Indians showed us his pipes, his bows and arrows, his gun and his little curiosities. He admired our guns, which we had kept loaded, removing the percussion caps before entering the lodge. The sergeant interested them with a pack of cards, while I amused the younger squaws by drawing pencil sketches for them, and showing them my watch.

I began to wonder what the arrangements for sleeping would be when I noticed one of the squaws make a bed of buffalo robes and other skins on one side of the lodge for us, while directly opposite on the other side of the fire which was in the center of the floor, she put the two young squaws to bed. First she wound a horse hair rope many times around the lower limbs of each, to prevent them from running away with us I suppose. As a further precaution she lay down at their side next to the fire. The Indian with the other squaw slept opposite the opening to the lodge. The two children slept at the foot of the young squaw's bed next to the door, while the old squaw was left defenceless and alone to sleep at our feet on the other side of the door. They all lay down with their clothes on so we did the same, taking off only our coats. Our guns we laid next to the side of the lodge where I slept, the sergeant sleeping in front next to the fire.

I was tired and soon went to sleep. A noise awoke me during the night, but it was only the old crone putting a few fagots on the fire to keep it lighted. We arose soon after daylight. The two girls had been unwound before we got up. We had breakfast and departed, not forgetting to invite the family to visit us at Fort Randall.

We resumed our hunting, and soon had all of the ducks we were able to carry. Then, after a lunch by the lake, we took up our tramp to the fort, where we arrived in the evening.

The Indian and his family hunted us up in a few days at the fort, but the old squaw and the two children were not with them. They came mounted on ponies. The sergeant and I got them something to eat, and bought the squaw a few things in the sutler's store. We gave a plug of tobacco to the buck to repay his hospitality and they all went away satisfied.

The river closed early, and cold weather was soon upon us. We passed our time as we had done the previous winter. Nothing disturbed our tranquility, until suddenly in the early part of January Company I and my company were ordered to go at once to Niabrara. Four army wagons mounted on runners were prepared to carry our provisions and baggage. One of them was fitted up with a sheet iron stove for the officers to ride and sleep in. It seemed that the Ponca Indians, whose village was close to Niabrara, had killed one of the citizens and committed depredations on the settlers. The villagers had asked the commandant of Fort Randall for protection. The commanding officer sent a message to "Big Drum," the chief of the Poncas, and the head men of the tribe to come to Fort Randall, but they paid no attention to it. After waiting a reasonable time he ordered the two companies to go and punish the Indians.

The captain of Company I, who commanded the expedition, was a corpulent, elderly man, with a large family. He loved his ease and had lost his stomach for fighting. When the Civil War broke out he soon resigned to spend his declining years peacefully keeping a store in a western town. The other officers of our little expedition were Captain Gardner and Lieutenant O'Connoll of my company and a lieutenant of Company I.

We started our march in the forenoon of a very cold but bright day and climbed the hills below Fort Randall. The snow was deep, and the thick crust on it made marching hard and tiresome. It was quickly discovered that our customary way of marching by fours was impracticable. We were reduced to twos, and as soon as the two leading men were tired out breaking a path in the deep snow, they stepped to one side, and waited to fall in line again in the rear. The officers rode their horses, but at times took to the warm sleigh which the commander hardly ever left. The days were short, and I think we accomplished only a little more than six miles on the first before darkness overtook us. We went into camp on the spot where we halted on top of a bleak hill, and waited a while for the sleighs with our baggage to come up.

It was bitter cold, probably thirty degrees below zero at least, but we had no thermometer to tell us that. We shovelled away some of the deep snow and tried to put up tents but found it impossible to drive wooden tent pins into the frozen ground. We therefore banked up the snow high to the windward, and made our beds on the frozen ground. Fortunately we had plenty of robes and blankets. I slept in the middle with three in the bed, and felt warm all night.

The cooks started a fire with wood obtained from a nearby

ravine, but for water they had to melt snow. We had coffee before we went to bed, which helped to warm us up and the fire was kept burning all night. Snow had to be melted to water the horses and mules, and to make our coffee in the morning. We slept in our clothes, removing only our overcoats and boots. When we arose we found that the exhalation from our bodies had caused a thick crust of ice to form on the topmost robe, while the lowest one was frozen fast to the ground. I had imprudently left my boots and buffalo hide overboots outside of my bed. In the morning they were frozen as stiff as sheet iron. I could not put them on until a comrade had thawed them at the fire for me.

The four officers slept in the sleigh as best they could. I overheard Captain Gardner remark to another officer next morning while they warmed themselves at the fire before mounting their horses, that he had the courage, but not the constitution to stand such a march. Our corpulent commander did not leave the sleigh, and had his breakfast cooked and brought to him by his "dog-robber," as the men called an officer's soldier-servant.

We had a hard day's march the next day, for we kept near the river where it was hilly and made about twelve miles. We fared better on that and on subsequent nights, as we camped at the edge of woods where we could build roaring fires. Fortunately we had no snow storms to add to the rigor of the intense cold. We did not put up any tents during the march.

I think it was on the forenoon of the fourth day, just as we got to the brow of a hill, that about fifty mounted Indians appeared over the crest of a hill more than half a mile away. They seemed astonished on seeing us and halted for a moment. An excited soldier discharged his rifle at them without waiting for orders to fire. This caused nearly a dozen others to fire before the officer could stop them. At the first shot the Indians fled down the hill and were out of sight in a few seconds. They did not reply to our firing, which had done them no harm. We learned a few days later that this was a party of Ponca Indians on a peace journey to Fort Randall.

On the evening of the fifth day we arrived at the wooded bluffs overlooking the Niabrara River, near its junction with the Missouri. On the other side of the river was a small settlement of about a dozen houses and a hotel called "The Niabrara." Next morning we had a hard time getting the sleighs down the steep bluffs to the frozen river. The mules were unhitched, and the sleighs were slid down one at a time with ropes hitched around trees to prevent them from descending too fast. We got them all down safely, crossed the river and camped close to the settlement. With great difficulty we put up our "Sibley" tents, using steel picket-pins to drive holes in the ground before we could insert the wooden tent pins. We got brush in the woods to cover the ground inside the tents, and built fires in the company streets, as a fire within the tent would have thawed the frozen ground, and reduce it to a quagmire. The officers occupied rooms at the hotel and messed there.

The large Ponca Indian village was but a mile or two away, and the next day after our arrival orders were sent to the Indians to attend a council on the following morning. But that night a blizzard which lasted for forty-eight hours swept down upon us and caused intense suffering. The wind blew the drifting snow so fiercely that no fires could be kept going. It was evening before the kindly proprietor of the hotel sent for our cooks and allowed them to make some hot coffee for us in his kitchen. The next day the storm continued with unabated fury. All we could do was to lie in our tents covered up with our blankets and buffalo robes to keep from freezing. But we had hot coffee twice and some warm soup on the second day, which put some life into us.

The hotel at Niabrara must have been built with an idea that the settlement would grow rapidly like Sioux City. But it had failed to do so. The place seemed as large as one would expect to find in a western town of two thousand inhabitants. It was a frame building, clapboarded, three stories high with a shingled gabel roof. There was a kitchen and dining-room on the first floor, also a good sized bar-room and a sitting-room. The first two stories had been plastered, but the third was left unfinished, and had only the clapboards and the shingles as a protection against the weather.

I do not know whether it was an arrangement made by our officers, or an offer from the proprietor, influenced perhaps by the fact that at this time there were no guests at the hotel, and that all of the soldiers seemed to have money. At any rate, when the blizzard was over, we took down our tents and moved to the unfinished third floor of the hotel, which was just about large enough so that all could lie down at night. There were only about seventy of us, counting cooks, teamsters and "dog-robbers." It was very cold up there on the top floor at night, but we had plenty of bedding and during the day we were allowed to sit in the bar and the sitting-room, where there were stoves. We found it an agreeable change from the camp.

We cooked our own meals and ate them where we could, but the proprietor, who seemed a very shrewd sort of person, served some meals in the dining-room at fifty cents per head, at which we got fried bacon, corn bread, flap jacks and coffee sweetened with molasses, which was all he had to offer. He had some soft drinks at the bar, cigars and tobacco and a few candies and crackers. I do not know whether he had any liquor. If he did, he never sold any of it to the soldiers. He had his cook make large quantities of corn bread and often came into the bar-room with slabs of it, shouting: "Who'll have another section for a quarter!" Our officers occupied rooms on the second floor of the hotel, and had their meals served there.

The council with the Ponca Indians was held on the day after we had moved into the hotel. All the soldiers not on guard or other duty to the number of about fifty, were drawn up under arms in front of the hotel, when we saw Big Drum and his braves approaching. All of the officers and soldiers knew the chief. They had also met some of the other Indians, who had often been at Fort Randall, which was but "one sleep" (two days ride) from the Ponca Village. The chief, a man of about fifty years, was the tallest and most powerful member of his tribe. He was a typical savage in appearance with a large head and face strongly pock marked. I had seen him at the fort considerably under the influence of "fire water," which had been given to him by some of the officers or the sutler.

We noticed that the Indians had come to the council, contrary to custom, almost fully armed. Some had guns with them, which were but ill concealed beneath their robes or blankets. Their weapons were probably loaded, while our guns were not.

Our officers with a few citizens and some interpreters formed a group about twenty paces in front of the center of our little battalion, and faced the Indians who out-numbered us more than two to one. While the "talk" progressed the Indians spread around the flanks, and in rear of the officers, practically surrounding them. Had any trouble occurred we would have had to fire in their direction, and perhaps kill our own officers. We wondered at the unwise and negligent arrangements of our corpulent commander. I think the other officers noted it, for when the council was continued on the following day, our guns were loaded, our officers kept close to the front of our ranks, and the Indians were not allowed to spread around the flanks. At the close of the second day of the council Big Drum surrendered four Indians as prisoners. They were disarmed, and put in the guard house, which was a small out-building belonging to the hotel.

About three days after the council, we commenced our return march to Fort Randall, taking with us the Indian prisoners, who marched in rear of the column with the camp guard. We crossed the Missouri on the ice and marched up on the east bank, where the land was more level and the distance somewhat shorter owing to the curvature of the river towards the west. We crossed the Vermillion River, almost without noticing it, where it passed through a piece of prairie. The snow being so deep that the banks were scarcely distinguishable. We accomplished the distance in three days' marching, and were fortunate not to encounter a snow storm.

About noon on the last day of the march, I succumbed to the severe fatigue of marching through the deep snow for the first time during my service. I was exhausted and unable to go further. I was put into one of the sleighs, hauled by six mules, into which some other worn out and half frozen soldiers had preceded me. We arrived at the fort after dark, where I discovered that some of my toes on both feet were badly frozen. It was about three weeks before I was able to do duty again. A number of the soldiers had been frostbitten, but none seriously.

After a while Big Drum, accompanied by some Indians of his tribe, came to the fort, and remained for some time. He had several interviews with the colonel in command, which finally resulted in the four Indian prisoners being set free.

No further trouble occurred during the remainder of the winter. I began to count the days that remained before the expiration of my service on March 31, 1859. When the day arrived I received my discharge from the service, but remained with my company as their guest until I could get transportation to the States. A soldier of my company whose term of service had expired about the same time as mine, had built himself a staunch boat with two paddle wheels to be worked by hand power. He proposed to descend the Missouri in this boat to St. Louis, and invited me to make the journey with him. However, I preferred to wait for a steamboat. He started on his trip alone about the middle of April, but we never heard how he got along.

The ice in the Missouri broke up about a week earlier than usual, and the latter part of April I began to make frequent ascents of some of the highest hills about Fort Randall. From their summits I could look for many miles down the river and watch for a steamboat, for I was impatient to return to civilization. Finally the boat arrived on the evening of the first day of May, somewhat sooner than we had expected her. On this boat came Major James Longstreet, who was a paymaster in the United States Army and destined to become a Lieutenant General in the Confederate Army, and a conspicuous figure all through the war of the Rebellion.

Major Longstreet, with the assistance of his clerk, J. T. Bradley, paid off the troops at the fort next morning. I received all my due pay, and my retained pay of two dollars per month. The retained pay was the amount held back by the Government from each soldier since the pay had been raised in 1854, to be given to him at the expiration of his service. I also received more than fifty dollars, which I had saved on my clothing allowance and mileage to New York City, the place of my enlistment. All this amounted to over three hundred dollars—quite a sum of money for a boy not eighteen years old. It made me feel wealthy. From the pay of every soldier throughout his service there was a monthly deduction of twelve and a half cents, which went towards the maintenance of the Soldiers' Home at Washington, D. C., an institution of great benefit to old and indigent soldiers.

I engaged cabin passage on the steamer to St. Louis, as did a few other discharged soldiers, among them Sergeant John Brown of my company, whom I had first met as cockswain of the Governor's Island barge. Sergeant Brown had re-enlisted, and was going on a furlough. Later on he was made an Ordnance Sergeant. A few other discharged and furloughed soldiers took deck passage. I had sold or given away my clothing and bedding, and bought a suit of citizens' clothing at the sutler's store—regular wild western store clothes. I took with me a collection of Indian pipes, mocassins, bows and arrows, etc., and about three days after the arrival of the steamboat, I bade farewell to my comrades

TEN YEARS IN THE RANKS U.S. ARMY

and to the officers of my company, receiving some good advice from Captain Gardner.

Many of my comrades advised me to remain in the west, and grow up with the country; and I came near doing so, but a strong desire to go to New York and see my mother overcame all other considerations. I was still very young, hopeful and ambitious to succeed in civil life, and I was strong and healthy in spite of the hardship and sufferings I had endured in my tender years.

I little thought at that time that in a year I should re-enlist and serve in the same company throughout the Civil War, in the Army of the Potomac. Neither did I think that I was too young and inexperienced at that time for success in civil life, or that it would require another term of service of harder experience to mature and prepare me for a permanent career outside of the army.

There were a few furloughed officers on the steamboat, among them Brevet Major Henry W. Wessells of my regiment, an estimable officer who was taking his eldest son, H. W. Wessells, Jr., whom I knew very well, to place in a school at Danbury, Connecticut. Young Wessells became a Second Lieutenant in the Army in 1865, while his father was retired as a Lieutenant Colonel and Brevet Brigadier General in 1871.

We took many passengers on the way down the river, some of them very interesting and talkative people, but Major Longstreet and his clerk, Bradley, led the conversations at the steamer's public dining-table. They were not only the most interesting talkers but received the most respectful attention.

I had not been many days on the river, when I was afflicted with the chills and fever again, and had to keep to my berth a great part of the time. It seemed as though I was to suffer from that or dumb-ague every time I traveled on this river. There was no doctor on the boat, but an elderly colored man, the chief steward, heard of my illness and came to see me. He assured me that he could cure me with three doses of medicine, so I would never have the fever again. For this he sagaciously demanded five dollars in advance. I was desperate, so I gave him the money and told him to go ahead. He brought me a dose of medicine, which was the vilest stuff I ever tasted and made me feel very sick. After an interval of a day he brought me another dose, which tasted so much worse than the first and made me feel so ill that no amount of his persuasion could induce me to take his third dose. I vowed that I would rather have the ague for ever after than to take his medicine. About this time we had reached Leavenworth, where I spent about half a day on shore. I began to feel better, and before I reached St. Louis I was entirely well.

At one of the towns along the river a gentleman and his son from Cleveland or Rochester, who were traveling on business in the west, took passage for St. Louis and struck up an acquaintance with me. The elder man seemed to be greatly interested in my experience in the Indian country, and before we reached St. Louis he invited me to visit him. He hinted that he would charge himself with my future, if I would go with him; but I declined. I was too much bent on getting back to New York, where I hoped to build up my future by my own efforts.

The river was high, and we had a quick passage to St. Louis, where my companion, Sergeant Brown, and I stayed for two days, seeing, after so long in the wilderness, the sights of a large city. We left St. Louis for New York on a Saturday afternoon, and arrived at Cincinnati on Sunday morning, where we had to lie over until midnight as no trains went out on Sunday. With a few changes of cars, we reached New York, where we separated, and I went home.

PART VII.

RE-ENLISTMENT AND RETURN TO FRONTIERS, 1860.

IT is not my intention to describe in detail my experiences as a civilian during the period between my first and second enlistments, but to restrict this story to my army career. I will only state here that my lack of knowledge of civil life made it hard for me to obtain any remunerative or permanent employment. I made all kinds of efforts, answering advertisements by letter or in person; in the latter case often finding a crowd of applicants ahead of me, most of whom had some experience in the kind of work offered. I often walked the streets looking for work and felt heartsick and discouraged at my failure to find employment. My little stock of money diminished day by day although I practiced the strictest economy, spending a few pennies for a mid-day meal when I was tramping about the city. After a time, during the summer, I found occasional employment; but it was not until fall that I secured a steady job where, however, the hours were long, the pay small and the work uncongenial.

About the midde of March, 1860, I was visited by two discharged soldiers from my company who had also come to New York, their former home, in search of employment, but without success. They had made up their minds to re-enlist and asked me to join them. I considered the matter carefully, and seeing no prospects for advancement, finding myself poorer financially than if I had remained in the service, and having a real fondness for a soldier's life, I decided to give up my employment and try my fortune once more in the military service.

On the twenty-fourth day of March, 1860, my two comrades and I re-enlisted to serve for five years in the United States

Army. The recruiting office was in Chatham Street (now called Park Row), New York city. First Lieutenant Thomas W. Sweeney of my old company was the recruiting officer. He remembered us, seemed glad to have us return to the service and promised to see to it that we would be restored to our former regiment and company. It was just one year, lacking a week, since I had been discharged at Fort Randall, Nebraska Territory. My age at my re-enlistment was nineteen years, less three months.

We passed the medical examination, were sworn into the service by a notary, and on the same day were sent to Governor's Island, New York harbor. As I was no longer a musician I was assigned to quarters in the upper casemates of Castle Williams, along with a number of raw recruits. I found no changes or improvements on the island since I had left it more than five years before; it seemed the same as I have already described it, only the officers had all been changed. Major T. H. Holmes of the Eighth Infantry was in command.

In a few days I drew my kit and clothing at the quartermaster's stores and had to commence drilling along with other recruits who were being instructed by the drill-sergeants in their facings, marching, etc. The officer in command of the drilling squads soon discovered that I was well versed in all that was to be taught the recruits and detailed me to take a few of the stupidest of the lot to one side and try to instruct them. I disliked drilling this awkward squad, as it was very trying to my patience. They did not seem to know the left foot from the right; and when ordered to keep their heads up, out would go their stomachs. When it came to an "about face," some of them fell over themselves.

One afternoon a comrade and myself were detailed for fatigue duty to dig a grave for a soldier who had died in the hospital. We were supplied with pick and shovel and conducted to the island graveyard by a sergeant who marked out the location and the dimensions of the grave and then left, after admonishing us to be sure to have the job finished before two o'clock in the afternoon, when the funeral was to take place. Neither my comrade nor I had ever handled a pick or shovel before and we found the work hard. It was a warm day in April. We soon grew tired and felt very hot and dry. Opportunely the sutler's store was close by and beer by the glass was sold there. We found it necessary to refresh ourselves several times during the forenoon and to take a good long rest at noon-time. At two o'clock we were still digging when we heard the drums and fifes playing the dead-march and saw the funeral approaching from the hospital close by. The procession entered the graveyard and lined up at the grave; the corpse was ready, but we were not, for we had dug a hole only about four feet deep. After a scolding we were ordered to quit—much to our satisfaction. A couple of strong and husky Irishmen soon dug the hole to the required depth of six feet and the ceremonies were completed.

After a few weeks I was transfered from the castle to the garrison, where both the quarters and food were better. As I understood all the necessary drill, a rifle and accoutrements were issued to me and I had to take my turn at guard duty twice a week. I well remember that, the first time I was a sentinel on post, I was stationed on the shore facing Brooklyn, in front of some store houses, where I paced for two hours at a time and then was relieved and had four hours off before going on post again. In the day-time I could interest myself in watching the movements of steamboats and small craft on the river, but at night it was lonesome and the time on post seemed much longer. We had a little rest at night, during the four hours off, when we lay down on a hard wooden platform in the guard-house which was built for that purpose. We had to keep all our clothing and accoutrements on, and were generally disturbed after midnight by sentinel number one in front of the guard-house calling out, "Turn out the guard for the officer of the day" when we hurried out, formed ranks and were inspected by the officer of the day, who usually made the rounds of all the sentinels on the different posts at that hour.

There was on the island at that time a sergeant with a Polish name who had the immediate charge of the raw recruits. He was a martinet, a tyrannical bully in his treatment of the poor and ignorant recruits, who feared and hated him, but he was artful enough to keep aloof from the old soldiers who understood their rights and privileges. He seemed to be the most detested non-commissioned officer in the army.

I was impatient to rejoin my regiment on the frontier and to get away from Governor's Island, where my former experience was not a happy one; but it was not until early in June that a detachment of recruits for the Ninth Infantry, then serving in Oregon, was ready to depart. With this detachment of one hundred and fifty, another of fifty, destined for the Second United States Infantry, stationed in Dakota Territory, was to travel a part of the way. I secured a pass to be absent for forty-eight hours and went to the city to bid farewell to my mother and friends. One morning a few days later we formed on the parade ground, fully equipped with knapsack, haversack, tin cup, tin plate, knife, fork and spoon, a canteen and three days' rations of boiled salt pork and hard bread stowed in our haversacks; but without arms. We were escorted to the wharf by the post band, playing the usual airs, and embarked on a steamboat for the Erie Railroad depot in Jersey City.

Upon our arrival at the railroad depot we found a special train waiting to take us out West. The soldiers traveled in emigrant cars with bare wooden seats, very uncomfortable to ride in and very fatiguing, as we could sleep but little in our cramped positions. My experience on this journey was similar to that of my first trip West five years before. We lived on our rations with a quart-cupful of hot coffee with milk twice a day at some of the stations.

Upon arriving at Chicago the fifty recruits for the Second United States Infantry, of whom I was one, changed cars for St. Louis, Missouri, while the larger party kept on West as far as the railroad went and then had a long march across the plains to Oregon. From St. Louis we went South a few miles by cars to Jefferson Barracks, on the west bank of the Mississippi River, where we arrived about the middle of June. There were few soldiers at the barracks at that time, about a dozen re-enlisted men awaiting an opportunity to rejoin their regiments, like myself, and a few score recruits in addition to our detachment. The barracks was pleasantly situated on high ground overlooking the river and was quite extensive. The country round about was sparsely settled, with large stretches of still uncultivated land and woods. A good road led to the village of Carondelet about half-way to St. Louis. Midway between the barracks and the village was a tavern called "The Stone House," which was much frequented by the soldiers.

I was appointed lance-corporal and helped to drill the recruits. I was also corporal of the guard about once a week and, as such, posted and relieved the sentinels. This gave me plenty of spare time for roving about the country, and for fishing and swimming in the Mississippi River. I was exceedingly fond of swimming and for nearly three months, except when on guard, I had a swim immediately after the reveille roll-call before breakfast, rain or shine. The weather was very hot that summer and I went into the water generally twice more during the day and always had a short swim in the evening after sundown to fasten a fish-line to a snag in the river about fifty yards from the shore, where I often found a catfish when I examined the line in the morning. It was pleasant to sit in the cool shade on the river-bank and see some of the famous Mississippi river steam-boats racing by, for at that time there were still many boats plying the river and the levee at St. Louis was crowded with them. Several times I secured a pass for a twenty-four hours' visit to St. Louis, and walked six or seven miles to Carondelet a few times without a pass.

Farm produce was very cheap; we improved our rations at very little expense and lived fairly well during the summer.

Early in September about sixty-five of the recruits destined for the Second United States Infantry, myself among the number, received orders to proceed to St. Louis and there to embark on a steamboat for St. Paul, Minnesota. We boarded the cars of the Iron Mountain Railroad at the barracks station and rode to St. Louis. It was a long distance from the railroad depot to the steamboat, which was near the north end of the levee; the day was hot and I staggered along under my heavily loaded knapsack and was ready to drop when we reached the steamer. My excessive swimming had weakened me to an extent that I was not aware of.

The steamer was a regular passenger and freight boat of the usual type; there were no bunks nor any kind of accommodations for us and we had to stay on the lower deck with the freight, spreading out blankets and sleeping any place we could find room. This proved to be a great hardship for me, for on the second day of our journey I became ill with a violent attack of what we called dumb-ague, which lasted until we reached St. Paul. It seemed that every time I traveled on the Missouri or the Mississippi rivers I was to have a fever of some sort. Dr. Andrew K. Smith, our surgeon, dosed me so liberally with quinine that I was in a stupor, so that my memory is almost a blank regarding this trip up the river. I could not eat the rations, but, fortunately, had some money and could bribe the cabin cooks to give me nourishing soup and a few delicacies, for which I was grateful. When we landed at St. Paul I felt better and was able to march to a camp prepared for us a few miles from the city, where Sibley tents had been put up and a train of about twenty army wagons with their six-mule teams were ready to load up with commissary and quartermaster's stores for Fort Abercrombie, Dakota Territory, which was our destination.

In a few days we started on our long march, passing through Minneapolis, and then in a northwesterly direction through a sparsely settled country to the town of St. Cloud, on the Mississippi, which dwindled to a small river at that point. Captain Deluzier Davidson, together with a lieutenant and a surgeon, were the officers of our detachment. I was still weak, but improved rapidly under the influence of the healthy atmosphere and the out-of-door life. I could not make a full day's march, however, although we carried no knapsacks; sometimes I rode the doctor's horse when he wanted to walk, or rode in one of the wagons when I was tired out. We did not attempt hard marches, but started at sunrise and generally encamped in the early afternoon, for Captain Davidson loved his ease and comfort, and there was no necessity to rush us along. At St. Cloud we rested for a day and washed our clothing in the river.

A day's march after we left St. Cloud all signs of settlements disappeared and we saw no more until we came to the town of Alexandria, a cluster of houses on a lake, about half-way between St. Paul and Fort Abercrombie. We were now in a country full of lakes, large and small, some of them were beautiful—the water clear and teeming with fish. When we arrived at the Otter Tail Lake, which was larger than any we had seen, we rested for another day and were amazed at the countless numbers of pelicans that we saw. These birds, when not fishing, rested on the islands in the lake, completely covering them, and from a distance it seemed as though they were covered with snow. We made a sort of seine out of feed bags, sewed together end to end, about twenty-five feet in length, and fastened to a stick at each end. Two men would wade into the lake for a short distance, extend this seine and drag it towards the shore, bringing with them many fish that struggled and wriggled when they got into shallow water, where we picked out with our hands such of them as we fancied.

Although we were in the country of the Chippawa Indian, we saw none of them until we reached Breckenridge, an old trading-post, where we met a few of the savages. Breckenridge was an easy day's march from Fort Abercrombie. We had just finished establishing our camp there for the night when several wagons and a small escort of soldiers arrived and halted for a while. They were from the fort on their way to St. Paul, and with them was Captain William M. Gardner of my company, going home on a six-months' furlough, accompanied by his wife and negro servants. They rode in a spring wagon (about the size of an ambulance) drawn by two horses. The captain was somewhat surprised to find me back in the army again. He talked with me for a long while and mentioned that he would make me a non-commissioned officer as soon as there was a vacancy in the company. He advised me to study with a view to being admitted to the military academy at West Point, and promised to use his influence, along with that of some other officers, to obtain for me an "appointment at large" from the President when I could qualify for admission. Much to my regret, I never saw Captain Gardner again. He resigned his commission before his furlough expired (while at his home in Georgia) and joined the Confederate Army.

The next day we arrived at Fort Abercrombie. The fort was situated on the west bank of the Red River of the North, which here marked the dividing line between Dakota and Minnesota Territories. This river flows north and empties into Lake Winnipeg in the British possessions, while the Mississippi, but little more than a hundred miles to the east, flows south. The Red river was but a small stream, navigable for canoes only. The most interesting thing about it and the Wild Rice river, a tributary a few miles away, were the dams built by beavers, which were plentiful on both rivers. Muskrats were also abundant.

The place was a fort in name only; it was in a bend of the river, whose course was marked by a fringe of woods in places, while all else was a bleak, level prairie as far as the eye could see. Two companies of my regiment had arrived here from Fort Randall in the spring and had built the customary log huts, which they were now occupying, in the woods on the low bottom-land of the river. Two other companies made the long march from Fort Laramie, via Fort Randall, and had arrived here in midsummer. These companies were engaged in building permanent quarters of hewn logs, with board floors and shingled roofs, on the plateau which formed the edge of the prairie. The soldiers' quarters consisted of one large room to house an entire company with a wing for the kitchen and mess-room. These buildings had not yet been completed upon our arrival and the two companies were in camp in Sibley tents. It was the end of September, the nights were getting cold and we had an occasional white frost in the morning; we were a few degrees further north than at Fort Pierre and on a higher elevation.

Our detachment of recruits was apportioned to the different

companies and I rejoined Company D, in which I had served during my first enlistment. I missed a number of my old comrades—they had been discharged and had scattered throughout the West—but most of the former non-commissioned officers had re-enlisted. The first, or orderly sergeant, as he was also called, had me appointed as company clerk, which was an easy job and excused me from guard duty and from work upon the new quarters. This lasted for about two months, when we had a dispute and I was ordered back to do duty the same as any other private.

Fort Abercrombie was a dreary, lonesome place. The Chippawa Indians seldom came there and only in small parties and for a short stay. Their villages were much farther north—as far as Pembina, near the British lines.

A paymaster arrived at the post shortly after we did, accompanied by Major Irving McDowell, who was an assistant inspector general. He was a fine looking and apparently genial officer. He made a thorough inspection of the post and the soldiers. I little thought then that I would next see him in Washington after the battle of Bull Run, a defeated general. The commander of the post was Major Hannibal Day of the Second Infantry, a dignified old gentleman with long white hair and beard and a cold austere look in his eyes. The company commanders were Captains Christopher S. Lovell and Deluzier Davidson; a first lieutenant was in command of the third company, and my own was commanded by Second Lieutenant Wm. H. Jordan of the Ninth Infantry, who was temporarily attached to my regiment, our captain being absent on furlough and the first lieutenant on recruiting service in New York city. A few other second lieutenants and the surgeon made up the complement of officers at this time.

In October we began to have frosts and some snow; the Sibley tents were cold and uncomfortable, as no sheet-iron stoves had been provided and when we attempted to build fires in them the smoke drove us out. This led to various contrivances to warm our tents. In my own we dug a deep pit on one side and a covered trench with two lateral branches extending from it under the dirt floor, with openings outside of the tent for the smoke to escape from the fire which was built in the pit. This system of heating kept the tent comfortably warm except when the wind was contrary.

A great snow-storm and blizzard struck us in November and caused much suffering. Fortunately our quarters were completed about the end of the month; we moved in and enjoyed the comfort of sleeping in bunks on bedsacks filled with dried leaves, and warming ourselves at the two stoves with which our quarters were provided, although the large room except directly around the stoves was freezing cold. In January and February the thermometer sometimes fell to more than forty degrees below zero. We had a number of frost-bite cases in our little log-house hospital—some of them very severe—before our unsympathetic post commander issued an order to relieve all sentinels except Post No. 1, in front of the guard house, who, with the temperature twenty degrees minus zero, was to be relieved every thirty minutes.

I had to take my tour of guard duty about once a week and was on post for two hours at a time with four hours off. I was warmly clothed, but when the temperature was down to thirty or lower I was chilled to the bone in less than an hour. In the night I often leaned my gun against a snowbank and beat my hands against my shoulders vigorously and ran to and fro the extent of my beat to keep my feet from freezing. On my hands I wore a pair of heavy woolen gloves and over them mittens made of buffalo skin with the hair on the inside, yet my fingers became so numb with the cold that, if I had had occasion to fire off my gun, I could not have reloaded it. From a board fence close to my post the intense cold forced out nails, which whirred through the air with a whizzing sound.

Wolves were plentiful; they came howling around our kitchens at night and close to the sentinels—less than a hundred feet away sometimes, when I shouted and rushed at them with my bayonet to scare them away. When a horse or a mule died, he was dragged out on the prairie a short distance and there devoured by the wolves. Traps were set in the snow about the carcass and many wolves were caught, while the others picked the bones clean.

I was frequently excused from the severe guard duty by being selected as commanding officer's orderly. This was a reward for the soldier whose clothing, arms and equipment the adjutant considered the cleanest and neatest. A speck of rust or a small spot on the clothing often put a man out of the race. There was great rivalry for this selection among the soldiers, for the orderly had an easy time. He could sit in a warm room in the commanding officer's quarters, carry a few messages during the day and sleep in his own bunk all night.

During the long, dreary winter we kept within doors, when not on duty, for the inclemency of the weather permitted but little out-of-door exercise. In compliance with Captain Gardner's advice, I borrowed text-books from Lieutenant Jordan, who was but lately from West Point, also from some other officers, and studied them all through the winter during my spare time. Some soldiers read papers and magazines, but the favorite pastime was playing checkers and cards; the games were euchre, seven-up, forty-five and poker, at which the stakes were dried beans instead of money.

An enterprising citizen established an express service between St. Paul and Fort Abercrombie with way-stations for the changing of drivers and horses. This gave us a mail service once a week, when the weather permitted, and kept us in touch with the world. The expressman took orders from us for any articles we wished from St. Paul and brought up the packages, as well as goods for the sutler.

There was a Scotchman in my company, whom we called Sandy, who was an excellent cook and a born caterer. During the winter he proposed to get up a dinner to be followed by dancing in the company's mess-room. Permission was obtained for "Sandy's ball," as we called it; most of the company subscribed, as well as some soldiers from the other companies. Sandy shrewdly collected the cash and gave no credit, then he sent to St. Paul for stone china dishes, for we had only tin cups and plates in our mess-room. He ordered hams, tongues, sardines, pickles, preserves, lemons, etc., not forgetting a few dozen bottles of American champagne, which had been carefully packed with sawdust into barrels both for safety and concealment. These goods arrived in due time and Sandy was a busy man, cooking hams and venison and baking pies and cakes. We helped him put up a few decorations and a lot of candles around the walls.

All was ready when the eventful evening arrived. The dinner was to be at eight o'clock, followed by dancing until midnight, with two fiddlers and a flute player to furnish the music. A half dozen soldiers' wives were the only ladies present; but we had as many more of the younger men dressed up in borrowed female clothes. The dinner was voted a great success and we lauded Sandy. We had bottled ale from the sutler's and topped off with whiskey punch, which continued to be served throughout the evening. Then the tables and benches were moved into a corner, the dishes piled on them, and the dancing commenced.

Everything went well for a while and we had lots of fun, until trouble started between the fiddlers. One of them, Mike Burns, had partaken of too much punch and wanted to play an Irish jig, while his German partner held out for a waltz. This enraged Mike so that he exclaimed, "Oi despises no nation, but damn the Dutch!" and smashed his fiddle over his partner's head. The combatants were separated, Mike was put out, order restored and the dancing resumed. While the dance went on Sandy had been busy in the kitchen selling Ohio champagne to the soldiers at steep prices. This, together with liberal quantities of whiskey punch, began to show its effects and the fun became fast and furious, until near midnight a fight started in one end of the room and in a moment a dozen or more of the soldiers were in the midst of it. Bottles and dishes were thrown about the room; the women screamed and rushed for the door; Sandy was up on a table waving his arms and shouting, "Quit yer fechting! dinna be breaking me dishes, I'm a puir mon," when the table upset and he went down to the floor among his broken dishes. The officer of the day and a few files of the guard, together with the corporal, now made their appearance and quelled the disturbance. All those who showed marks of having been fighting or were drunk were marched off to the guardhouse and all others ordered to their quarters.

Sandy's ball had a sad sequel for him. He was a canny Scot and took good care of his bawbees (pence), saving much of his pay for some years, and it was assumed that he had made money out of the ball. A few weeks later, during midwinter, Sandy was missing for nearly a week and when he was at last brought back to the post in the express sleigh he had to be put into the hospital with his feet so badly frozen that all of his toes on both feet had to be amputated. He remained in the hospital until spring, when he was able to go about on crutches. He was then dishonorably discharged, forfeiting his pay due and all allowances. In the woods close to the post we built a shack for him to live in, also a stable, for he bought some cows and had them sent up from the settlements. There he made his living by selling milk and butter to the soldiers and ice cream, at which he was an adept. By the time we left the post he had discarded his crutches and was able to hobble about on his stumps.

Newspapers kept us informed of what transpired in the southern states after Lincoln's election to the presidency in November; how the violent threats of the south culminated in the secession of South Carolina from the Union on December twentieth, 1860, soon to be followed by other southern states. We read how Major Anderson transferred his small force from Fort Moultry to Sumpter, and about the firing on the steamer "Star of the West" with reinforcements for Fort Sumpter. We also heard that the Secretary of War, John B. Floyd, was accused of robbing the Indian Trust Funds and of depleting the Northern arsenals of arms and ammunition and of sending them south while still in office; also how in February General Twiggs traitorously surrendered the Seventh United States Infantry and other troops serving in Texas to the Confederacy; and how the rank and file refused the inducements held out to them to join the Confederate army, but were paroled and later on exchanged and did valiant service in the Union army, while a large number of their officers joined the standard of the enemy. We discussed these events earnestly and were much stirred when we learned that Fort Sumpter had been bombarded on April twelfth and evacuated by Major Anderson. We then understood that this was the commencement of war.

Militia soldiers from Pennsylvania reached Washington a few days later and on the fifteenth of April the President called out seventy-five thousand volunteers to serve for three months. Another proclamation of the President, dated May third for an increase of the regular army by twenty-two thousand and of the navy by eighteen thousand, was read to us on dress parade. In the meantime hundreds of the officers of the regular army had resigned their commissions and nearly all joined the Confederacy, among them my captain and some other officers of my regiment. To the credit of the rank and file be it said that, with very few exceptions, they remained loyal to the Government in the hour of its need. We began to wonder whether we were likely to take any part in putting down the rebellion before it was over, or whether we were to remain here in the Indian country.

Spring had come. When the snow had melted and the prairie became dry, we began to drill from three to four hours each day except on Saturday afternoons and Sundays. We had company, battalion, skirmish and bayonet drills, as well as target practice, and in a few months we became very expert in all of them. I was fond of the free action in skirmish drill, but did not like drilling in close formation. I also liked the bayonet exercise, and at target practice few could show a better score.

When not on duty we spent much of our time at the river, fishing, and swimming after the water had become warm enough. A favorite diversion was to go up the river a few miles and build a small raft of sticks to hold our clothes, swimming and pushing the raft before us down the current which flowed through shady woods. A small party of Chippawa Indians and squaws appeared a few times during the early summer and danced for rations, which was the only thing that relieved the monotony at this post.

TEN YEARS IN THE RANKS U. S. ARMY

We read of small engagements that had taken place between the opposing forces in various parts of the country and that an army was being concentrated at Washington, where two companies of our regiment from Fort Snelling, Minnesota, had gone. We envied these companies; they had a chance to see something of the war, which would soon be over, as we imagined, while we fretted and chafed in this lonely, far-off place, seemingly forgotten by the Government. At last, about the middle of July, we received the joyful news that two companies of the Second Minnesota Volunteers were on the way from St. Paul to relieve us and that we were ordered to Washington. In a few days the two companies arrived, weary and footsore from their long march. Most of them were very young lads who, though strong and hearty, were unaccustomed to marching on the burning hot prairies in midsummer. They had arms and accoutrements, but as yet no uniforms. We gave them a hearty reception, fraternized with them and helped to make them comfortable in their camp until they could occupy our quarters.

We packed our dress uniforms, hats and surplus clothing into packing-cases from the quartermaster's department, which were received some time after our arrival in Washington. In a few days our wagon-train was made up, we put our knapsacks on board, and left Fort Abercrombie without any regrets, early on a forenoon, amidst mutual cheering and a salute of "Present arms!" from the battalion of volunteers. All of the officers' ladies, as they called themselves, and the soldiers' wives and children went with us, riding in ambulances and in the army wagons.

Our first day's march ended at Breckenridge; our second day's march was a much longer one—we pursued about the same route as in the previous fall when we came up from St. Paul, but did not have the short marches we had enjoyed with the easy-going Captain Davidson. We soon found out that Major Hannibal Day was forcing us along at a rate of from twenty-four to thirty miles a day, which was very severe in the scorching heat of a July sun on the prairies. A number of men gave out on these long marches and were picked up by the rearguard and put into the wagons. To be sure, we were anxious to get to Washington before the war would be over, but we did not want to kill ourselves in trying to get there. The men cursed the Major for an old tyrant, not loud but very deep.

We had completed about one-half of our journey to St. Paul when we encountered the express wagon carrying the mail to Fort Abercrombie and from newspapers received learned of the disaster and rout of the Union Army at Bull Run. This sad news staggered us—we could scarcely believe it. The northern press, from which we derived our information and shaped our opinions, had boasted so much about the patriotism and valor of the militia, who so promptly responded to the President's first call for troops, that we had fondly believed a single real battle would be enough to give the Confederacy a terrible lesson and break up the rebellion. We were indignant at the conduct of some of the Union troops, as we then understood it, the news of Bull Run cast a deep gloom over our battalion and we realized that we were likely to arrive at Washington in ample time to see something of the war.

Major Day, upon whom we looked as a very unfeeling man, allowed us some unusual privileges on this march. At St. Cloud a brewery had been erected, and when we were within four days' march of the town one forenoon we met a two-horse wagon loaded with kegs of lager beer, packed in ice and carefully covered over to shield it from the fierce rays of the sun. There was a man on the wagon beside the driver who, we noticed, had some talk with the Major and then turned the wagon around and followed our column until we halted for a rest, when we learned that each man who desired to do so might purchase a quart cup of beer for ten cents (a non-commissioned officer saw to it that no one got more than a quart). A rush was made for the beer wagon and keg after keg was tapped. It tasted delicious and cheered us. The officers also drank it, sending their servants for it; indeed, old Major Day, himself, did not disdain it. The beer wagon met us every day thereafter, near noontime, all the way down to St. Paul, and when it appeared we halted for a longer rest at the next convenient place and ate our lunch.

The Union sentiment was strong in the few small settlements through which we passed. At St. Cloud, where we encamped about a mile from town and rested for a day, the citizens gave us a generous welcome. A lady named Jane G. C. Swisshelm, who edited a newspaper there called "The Visitor," assisted by a committee of citizens and accompanied by the St. Cloud band, drove out to our camp, bringing with them a fine lunch and kegs of beer, for which we were very grateful. We gave her and the citizens of St. Cloud three rousing cheers when they departed.

The last day's march but one brought us to Minneapolis, where we encamped for the night on some fields just outside of the town, too tired and worn out to care for anything but to lie down and rest. This had been the hardest day's march of all—Major Day had made us cover thirty-two miles. Many men dropped out along the dusty road, overcome by the heat and fatigue; some fell asleep in shady places and did not reach camp until midnight. I was one of only a third of my company that was able to keep in the ranks until we reached camp. As the race is not always to the swift, so marching is not always the forte of the biggest and strongest men in a company of soldiers.

Next morning we resumed our march somewhat later than was customary, passing through Minneapolis, which was but a small town then, on to St. Paul, about ten miles away. The road between the two places had only farms and a few clusters of houses scattered along it. Upon arriving at St. Paul we marched to the steamboat wharf with closed ranks and received much attention and cheering from the citizens. When our wagon-train arrived, we got our knapsacks and the four companies boarded a steamboat which was waiting for us; we stowed ourselves away wherever we could find room, except on the cabin deck, which was reserved for passengers. There was no railroad at St. Paul then. We were to go down the Mississippi as far as La Crosse, Wisconsin, and take the cars there.

We sailed in the early afternoon; the boat was crowded and the weather very hot. When night came on my bunkie and I, along with others, spread our blankets on the hurricane deck back of the smokestacks. We took off our shoes and blouses, used our knapsacks for pillows and the starry sky for a covering. Being very tired, we were soon in a deep sleep. During the night I was awakened by a terrific yell and saw that my bunkie was sitting up, clutching at his chest and roaring with pain. I was confused, and for a moment I imagined the boat was on fire, as I saw fiery sparks in the air. We soon discovered the cause of the trouble. A large red-hot cinder from the smokestack (the boat burned wood for fuel and had high-pressure engines) had lodged on his bare breast through his open shirt and burned him severely enough to raise a large blister. We moved our bed to a safer place and slept peacefully for the remainder of the hot night.

Early in the afternoon on the following day we disembarked at La Crosse, where we noticed a train made up of one passenger car and a lot of empty box cars which was apparently waiting for us. We were indignant and loudly expressed our determination not to enter these cars and travel like cattle. The officers who, no doubt, overheard us, must have been of the same opinion, for we were not ordered into the cars but stacked arms and waited about three hours until a number of cars with hard wooden seats came along to replace the others. We embarked and started for Chicago.

After a weary night we arrived in Chicago the next day, where a change of cars was made, much for the better, as we got cushioned seats this time. We remained there about two hours and during that time crowds of citizens surrounded us and served us with coffee, sandwiches and pies, and presented us with cigars and tobacco. At Chicago we lost two men by desertion—the only ones on the entire trip. We also lost Captain Davidson, who remained behind and later on resigned his commission. He was an elderly man, very corpulent and unable to stand the hardships of a campaign.

All through the loyal western states across which we

traveled there had been an uprising for the Union. The people were enthusiastic and gave us a hearty welcome wherever we stopped. At a town in Indiana, where we arrived near midnight, the citizens must have been informed of our coming. The station platform was crowded with people and they had a band playing patriotic airs. A group of young ladies, all dressed in white and wearing red-white-and-blue sashes, sang "The Star Spangled Banner" for us. Since the news of defeat at Bull Run the people were ready to make any sacrifice; the Northern papers clamored for the formation of a new army and an immediate advance "on to Richmond." It must have been during the time of this national excitement and enthusiasm that Josh Billings wrote the memorable words, "The Union must and shall be preserved, if I sacrifice all my wife's relations."

On our arrival in Harrisburg, Pennsylvania, in the forenoon, the depot was jammed with people. Provisions enough for a feast and baskets of fruit were brought into our cars; it seemed as though everyone in the crowd wished to do something for us. After leaving Harrisburg we received orders to load our rifles, for there were rumors of expected trouble in Baltimore while the troops were traversing the city from one depot to another, for at this time the trains did not pass through to the Washington depot and it was necessary to march a long distance through the streets of the city. We reached Baltimore about four in the afternoon, formed ranks in the street, fixed bayonets and marched by fours in close order with the venerable Major Hannibal Day leading us. We carried our knapsacks, haversacks and canteens; we were dusty and dirty and bronzed by the hot sun on our recent march across the prairies. There were four companies of us and we looked more seasoned and determined than the militia troops that had passed through Baltimore before. We marched silently, only words of command being heard. There were many people on the streets regarding us with close attention. Sometimes a ruffian yelled out, "Bull Run!" which provoked no reply from us. A large, red-headed woman leaning out of a third-story window shouted,

"Three cheers for Jeff Davis!" but got very scant encouragement from the people in the street.

We reached the depot without having any trouble, but were kept waiting there a long time and it was quite dusk in the evening when we embarked for Washington, arriving at the national capitol late in the evening. In Washington we formed ranks and marched to the "Soldiers' Rest," a large shed-building north of the capitol and but a short distance from it, where newly arrived troops received food and rested for a short time before going to their camps or quarters. The place had a board floor on which we spread our blankets. We were glad to stretch ourselves for we were very tired and stiff after our ride of three days and nights in a cramped position on the narrow seats of the cars. I think I fell asleep as soon as I lay down, and no ordinary noise could have waked me up before morning.

PART VIII.

SERVICE IN WASHINGTON AND GEORGETOWN, D. C., 1861-1862.

WHEN I awoke on my first morning in Washington, I hastened out of doors to have a look around. The first prominent object I saw was the great white capitol building, the steel ribs of its unfinished dome strongly outlined against a clear sky. I took a long look at everything in view and then answered roll-call and had breakfast in the "Soldiers' Rest," after which we formed ranks in the street, where we "stacked arms" and waited for orders, watching meanwhile the arrival of some volunteer troops who had just come in on the cars and marched into the "Soldiers' Rest." Troops were beginning to arrive daily in large numbers in response to the President's call for "four hundred thousand more." About ten o'clock in the forenoon we received orders to "fall in" and the four companies separated, being sent to quarters in different parts of the city.

My company marched up Pennsylvania Avenue toward the White House. On the way some ladies presented each man with a Havelock, which is a cover for the forage cap and was made of white muslin and with a hood to protect the back of the head and neck from the sun's rays. They had been much worn by English soldiers in India during Major-General Sir Henry Havelock's time, and looked very fine when an entire regiment wore them on parade; but in less than a year their use was abandoned, as they were too conspicuous and kept the air from our necks. Our march ended at a house on the north side of K, near Eighteenth Street, which was to be our quarters. It was a three-story and basement private dwelling of the usual type and was devoid of any furniture. It belonged to a secessionist and, like a number of others, had been taken charge of by the Government. We drew rations and did our cooking in the basement and used the upper floors for sleeping, at night spreading our blankets on the bare floor. We had only light duties to perform, which left us plenty of time to wander about the city, visit the capitol and other public buildings. Only the principal streets in Washington were paved at this time, the remainder were mud roads rendered almost impassable in rainy weather by the artillery and army wagons.

It was the first week in August; most of the three-months' warriors had left for their homes and order was being restored. The streets were patroled by regulars and all soldiers found in the city without permission were arrested, taken to a central guard-house and then returned to their respective commands. General George B. McClellan had been called to Washington immediately after the battle of Bull Run and placed in command of the Army of the Potomac. He was busy with his staff in organizing a great army. Our quarters being but a short distance from the headquarters of General McClellan, I had frequent opportunities of seeing him there and also riding through the streets, followed by a brilliant staff, among whom were a number of foreign officers in showy uniforms adorned with decorations and much gold lace. I also saw President Lincoln on the avenue a few times and saw his boys in Zouave uniforms "playing soldier" with some companions on the lawn in front of the White House.

There were probably not more than fifty thousand troops in and about Washington upon our arrival, but they soon began to come in at a rate of forty thousand a month, so that by the first of November, 1861, the numbers had reached one hundred and seventy thousand. They were young men who enlisted for three years or the duration of the war; they were patriotic and earnest and were not tempted to enlist by the payment of bounties. These soldiers became the flower of the Army of the Potomac and, I think, were not equaled by any subsequent levies.

A thousand regular soldiers had preceded our small command

to Washington and about eight hundred of them had been in the engagement at Bull Run, including some marines. Among them were also the two companies of our regiment previously mentioned. From them we learned many details of what occurred on that disastrous day. This small body of eight hundred regulars and marines were unaffected by the panic and covered the retreat of the Federal Army. Many of the regulars were quartered near the then outskirts of the city on the north side in hastily constructed wooden buildings, which were called Kalorama Barracks. There were at that time six companies of my regiment in Washington, also the regiment headquarters and the band. Four other companies were with the western armies and remained there throughout the war. During my entire ten years' service I never saw more than six companies of the regiment together at one time.

After a stay of about two weeks in the K Street house in Washington my company (D) and Company A were ordered to Georgetown and quartered in Forrest Hall, a large sized building on the corner of what were then called High and Gay Streets. This building is still standing at this date (1913). There was a large entertainment hall on the second floor with a raised stage at one end and many wooden benches on the floor. Company A occupied this apartment, while my company took the third floor, which was divided into rooms. We slept on the bare floors, as we had done in K Street, but had the additional comfort of some of the wooden benches to sit on. The first floor was used for a guard-house with a large room for prisoners brought in by the patrols; the basement, which had an alley on the rear leading out into Gay Street, was used for our kitchen.

On the hot day that we moved into this building a severe thunderstorm broke out in the afternoon and the rain fell in torrents. We thought this a good opportunity to get a refreshing bath, and as the high roof of the building could not be overlooked from any of the houses in the neighborhood, a number of us took off our clothing and ascended to the roof and remained there until the storm was over; later on we took our baths in Rock Creek and our swims in the Potomac above the Aqueduct Bridge.

It was the custom then in the regular army for every private soldier to serve a term of two weeks as company cook. There were two cooks to each company, a head cook and an assistant. After serving as assistant for a week, one then became chef, unless the chef was satisfactory and desired to remain longer. It often happened that both of the cooks remained for months; they got no extra pay, but were relieved from all other duties and had some perquisites in selling soap-grease, if there was a market for it. It was my hard luck to be detailed as assistant cook after we arrived at Forrest Hall, much to my disgust. After a week's service I was declared to be a failure and returned to company duty.

A few days later a vacancy occurred and I was promoted to corporal with two dollars per month additional pay, making fifteen dollars per month, for the pay of the army had been raised from eleven to thirteen dollars per month for a private soldier. About this time we received four months' pay in greenbacks with coupons attached to the larger notes—the ten and twenty dollar bills, I think. Heretofore we had always been paid in gold and silver.

We were busy while in Georgetown; we kept a main guard with a sergeant at the hall in charge of the prisoners, a corporal and six privates at the Aqueduct Bridge, and the same at the foot of High Street, where there was a flat-boat rope ferry to Analostan Island in the Potomac opposite Georgetown. The two companies in Georgetown did not have their full complement of men; some had been detailed as clerks in the War Department, and others as orderlies at army headquarters on "extra duty," as it was called. This made us somewhat short on the "present for duty" number and caused a tour of twenty-four hours on guard every three days or less. We also did considerable drilling in company and skirmish drills, sometimes brigade drills and a few reviews for General McClellan and staff. We had to patrol the streets of Geogretown from eight A. M. till ten P. M. for two hours on and two off. The patrol was a squad of eight privates under a sergeant or a corporal, often accompanied by an officer in the daytime. This patrol had authority to enter saloons and other places and search them for soldiers and demand their passes; every soldier on the street was halted, and if he had no pass or a poor excuse he was told to fall into the ranks and march with the patrol until it repassed or returned to the main guard, where he was turned over to the sergeant, who recorded his name, company and regiment and then locked him up. There was, however, considerable leniency both on the part of the officers and the non-commissioned officers in command of the patrol; if the soldier were sober and had some sort of a plausible excuse, he was often simply ordered to get out of town quickly and return to his camp. It was the drunks that gave us trouble, when we tried to march them in the ranks. In some extreme cases we took them to the guard-house in a borrowed hand-cart. One day the patrol arrived just in time to save the "Eagle Bakery," where a drunken soldier was wrecking the place because he failed to get a baked eagle he had ordered.

About this time a very young officer named William Kidd, who belonged to a prominent New York family, joined my company as second lieutenant. He was a civil appointee and knew very little about drill or military matters in general, but was trying to learn. He was well liked by the men for his genial nature. Often when I was on patrol with him he would say, "Now, Corporal, you head her in any direction you like and don't march too fast." He let many a soldier off with a reprimand such as, "If I catch you in town again without a pass I'll have you court-martialed and shot before sunrise." Sometimes he stopped at a cigar store and bought cigars for the patrol, which he handed to us when we were dismissed. Lieutenant Kidd, to our great regret and sorrow, was killed in less than a year at the second battle of Bull Run.

One evening I received word from a friend, a sergeant of a New York regiment which was encamped a short distance from Georgetown on the Tennalytown road that he had been arrested by the patrol and wished me to try and have him released so that he might return to his camp that night, as he feared that if he was returned to his regiment from the central guard house it would mean the loss of his sergeant's stripes and reduction to the ranks. I implored the sergeant of our main guard to release him, but he refused as he had just reported the number of his prisoners to the officer of the day. He agreed, however, to make an exchange with me if I brought him another prisoner when I went out on patrol from eight to ten that evening. I started out with my squad at the appointed time. It was a stormy night, the wind howled and the rain beat fiercely upon us; the streets seemed deserted and there were no soldiers in sight. Instead of resting at times in a sheltered place, as we were accustomed to do in bad weather, I kept my patrol moving and visited most of the places where soldiers were in the habit of congregating, despite the grumbling of my squad. Our time was nearly up and I had encountered but two or three soldiers, whom I could not arrest as they showed me passes. I was in despair, when suddenly, while passing along Bridge Street on our return to the guard house, I caught a glimpse of a blue uniform in the back room of a saloon, through a partly opened door. I halted my squad and went into the saloon, where I found a soldier asleep on a chair. I shook him and demanded to see his pass. He was mildly inebriated, but managed to explain that he was on duty as a nurse in the hospital close by and did not require a pass in Georgetown, but not having a pass was enough for me. I took him out, put him into the ranks and turned him over to the sergeant of the guard in exchange for my friend, who hurried off to his camp. The man I arrested was soon released by the sergeant when he satisfied him as to the truth of his story.

Every morning at eight o'clock when the guard was relieved, the old guard was obliged to take the prisoners picked up during the twenty-four hours and march them to the Central Guard House in Washington, situated just off Pennsylvania Avenue near the market. This was a long and tiresome tramp after a night on guard. We often had a couple of dozen prisoners, some of them unruly and others scarcely able to march after their spree. After our return from the Central Guard House the old guard was excused from duty and rested until retreat that evening. The men whom we arrested in the streets were volunteer soldiers, almost without exception, from the different camps about Washington.

Occasionally I was corporal of the main guard at Forrest Hall and was surprised to observe the effect of drink on the prisoners at different times. They were all locked up together in one large room with a sentinel outside of the door. The prisoners from our own command, when we had any, were confined in a smaller room. In the large room the prisoners were sometimes hilarious and noisy with laughter, while at other times they were sad and melancholy, many of them crying for "home and mother," and others shedding silent tears. At still other times they seemed to have imbibed fighting whiskey and were quarrelsome, fighting fiercely among themselves or against the guard who had to go in and separate them; some we could only subdue by tying their limbs. It was a job we did not relish. Some of them threw bottles at the guards and other objects which had escaped the sergeant's search at the time of their admission.

Our two companies had the free run of Georgetown to go where we pleased when not on duty, but if we crossed the Rock Creek bridge and went into Washington without a pass, we were in turn liable to be arrested by the provost-guard's patrol and put into the Central Guard House. We were well posted on the time and route of the patrols and knew how to elude them.

Another of our duties was to furnish an escort to the cemetery for all the soldiers who died in what was called the Seminary Hospital located at Georgetown. The cemetery was in the grounds of the Soldiers' Home, a long way from Georgetown, a very tiresome march over a poor road. At these funerals there was no music or ceremony of any kind; no one but the escort of eight privates and a corporal marched with the ambulance which carried the corpse. On the arrival at the cemetery we found only grave-diggers constantly busy digging graves for the many soldiers who died in the hospitals or camps in or about Washington. The coffin was unloaded and left on the ground beside the grave to await the leisure of the gravediggers; the escort fired the three customary rounds of blank cartridges over the coffin and hurried away. At some distance from the cemetery, where the road was lonely, we climbed into the ambulance and rode to the outskirts of Georgetown. During the winter when the weather was bad and the mud ankle-deep on the road, the escort took their chances and halted the ambulance near a road-house about half-way fired the three rounds and waited at the road-house playing cards until the driver, whom they bound to secrecy, passed on his return. This went on for some time until one day a firing squad was discovered at it and punished.

Towards the close of 1861 many changes had taken place among the officers of my regiment. Aside from the few who had resigned to join the Confederate army, nearly all were advanced in rank; colonels and majors and some captains became brigadier-generals or colonels of volunteers. The twelve new regiments added to the regular army absorbed many of our captains and first lieutenants who gained a step in rank by the transfer. The lower grades were filled mainly by civilian appointments, many of them through influence more than any adaptability for a military life, as was demonstrated later on. The Government began to make some appointments from the ranks and later on increased them. These men, appointed from the ranks, as a rule made efficient and reliable officers, whom the rank and file could respect. Dixon S. Miles became colonel of my regiment and remained so until he was killed at Harper's Ferry in 1862, but we never saw him, as he had a higher volunteer rank. All of our former field officers were promoted and replaced by others, some of whom we never saw. The regular army, small in numbers, was stripped of many of its best officers. All through the war, companies were largely in command of first lieutenants and regiments were often commanded by senior captains. My company was particularly unfortunate at this time in having for its captain, and serving with it, the lieutenant who had joined the regiment in 1857 at Fort Randall whom we had dubbed our "Alcoholic Lieutenant," and whose name I withhold because I cannot say anything to his credit. He had gained the rank of captain by seniority because of the general promotions at this time. Our first lieutenant was William H. Jordan of the Ninth Infantry, who had never as yet seen his own regiment in the West since he left West Point in 1860. He was an estimable officer, who remained with my company until he was severely wounded at the battle of Gaines' Mill in 1862. Our second lieutenant was William Kidd, who was killed in battle, as previously mentioned. Major William Chapman was in command of the six companies of my regiment in Washington at this time; he was well along in years and retired early in the war. He was a good disciplinarian and an excellent drill-master.

In the late fall of 1861 the regular troops in Washington, old and new regiments, had been augmented to nearly three thousand and were formed into a brigade under the command of Major George Sykes of the Fourteenth Infantry, who held the rank of brigadier-general of volunteers and later on became a major-general. I think he was one of the best tacticians in the army and a very capable officer. He drilled the brigade in line of battle manoeuvres occasionally on a large field near the Kalorama Barracks. We made a fine appearance in full uniform, marching down Pennsylvania Avenue and out Seventh Street to the drill ground, with our bands playing and colors flying. I liked this parade and drill; when we turned the corner of Fifteenth Street and I looked down the avenue and saw a great mass of bayonets glittering in the sun ahead of me it was impressive—a sight I had never witnessed in my previous service. Major Chapman, who commanded our battalions, never made an error in executing General Sykes's commands in these brigade drills, but, alas! some of the new fledglings of first lieutenants in command of companies often got tangled up; this angered the major and caused him to say sharply, "Mr. Long, face your company to the front! Mr. Freeman, bring your company on the right by file into line!

Mr. Goodrich, you are obliquing your company to the left instead of to the right," etc., all of which was very annoying to me, for it destroyed the movements of other companies and hurt the pride I always had in marching and drilling correctly. Our first sergeants were able to coach the inexperienced officers and did so quietly on parade. Fortunately for my company, our captain never appeared at brigade drills and Lieutenant Jordan put us through our paces very creditably. The brigade drills ended with a "Pass in review!" before General Sykes and his aides-de-camp. This movement was often executed in "double quick time," which gave rise to a story that the general made us double quick because his little daughter used to say to him, "Pa, make 'em twot!" which amused her greatly. The general lived with his family in a house overlooking the parade ground where they could see all the manoeuvres of the troops. We were also reviewed on the same parade ground by General McClellan and staff, but upon that occasion did not have to *trot*.

I was often on guard at the Aqueduct Bridge and at the Ferry and liked that duty much better than guarding prisoners. The Chesapeake and Ohio canal crossed the Potomac river here on its way to Alexandria, Virginia, by means of the Aqueduct Bridge. At the breaking out of the war the water had been shut off and the bridge solidly planked over to serve as a roadway for pedestrians and vehicles. A small guard room had been built for the shelter of the six men and corporal composing the guard on the Georgetown side. A sentinel was stationed on each side of the entrance to the bridge. Our orders were to permit no soldier to pass or repass the bridge without a properly signed and countersigned pass, and no civilian without a pass from the provost-marshal's office in Washington. Officers unaccompanied by troops were also to show passes, except those of high rank who were supposed to be known to us.

We were also to search for and to prevent the smuggling of liquor to the soldiers encamped on the opposite side of the river; but I am afraid we were somewhat lax in carrying out that part of our orders, as we did not like to act as customhouse inspectors, considering that unmilitary. If the person halted carried a package or basket we generally took his or her word for it that it contained no liquor and passed them on without examination, except in cases of inebriety or when they were insolent to the guard.

I think women did more smuggling of liquor than the men. Many got passes from the provost-marshal to visit their soldier relatives or friends encamped on the other side of the river. They generally came on foot and carried baskets or packages containing food and articles of clothing for the soldiers, as they invariably informed the guard, and some became indignant when they were asked the usual question about liquor. One day as I was examining the pass of a large, good-natured-looking woman with a fine broad smile, I heard a tinkling sound with every movement she made and noticed that she wore unusually large hoop skirts which made her look like an animated haystack from the waist down. I asked her if she carried any liquor about her and was met by an emphatic denial. I put my hand on her waist and gave the skirt a shake which caused an audible jingle of bottles, and asked her, "What's that, Mama?" "Whisth! Sergeant, dear, shure it's sody-wather for the bys!" she said laughingly. I was in a dilemma. She evidently had bottles of liquor strung all around her waist beneath the large hoops she wore; but I could not take them from her without undressing her, which was inconvenient at the time and place; besides it was such a clever trick that it deserved success, and I let her pass.

Some sutlers had permits to carry liquor for officers' messes in their wagons; others carried barrels which they declared contained beer or cider, which we were allowed to pass, as we had no means of testing it anyway.

We got to know many of the sutlers by sight; their wagons bore the regimental designation to which they belonged and, as we knew they had passes, we did not always halt them. Occasionally some of them tossed a package to the guards containing cigars, tobacco, crackers and cheese or a can of preserved fruit. The sentinels halted every passenger and vehicle, with this exception, looked at the pass and in cases of doubt called on the corporal of the guard for his decision of the case.

Sometimes General McClellan, who, since General Scott's retirement, was commander-in-chief of the United States Army, passed over the bridge with his staff to review troops or examine defences on the other side. It was here that I first saw the Orleans princes, the Duc de Chartres and the Comte de Paris, who were aides on his staff. The Duc was a very young looking man.

The Fourteenth New York Volunteers, better known as Colonel Fowler's Fourteenth Brooklyn Regiment, were encamped on Arlington Heights and guarded the Virginia end of the bridge. We became acquainted with many of them and were on friendly terms, often letting some of them pass into Georgetown at night, cautioning them to look sharply for the officer of the day on their return.

When my guard was relieved in the morning, we discharged our rifles into the river, firing at some floating object, instead of drawing the charges; sometimes I threw an empty bottle into the river and frequently knocked off the neck with a ball from my rifle.

While on guard at the bridge I had many opportunities to observe the uniforms, arms and equipments of the volunteer soldiers who crossed and went into camp on the other side. A few of the regiments were armed with Springfield rifles, as we were, but the greater part of them had arms of foreign manufacture; there were English rifles, Belgian and Austrian muskets and even some of the old "smooth-bores" of the Mexican War time, which the traitor, Secretary of War Floyd, had not deemed worthy of removal from the Northern arsenals. The Government had hastily purchased these arms abroad and as all the calibres differed, serious confusion resulted sometimes through issuing the wrong ammunition. It was more than a year before there was anything like uniformity in the arms of the infantry regiments. Their uniforms were also diversified; many still wore the gray uniforms issued to them by the states they came from; some had a sort of German uniform; and the Garibaldi Guard, an Italian one; the Fifty-fifth New York Volunteers, Colonel De Trobriand, wore a distinctly French uniform, including the red breeches and "kepi." Another distinct uniform was that of the Chasseurs d'Afrique, and there were others; also a number of Zouave regiments, some with red breeches and some with blue, some wearing white turbans and some only a red Fez cap on their heads. In the course of a long time this was remedied and all wore the regulation uniform, except some of the Zouave regiments, who were permitted to retain theirs to the end of their term of service. In the month of September at Fall's Church, Virginia, one of our gray uniformed regiments was fired into by another of our regiments who mistook them for "graybacks" (rebels) and sixty or so were killed and wounded before the mistake was discovered. Lamentable errors like this occurred in various parts of the country at this time.

The neatness of the uniforms, the polished buttons and the bright looking arms of the regular soldiers was often a matter of interest to the volunteer officers. One day while on guard an elderly captain, who unquestionably hailed from one of the New England states, said to me, "Where be you men from? I see you all got brand new guns!" I explained to him that we were regular soldiers and had used these guns on the frontiers for years. He exclaimed, "Dew tell! Our boys got new guns but they're all rusty. What do you clean yours with?"

In October happened the unfortunate engagement with the Confederates at Ball's Bluff, some distance up the Potomac, where Colonel Baker was killed, and we lost nearly a thousand men—killed, wounded and prisoners; also by drowning. After the battle corpses floated down the river, some of them being washed ashore at Georgetown.

We preferred to do guard duty at the ferry to Analostan Island at the foot of High Street because it was easy, as it took the rope ferry boat a good while to make a trip and the traffic was small. This spot was the landing place for fishing boats and small sloops which brought oysters and vegetables to the Georgetown market from down the river. The watermelon season was still on and sloops came in loaded with them. We watched the boats for the owners at night and in return they gave the guard all the melons they could eat, and they were delicious. It was the same later on with oysters; and last came the sweet potatoes, the real Virginia or Maryland sweet potatoes, which we roasted and feasted on.

One day when I was corporal of the guard at the ferry, the sentinel called out, "Turn out the guard for the commanding general!" and immediately the general replied, "Never mind the guard!" He did not seem to care for my little command of six men. General McClellan was in a carriage along with his chief of staff, General Randolph B. Marcy, his father-in-law, but without any escort. Although I knew them both, I went to the side of the carriage, saluted and said, "Passes, gentlemen?" to which the General, returning the salute, replied, "I am the commanding general." I said, "Pass on, General," which ended the only conversation I had with him during the war. The General had to wait for about ten minutes before the carriage could be driven on the boat. During that time I could observe him closely, while he conversed earnestly with General Marcy.

A miserable looking tramp passed our little guard house at the ferry one day and seeing a pair of old buckskin gloves belonging to me, which I had left on a bench outside, promptly appropriated them. The sentinel saw him and called me. He ran, but I caught him, took the gloves from him and was about to give him a kick and let him go, when one of the town constables came up and insisted on arresting the man. Since the town had been policed by the soldiers, the few constables had had little to do and had grown rusty. This one seemed glad to have a case and would not let his prisoner go, although I entreated him to do so as the old gloves had no value. Next day I received a subpoena to appear as a witness at the court house at Four-and-a-half Street in Washington the following morning, and with the subpoena I was handed a dollar and a half, which was a godsend to me, as I had n't another cent at the time. I blessed that tramp! I was provided with a pass for all day, gave my evidence in court and heard the poor tramp sentenced to thirty days in the workhouse; then I started in to regale myself royally on the dollar-fifty. I had an oyster fry at Harvey's on the avenue, and something to drink and smoke. I spent the afternoon in the streets and I fear I was rather more extravagant than a man in my company who sometimes said, "Give me two cigars for five cents. I'm on a spree and don't care how I spend my money."

My captain resided with his family in a house on Bridge Street; the unmarried officers boarded around town; the married soldiers had located their wives and children in cheap apartments where some of them remained to the end of the war. Some wives never saw their husbands again after we went into Virginia. The captain in his capacity of commanding officer sometimes visited the guard late at night and had it turned out for him and put us through the usual formalities. I was always thankful that he omitted the inspection of arms, for at times I would have hated to trust him with the handling of a loaded gun. He sent for me occasionally to report to him at his house and when I appeared he put me through a kind of catechism commencing with, "Who made you a corporal?"

"The captain," I replied.

"Why did I make you a corporal?"

To which my answer was, "Because I was in the line of promotion, I presume."

"No! because I then believed you to be a good and reliable soldier. I see by the guard report that you were corporal of the guard at the ferry on Tuesday night when a lot of common soldiers were drinking in a saloon on Cherry Street and wrecked the place. Why didn't you go there and arrest them?"

"I could not hear the disturbance, it was too far away; besides, the regulations for the army forbid my leaving the guard without orders."

"I am the provost-marshal of this town and I make the regulations. Don't let this happen again. I will not allow any more common soldiers to go into saloons and will issue an order to that effect. Remember, I can break you. Go back to your quarters!"

He never issued that order—he couldn't; neither did he break me, although he used to send for me if there was any scrape in town; no matter if I didn't have the remotest connection with it, he suspected I was concerned in it.

A tragedy happened while we were quartered in Forrest Hall. A soldier of Company A was on post No. 2 on the Gay Street side of the building one winter night when Sergeant Brennan of his company, who was the sergeant of the main guard that night, went out of the guard-room and passed around the corner of the building towards sentinel No. 2. In a few minutes a shot was heard, and some of the guard running out found Sergeant Brennan on the sidewalk, dead, with a bullet through his heart, while the sentinel, with his gun in his hands, calmly stood there awaiting arrest. What transpired between them during the few minutes they were alone never became known. The soldier admitted shooting the sergeant, but made no explanation. It was well known, however, that there was a bitter enmity between them dating back to the time when they were on the frontier service. The body was carried up into the Hall and laid out on some benches on the second floor among the sergeant's sleeping comrades. A screen was erected around the body next morning and some nuns from Georgetown watched and prayed by it, until the next day when the funeral services were held in the Catholic church. The murderer was incarcerated in Washington and was speedily tried by a general court-martial which sentenced him to be hanged. A few weeks after the tragedy the entire regular brigade marched to a field on the north side where many of the finest houses are now built and formed a square about an elevated gallows which had a flight of steps leading up to the platform. The hangman (a soldier) was there adjusting and soaping the rope. Presently the prisoner arrived in a closed carriage, accompanied by a priest and a cavalry guard. The culprit mounted the steps unassisted, and when he reached the platform he stood erect, waved his right hand and exclaimed in a firm voice, "Good-bye, soldiers! Good-bye!" His limbs were quickly bound and a black cap drawn over his face; the trap was sprung and we saw the contortions of the lower part of his body. In a few minutes his struggles ceased and the soldiers marched silently back to their quarters.

We found the winter climate of Washington mild and agreeable, as compared with our experience in Nebraska and Dakota Territories. Our food was fairly good. We drew bread from the Government bakeries; fresh beef was issued to us at the foot of the unfinished Washington Monument, where all the beef cattle for the troops in or about Washington were slaughtered. Other provisions we drew from the general commissary depot.

During our stay of about five months in Georgetown we had become well acquainted with every nook and corner of it and got along well with such of the citizens as were not Southern sympathizers. At some of the houses to which we had been invited we played games with the girls. At one house in particular where a few friends and I called for a while I flattered myself that I was the daughter's favorite visitor; but, alas! "fair and false was she!" for she placed her young affections on a drummer of the band whose more gaudy uniform seemed irresistible to her.

About the end of January, 1862, my company was ordered to leave Forrest Hall and occupy a vacant two-story and attic house on Pennsylvania Avenue between Eighteenth and Nineteenth Streets, facing a small triangular shaped park. This house is still standing (1913) and is now numbered 1806. We lived there as we did in the K Street house. Our duties were much easier than in Georgetown; the only guard duty we had was one post in front of our own quarters. We picked up a few recruits in Washington and I had to drill them sometimes in the little park, to my chagrin and much to the amusement of the spectators, as one of them named Davis was as awkward a man as I ever tried to instruct.

Since the battle of Bull Run, the preceding July, the Army of the Potomac had been assiduous in drill and had gained much in discipline under that admirable organizer, General McClellan, all except the volunteer cavalry regiments. Many of the men could not ride horses when they were enlisted. The horses were untrained and were as green as their riders. In a few slight skirmishes with the enemy on reconnaissances the horses ran away at the first fire, in spite of the efforts of the troopers to make a stand. It was a standing joke in the army at that time that there was a reward of five dollars for any soldier who had seen a dead cavalryman. It takes a long time to drill cavalrymen and horses. It was not until after the second year of the war that they became really effective and after that they did splendid service.

The Northern papers were clamorous for the Army of the Potomac to make a move on the enemy. "Why doesn't the army move?" was the cry. In the West there had been some success; General U. S. Grant had captured Fort Donaldson, Tennessee, together with Generals Buckner and Tilghman and thirteen thousand prisoners. President Lincoln, impatient at General McClellan's delay and unwilling to agree to the General's plan of a campaign, appointed February twenty-second as the day for a general movement of all the land and naval forces; but nothing was done. We observed the day by hanging out a flag and by burning a lot of candles in the front windows of our quarters at night. We were tired of garrison duty and wanted to see some field service. Up to this time the small regular army had had but little representation in any of the conflicts and no share in what little glory there had been. All seemed eager for real service, even the man in my company who used to declare that he "enlisted to fight but was not quarrelsome."

We knew that a campaign of some sort would soon take place and began to prepare for it. All of our fancy uniforms and articles of no service in the field were packed into cases, turned over to the quartermaster's department and placed in storage in the then unfinished Corcoran Art Gallery, situated on Pennsylvania Avenue near our quarters, and none of us ever saw them again. Shelter tents were issued to us. They were an imitation of the "tent d'Abri" used in the French army and consisted of a piece of thin canvas supposed to be rainproof. It was about six and a half by five feet and had buttons and buttonholes along the edges, so that two or more pieces could be joined together and stretched across a ridge pole supported on two posts, and the sides fastened to tent-pins driven into the ground. This formed a small A-shaped tent, a "pup-tent," as the soldiers called it, but was open at the front and back. Generally three men got together and used the third piece of canvas to cover one of the open ends—the one to windward The little tents were so low it was necessary to crawl into them on hands and knees and we could barely retain a sitting posture. Tent and ridge-poles of light wood, made to telescope in convenient lengths, and small hardwood tent-pins were also issued to us. All this had to be strapped to our knapsack and increased the load to be carried on our back very considerably. The poles and pins we threw away after a few days' trial in the field and trusted to chance to pick up forked sticks and ridge-poles in the woods. For this purpose I provided myself with a small hatchet, and to even up loads my bunkie carried a frying pan for our use.

On March eighth Centreville was discovered to have been evacuated by the Rebels. Painted logs (Quaker guns) were found mounted in the enemies' earthworks. Manassas was also found to be evacuated; at last the Army of the Potomac was forced to move. General McClellan was relieved from the supreme command of the United States Army and appointed to command the Army of the Potomac. We received orders to cross the Potomac into Virginia. The six companies, headed by the band, formed on Pennsylvania Avenue in the forenoon of the tenth of March and marched to the "Long Bridge" by way of Fourteenth Street, after more than seven months in Washington and Georgetown. The day was clear but cold. It was my hard luck to be corporal of the guard bringing up the rear of the column with a few prisoners and some drunks who had been unable to resist the temptation of a final debauch. I had some trouble to keep them from frolicking with the negro wenches who had lined up on the sidewalks in large numbers to hear the band play and see us marching off. The captain, much to our satisfaction, did not accompany us. He managed to get a medical certificate excusing him from field service and remained in Georgetown on easy duty.

PART IX.

THE PENINSULA CAMPAIGN, 1862.

OUR real war experience commenced when we passed over the Long Bridge at Washington into the enemy's country—Virginia. It is not my intention to write a complete story of any part of the Civil War, nor to criticize the general conduct of the war, but simply to describe my personal experience and my observations, together with the impressions made upon me and my comrades at the time. A soldier in the ranks sees but little of a battle and, outside of his own regiment or brigade, knows less of events that have taken place or new movements to be made than a civilian can learn from the newspapers. We often read articles about the Army of the Potomac in papers several days old which contained information that was news to us.

After passing the bridge we marched along the Fairfax Court House road for a distance of about six miles, when we were ordered to halt and go into camp beside the road at the edge of a piece of woods. Our heavily loaded knapsacks began to be a burden on this short march and next morning we threw away things we thought we could dispense with. On the frontiers we had wagons to carry our tents, rations and knapsacks, which made marching easier, although we marched greater distances than a large army could. All through the Civil War the soldier in the ranks furnished his own transportation. In this camp we put up our little shelter tents for the first time, but as I was on camp guard and had to relieve sentinels every two hours, I sat on a log by a fire all night and dozed between times.

Next morning we broke camp and counter-marched to within about a mile of the town of Alexandria, where we went into camp on some high ground, carefully putting up our tents along lines forming company streets, as we expected to stay for some time. My bunkie and I gathered some pine-needle brush in the woods and spread it over the floor of our tent, as the ground was frozen and damp. The nights were still cold. We cooked our rations at fires which we built in the company streets and gathered around them evenings until tattoo. Nearly every soldier soon had the back of his blue trousers scorched a deep brown above the heels of his shoes from standing too close to the fire. There were encampments of troops all around us. The greater part of the Army of the Potomac was in the vicinity of Alexandria awaiting transportation to Fortress Monroe, Virginia. A fleet of boats was soon gathered from New York and Philadelphia to transport the army; they were of all kinds—tug-boats, towing-barges, New York ferryboats, excursion steamers and coast liners. Daily shipments were made, but our corps, General FitzJohn Porter's Fifth Army Corps, was held in camp until near the last.

I was on camp guard a few times and remember particularly a very distressing night at that camp. It had rained all day, soaking us to the skin; and at night it turned into snow and sleet. We had no guard tent to shelter us and were exposed to the storm all night, sitting on logs around a fire that would not burn and blinded us with smoke. In the morning the storm ceased and soon the sun came out and warmed us. Fortunately I had a change of dry clothing in my knapsack in the tent, which I put on as soon as relieved and experienced no ill effects from the exposure. Although we were experienced soldiers, we had much to learn, now that we were a part of a great army entering upon a campaign. One of the first things that forced itself upon us was that while on a campaign or on marches there could be no company cooks and every soldier had to carry and cook his own rations. This was necessary because companies were constantly divided. Some men were absent on picket or on scouting duty for days at a time. It was only while in a permanent camp or when the army was in winter quarters, as it was called, that we could receive full rations and have the luxury of company cooks and fresh bread instead of hardtack.

The daily ration of hard bread was increased from twelve to sixteen ounces per day and a few other changes were made in the soldiers' rations by law and regulation in July, 1861, to hold good during the war. We lived on what we called "short rations" when on a campaign or a march, the daily allowance being as follows: one pound of hard bread, twelve ounces of salt pork or bacon, or twenty ounces of salt or fresh beef; one and a quarter ounces of ground coffee; two and a half ounces of sugar; half an ounce of salt and sometimes a piece of soap. We generally drew three days' rations at a time, which fairly filled our haversacks. Sometimes we had to carry rations for five days and were obliged to stow away a part of them in our knapsacks. There were times when we had to get along with less than the above allowance.

The haversack was a canvas bag, the knapsack was of the same material—both painted black. The haversack had a canvas lining which could be removed and washed. We made small bags to hold our coffee, sugar and salt; the pork or beef we wrapped up in a piece of paper or cloth and stowed away in the bottom of the haversack, and then filled it up with the hard bread. Each soldier carried a quart cup and a plate made of strong block tin, also a spoon and a steel knife and fork. Those who did not provide themselves with frying pans used their tin plates as a substitute. Our canteens were of strong tin, covered over with thick felt cloth, and held three pints.

We soon learned to make several palatable dishes out of our limited marching rations. We would fry our pork until it was well browned, and after dipping some of the hard bread into water for a few minutes we fried that in the hot pork grease, which made it swell and softened it, for it was very hard bread indeed when eaten raw. At other times we broke the hard bread into small pieces and soaked it in water for an hour or more until it was thoroughly soft and then fried it in pork grease. We also had a way of making a stew in our tin cups, to which the soldiers gave a name that would not look well in print. This stew consisted of pork or beef cut into small pieces, with broken hard bread boiled in water; and if we were fortunate enough to obtain a carrot, a potato or an onion, we had a feast.

We had good appetites. On the third day we generally fasted to a more or less extent, having used up more than the just proportion of our rations on the first two days. If there was any man in the company who could not eat all his rations, he was much sought after by those who were hungry. We boiled our coffee in the quart cups. Sometimes we could buy condensed milk from the sutler when not on a march.

Porter's Fifth Army Corps received orders to embark for Fortress Monroe about March twenty-second, but it was two or three days later that the division of regulars broke camp and marched to a wharf in Alexandria, where we embarked on an old excursion steamer. The crowded boat made her way slowly down the Potomac and when in the afternoon we passed Mount Vernon, where the remains of General Washington repose, the ship's bell tolled and we were ordered to remove our caps as a mark of respect for the Father of his Country.

We found that the soldiers could do no cooking on this boat; some of them tried to make coffee by placing their cups on the hot steam pipes, but they could not get it to the boiling point. A few fortunate soldiers got the firemen of the boat to boil their coffee for them. I had to be content with washing down my frugal meals with cold water. At night we lay on the floor of the saloon and about the decks, wherever we could find room.

Next day we were in Chesapeake Bay, making slow progress, and arrived at Old Point Comfort a little before sunset. Here was an interesting sight—the harbor was crowded with all sorts of boats which had transported the Army of the Potomac and its supplies from Alexandria to Fortress Monroe. There were also several men-of-war and the Monitor—the little "Yankee cheesebox on a raft," as the Rebels called her—which had defeated the redoubtable Rebel ram, the Merrimac, only a short time before. We picked our way carefully among the many vessels and were within a half mile of the dock—a short distance north of the present dock at the Hotel Chamberlin—when suddenly there was a crash which threw us off our feet and caused an ominous creaking and straining of the timbers in the old boat. We had struck something, probably a forgotten wreck, and were beginning to sink rapidly. There was great confusion, with shrieking of whistles, blowing off steam from the boilers, and a rush in search of life preservers. In a few minutes tug-boats came to our assistance and began taking us off. All were saved, but had our boat been going at full speed when she struck, there might have been a heavy loss, even though we had assistance close at hand. We spent a very uncomfortable night, lying on the open dock wrapped in our blankets and overcoats. It was cold, the strong wind which was blowing made us shiver, and were thankful for daylight and the sun's warm rays. Through someone's negligence our three days' rations, exhausted on the previous day, had not been renewed and on this morning many were without anything to eat; I had a hardtack or two and a little sugar; these and a drink of water constituted my breakfast. There was much grumbling and dissatisfaction. One soldier in my company declared that it was enough "to make a dog strike his father." Soon after sunrise our officers, who had spent a more comfortable night at the Hygeia Hotel than we had on the cold dock, joined us and we took up our march to camp.

We passed the fort, crossed Hampton Creek and passed through the village of Hampton, which had been nearly destroyed by the Rebel general, Magruder, who had ordered it to be set on fire the previous year. A few miles further on we came to a flat plain near the James river, where we halted to camp. Many thousands of tents stretched away as far as the eye could reach in the direction of Newport News on the James river; the entire Army of the Potomac was here.

It was afternoon before we received any rations and wood to start fires with which to cook them, for there was no wood to be had in the vicinity and we had to go a long distance for water. After a great deal of trouble we secured some sticks with which to set up our shelter tents; for the officers a few wall tents and some A tents were provided.

It was at this camp that I first saw the Fifth New York Volunteer Infantry, better known as the "Duryee Zouaves." They arrived from Baltimore, where they had been engaged in constructing fortifications on Federal Hill during the fall and winter, and established their camp in close proximity to ours, which afforded us opportunity of much friendly intercourse. They were commanded by Lieutenant Colonel G. K. Warren, whom we had known in Dakota Territory as a lieutenant of topographical engineers, making surveys for the Government in 1855-1857. Colonel Warren had brought this fine regiment to a state of discipline, efficiency and drill that was not equaled by any other volunteer regiment in the Army of the Potomac. When on drill or dress parade they looked both splendid and formidable in their picturesque Zouave uniforms and white turbans. General George Sykes, our division commander, selected this regiment of all others for the third brigade of the second division of the Fifth Army Corps. The First Connecticut Heavy Artillery, serving as infantry, was presently added to this brigade, and later on the Tenth New York Volunteer Infantry. The "Duryee Zouaves" remained in Sykes's division until the expiration of their term of service.

The first and second brigades, amounting to upwards of four thousand men, were made up of regular soldiers. The second, to which I belonged, was composed of the following: Second United States Infantry, Sixth United States Infantry, Tenth United States Infantry, Eleventh United States Infantry, Seventeenth United States Infantry. The eleventh and seventeenth were new regiments raised since the beginning of the war; they were what was called three-battalion regiments, twenty-four companies but only one battalion of each; eight companies were ever present with us. The old regiments were ten-company regiments, but none of them had over six companies present. The commander of the brigade at this time was Lieutenant Colonel William Chapman, an old veteran of the Mexican War, who remained with us but a short time, when he was retired on account of old age and disability.

At this time—the beginning of McClellan's Peninsula Campaign—my regiment had but three or four officers present who had served on the frontiers with us and were West Point graduates. All of the first and second lieutenants, with the exception of Lieutenant Jordan, who commanded my company, and a few who were appointed from the ranks, were civilian appointees. Some had served in state militia and had some knowledge of tactics and discipline; some turned out to be good officers, but others could have been dispensed with, and that with no loss to the service.

I took a trip along the shore of the river one day towards Newport News and had a close view of the masts of the Congress and the Cumberland sticking up out of the water. These were the two United States frigates that were sunk by the Merrimac in the memorable conflict of March eighth, 1862.

The Army of the Potomac commenced its advance on Yorktown on April fourth, but it was nearly a week later before we left our camp near Hampton. General McClellan, while in command of the Army of the Potomac, made Sykes's division his reserve—a body of troops to be relied upon "at a critical moment," as he expressed it, in his report of the Peninsular Campaign; that is why, during his time as commander, we seldom took the initiative in any forward movements, but were more often used to cover a retreat, as at the first Bull Run, when the enemy pursued us.

When we left our camp about the tenth of April we found the roads in very bad condition from recent rains and badly cut up by that part of the army which had marched ahead of us. We passed through a place called Little Bethel and through Big Bethel, where the "Duryee Zouaves" had an encounter with a body of the enemy on June tenth, 1861. The breastworks marking the Rebel's position were still there. A few miles beyond, about half way between our former camp and Yorktown, we halted and went into camp in a field at the edge of some woods, in which there were a large number of huts or shacks, which had been occupied by some Rebel regiment during the winter. We found a number of pigs running around in the woods, some of which we captured and had fresh pork for supper.

During the night a rainstorm came on which lasted almost without intermission for more than forty-eight hours. My bunkie and I had taken the precaution to put a thick layer of pine branches on the ground and had dug a ditch around our tent; still, next morning the water soaked in, though we dug the ditch deeper, and for two days and nights we had to sit or lie on beds that were water-soaked. To add to our misery, the shelter tents were far from being waterproof; such a rain as this could not be kept out. As we lay in our tents we watched the globules of water oozing through the thin canvas; and to keep them from dripping in our faces, we would put up our fingers to touch the drop and guide it along the sloping side of the tent. The rain was so fierce that half the time we could not boil any coffee, as no fires could be kept up. The field in which we camped was soon turned into a quagmire through which we waded ankle-deep when we ventured outside the tents. The men named this place "Camp Misery," and it remained as such in our memories for many a day.

On the morning of the third day the sun came out, but the roads were in such a horrible condition that we could not move. It was not until the morning of the fourth day that we resumed our march and arrived at Yorktown in the afternoon. At Yorktown our camp was established a short distance from the front of General McClellan's headquarters and was known as "Camp Winfield Scott." There was a fringe of woods which screened us from the enemy in the fortifications of Yorktown about a mile and a half or more in front of us. When the first of the troops of the Army of the Potomac arrived in front of Yorktown they found their further advance checked by fortifications mounting heavy guns, with smaller works and formidable, well protected breastworks extending from the York river on the north across the entire peninsula to the James river on the south, where the Warwick river enters it. For a few days reconnaissances, which brought on some minor engagements, were made to find some weak spots in the Rebel defenses. Then General McClellan decided that a siege would be necessary to capture the enemy's works. Presently the Union Army of about eighty thousand men was busy making roads, building works for batteries of siege guns and trenches for the infantry.

The first work my regiment did was to assist in building corduroy roads between the camps and Shipping Point on the York river, where the army supply depots were. These roads had to be substantially built for the transportation of heavy siege guns and all kinds of army supplies. This work was severe and frequent cold rains added to our misery; but it had to be done quickly, regardless of weather conditions. Early in the morning a detail of about one-half the regiment, furnished with axes, picks and spades, marched to a part of the Shipping Point road and commenced work. We cut down trees, trimmed them and dragged the logs to their places; we filled in low spots and dug ditches to drain the water from swampy sections, often standing in mud and water to do it. At noon we were allowed an hour's rest to make coffee and eat our rations. About sundown we quit work and returned to camp, very tired and glad that we could rest all of the next day, while the other half of the regiment was at work.

The sick list increased while this work went on, but it was soon finished and then we furnished detachments to work on trenches which were a part of the siege operations of the investment of Yorktown, consisting of ditches and earth breastworks running in long zigzag lines, constantly approaching the enemy's works. New lines were always begun in the night, but strong works for mounting siege guns and batteries were hurried along night and day, in spite of the enemy's frequent shelling, which was answered by our gun-boats in the York river; and generally they were soon silenced by them. After sundown the soldiers who had been detailed for work on the trenches during the night formed ranks and marched to a place where picks and shovels were furnished us; then we neared the place where the work was to be done and concealed ourselves in the woods, which were abundant in the vicinity of Yorktown, and awaited very quietly until darkness had set in. We were then led out into the open fields in front of the Rebel works, where we found pegs driven and lines put up by the engineers, indicating the direction in which the new line of trenches was to be dug. We were cautioned to make as little noise as possible with our tools and no talking was allowed, for the Rebel pickets might be near. The men began digging a wide trench, throwing the dirt in front of them to form a breastwork; and they worked very hard indeed until they had dug a hole deep enough to lie down in, then they took it easier.

As a non-commissioned officer I did not have to do any of the digging; I superintended my section and kept them at work, but the nights were still cold and raw and I often relieved a tired private for a while to warm up; besides I was as much interested as any of them to make a hole in the ground deep enough to protect me when the enemy fired at us.

All through the night, at almost regular intervals of about fifteen minutes, a single gun in the forts at Yorktown fired a shell in our direction, which passed over us and exploded or buried itself in the ground somewhere behind us. On the half-dozen occasions when I was on such a detail I can recall only one shell bursting over us which severely wounded two men of a regiment working next to ours. When the gun was fired at Yorktown a mile or more away, there was a flash in the sky and a sergeant on watch called out "Lie down!" when we immediately dropped flat on the ground or into the trench. About the time we heard the report of the gun, the shell was passing over us. The interval of time between seeing the flash of the gun and hearing the report was just about sufficient for us to drop for protection. Occasionally the Union gunboats in the river fired a few rounds in the direction of the Rebel gun which was annoying us and had the effect of silencing it for an hour or two. At the first streak of daybreak we ceased digging and returned to camp, depositing our entrenching tools where we had received them. We were then excused from duty and rested all day; alternate nights the same detail went out to work on the trenches again. Similar work was done by the troops all along our front line.

We had a fairly good camping ground, which could be drained, but there was much rain at this season and our thin canvas shelter tents leaked badly, until we thought to give them a coating of pork-grease or melted tallow, which improved them for a time at the expense of their looks, for all the dust and dirt flying about clung to them. In this respect the volunteer regiments were better provided for than we; many of them had rubber ponchos—not furnished by the Government, but by the states from which they hailed. The ponchos could be used as a shelter tent and were waterproof; they could also be worn as a protection in rainy weather, while on the march or on picket, for they were slit in the center for the head to pass through. They had, however, the disadvantage of being much too heavy and excessively hot when used as tents in warm weather.

During our stay at Camp Winfield Scott, for about a month, we had no drum or bugle calls nor were any bands allowed to play, and after sunset all fires were extinguished. This precaution was taken to prevent the enemy from ascertaining the exact location of our camps, many of them being within easy distance of their long-range guns, only a thin strip of woods masked the camps in most places.

A large captive balloon near the army headquarters was in charge of the signal corps, a new branch of the service added since the beginning of the war. Some of the engineer officers made ascensions in this balloon for hundreds of feet and must have obtained a comprehensive view of the enemy's camps and defenses. Shells were fired at this balloon at times; we saw them burst in the air, but they never came close enough to endanger the occupants. There was also a telegraph corps at headquarters, which was an innovation in warfare. Insulated wire was used, wound on large reels mounted on trucks drawn by horses. The wires could be paid out quickly and were secured to trees or fences, or laid on the ground, and communications established between headquarters and commanders of the corps.

Not a day passed without some long-range artillery firing from both sides; sometimes a shell passed over our camp and over General McClellan's headquarters camp behind us. Picket firing also went on, and there were some casualties daily. It was at this camp that I saw Rebel soldiers for the first time; some prisoners, taken in a skirmish, were brought to headquarters. Only a few among them wore a complete uniform of gray; the others had a mixture of military and civilian clothing and wore slouch hats; they were taken charge of by the provost-guard.

An estuary of the York river extended close up to our camp. There were many oyster beds in it, which were soon exhausted by the soldiers. We washed our clothing in this water, which was brackish; our drinking water we obtained from springs and from wells which we dug. Encamped alongside of our brigade was the regiment known as Colonel Burdan's United States Sharp Shooters, an independent organization belonging to no particular state. This regiment was much used as skirmishers and on picket. Many of the men had their own private arms, rifles with telescopes, hunting rifles and other superior arms; some had powder horns and cast their own bullets rather than use any fixed ammunition. A detail from this regiment was sent out and remained in the rifle-pits or were concealed in the branches of trees from daybreak till dark for the purpose of taking shots at the Rebel gunners in the fortifications of Yorktown.

About the first day of May Battery Number One on our right, the largest of our batteries, was completed and began firing occasional shots from its one-hundred and two-hundred pounder siege-guns at the Rebel fortifications at Yorktown and Gloucester Point on the opposite side of the York river. The noise caused by the firing of these great guns and the explosion of the shells was deafening. Siege mortars were also fired. At night we could plainly follow the course of the mortar shells by their burning and sputtering fuses as they curved high up in the air in their flight towards the enemy's works. It was expected that in a few days, as soon as all of our batteries were ready, a general bombardment all along the line would take the place of desultory firing. For several days the enemy replied but feebly to our rambling fire, but on Saturday evening they commenced a furious fire all along their line and kept it up until long after midnight.

At daybreak on Sunday morning, May fourth, it was discovered that the Rebels had evacuated Yorktown and were in full retreat up the peninsula toward Richmond. There was great cheering in all the camps as they received the news, the bands, silent for a month, played patriotic airs like mad, and as though they would never have another chance to play. We seemed to be celebrating a great victory and forgot our tremendous and now useless labor during the siege operations. When General McClellan and some of his staff appeared among the camps on their way to Yorktown, we threw our caps into the air and cheered him to the echo, for he was our "Little Mac," our "Napoleon," our "Little Corporal." The soldiers were very enthusiastic and cheered him along the line of march, whenever he appeared; they had the greatest confidence in him and would have followed him anywhere. No future commander of the Army of the Potomac inspired the rank and file with the same affection; they idolized him. But we were inexperienced in war and too easily enthused at this time; we expected our commander to lead us to certain victory. Of the future commanders I think that General Joseph Hooker was next to McClellan in the affections of his soldiers, but to a lesser degree.

Immediate pursuit of the enemy followed by a cavalry brigade which met with some loss from percussion shells planted on the road leading from Yorktown to Williamsburg, before they overtook the enemy's rear-guard and had a skirmish with them. The cavalry was followed within a few hours by the infantry of the fourth and a part of the third army corps, which pushed on vigorously until near night, when they encountered a large force of the enemy strongly posted in a work called Fort Magruder and about a dozen redoubts and many rifle-pits located about a mile or more east of Williamsburg.

Next day a fierce battle was fought all day; in our camps at Yorktown, where we were held in readiness to march at a moment's notice, we could plainly hear the heavy firing. That night the enemy abandoned their position and the road to the Chickahominy river was open. All the troops now began a forward movement, but we were among the last to leave, two or three days after the battle of Williamsburg. Transportation was limited, only one wagon being allowed our small regiment to carry the officers' tents, their baggage, mess-kits, etc. Nothing was carried for the soldiers, except the sergeant-major's and first sergeant's small desks or chests in which their books and papers were kept. By this time many of the officers had negro servants—soldiers not being allowed for that service while in the field; these they had picked up from among the many hundreds of General Butler's "contrabands" at Fortress Monroe. Many had broken-down mules, or old horses, on which they packed shelter tents, blankets, provisions and a few cooking utensils—a very convenient arrangement to resort to on a prolonged march, when the officers wanted some coffee, or when the baggage wagon failed to reach camp. These servants were mostly ignorant plantation niggers, but they seemed to fill the bill. They walked and led their animals; and in some way they managed to find or steal forage enough to keep them alive. The unfortunate ones who did not have animals to carry their burdens were obliged to make pack-horses of themselves. These camp followers, or "dog robbers," as we called them, kept up close with the command to which they belonged, except when they heard any firing going on in front, in which case they did not show up until all was quiet again.

Our first day's march was to Williamsburg, about twelve miles, where we encamped for the night near Fort Magruder on a part of the battlefield of three days previous. Not much of the struggle remained to be seen, the dead had been buried, the dead horses burned, but the woods and trees and the earthworks showed the effects of the rifle and cannon firing which must have been most severe. The road from our camps led through Yorktown; we passed by some of the Rebel fortifications which heretofore had been seen only from a distance. We noticed a number of small sticks with a piece of rag attached to them. These indicated places where percussion shells were supposed to have been buried by the Rebels. A squad of Rebel prisoners under guard were forced to dig them up. This was very dangerous work, as to step on the cap of the shell or to strike it with a tool was liable to cause a disastrous explosion.

The weather was very warm; the road was mostly through pine woods with an occasional clearing; the woods, set on fire by the retreating Rebels, were still burning in places and the smoke at times was suffocating. We found the road strewn with blankets, overcoats and other clothing and articles discarded by our troops who had marched ahead of us. Owing to the warm weather, the heat of the burning woods and the rough state of the roads, we felt the weight of our knapsacks on our backs more than ever before; and we also began to shed clothing. We reasoned that there was a long summer before us, during which we would need but little clothing in this climate; and if we were still alive in the fall we could draw more blankets and overcoats. My bunkie and I lightened our loads by discarding a blanket and an overcoat; the other blanket we cut in two, and cutting the cape off the remaining overcoat, we cast it away, together with half of the blanket and some other articles, all of which lightened our burden considerably.

All through the summer when on a march, we did not bother with putting up a shelter tent unless it rained. We spread one of the sections of the tent on the ground and lay on the half-blanket, covering ourselves with the blanket and with the other section of the tent if we expected a heavy dew. Sometimes we were caught in a shower during the night, but that did not disturb us much, as we were then too tired and sleepy to get up and erect a tent. We kept the overcoat for a while to be made use of when either of us was on guard or picket, but we soon threw that away, also. The country people who lived along the route of the army must have gathered a rich harvest in clothing and shoes at this time. There were a few men in every company who could not make up their minds to part with any of their property; some even picked up articles that others had thrown away and added them to their burden, although they staggered under the load.

The second day's march was a short one. We went only about six or seven miles beyond Williamsburg and encamped. In going through the town we saw but few citizens, except colored people; the stores were nearly all closed, the private houses had their blinds closed and were seemingly deserted. The ladies were evidently hiding themselves. The place was full of wounded soldiers from both armies; large hospital tents flying the yellow flag had been erected on the outskirts of the town. We passed the venerable buildings of William and Mary College, which, I think, were used as a hospital at that time.

Next morning, soon after reveille, I was handed an order for the admission of half-a-dozen sick soldiers from my brigade (whom the surgeon considered unable to stand a campaign) to a hospital at Williamsburg. I was directed to take charge of them, to march them there and rejoin my company as speedily as possible and as best I could. I secured permission to leave my knapsack in the regimental baggage wagon, keeping only a blanket which I made into a roll and carried over my shoulder. I started early, but it took my sick squad about four hours to travel the distance of six miles back to Williamsburg. I found the hospital tent, left my charges and was given a receipt for them.

The day was still young. I was puzzled whether to stay in the town and await the chance to return under the protection of some detachment of soldiers, or to go on alone. I decided on the latter course, for I felt fresh and vigorous and was a good marcher; I reasoned that I would be able to overtake my command before night, if they had not made too long a march that day; and, at the worst, I might find a wagon-train or some soldiers encamped along the road, among whom I might spend the night. I stayed in town only long enough to get something to eat and some coffee at the hospital, and then started off at a brisk pace which I kept up with only a few short rests until evening, when I began to look anxiously for signs of a large camp ahead. None was to be seen, and no one seemed to be traveling towards me, from whom I could learn how far it was to the next camp. The road was a very lonely one; much of it was through woods, and there were but few houses and cabins. The trail left by the army could be easily followed in the daytime, but after dark it would be more difficult when arriving at a cross or branch road to decide which way to go.

During the afternoon I was never any very great length of time out of sight of a wagon-train or some cavalry detachment, and I also met some stragglers, who had been foraging. They asked me to stay with them but I declined. Towards evening I saw no one and felt very lonely and uneasy. Shortly after sundown a small cavalry squad in charge of an officer overtook me. I was halted and the officer demanded to know what I was doing alone on the road. I showed him my receipt and explained that I was not a straggler. He advised me to hide in the woods in a hurry and to stay there until some detachment came along which I could join, or I would be shot by guerrillas. I had not heard guerrillas mentioned before in camp, but from the earnest way in which this officer spoke, I judged they were to be dreaded.

I quickly retraced my steps to the nearest woods, about half a mile behind me, and took a careful look up and down the road before entering, but saw nothing to alarm me. Within hearing distance of the road, I spread my blanket under a tree, ate a portion of my rations and took a drink of water from my canteen. It was growing dark and I was afraid to light my pipe and have a smoke, so I lay down on my blanket to rest, my loaded rifle beside me. I felt very tired, as I must have marched more than twenty-five miles since early morning, according to my calculation, and although I tried to keep awake and listen for any noise there might be on the road, sleep overcame me and I did not wake up until it was broad daylight.

After a careful survey I resumed my march and soon passed a house a few hundred yards off the road, in which no one seemed to be stirring yet. A few miles further on, I saw a cavalry picket post and, noting the blue uniform and yellow facings, I knew that I was safe. Here I learned that the camp was but little more than a mile ahead and soon heard the joyful notes of a bugle call. My regiment was waiting to take its place in line for the day's march and I reported to the commanding officer, who complimented me on my activity in making two days' marches in one, and ordered me as a reward to be excused from guard and picket duties for a month.

A short time later I knew better than to take the foolish chance I had in making that march alone. In less than a week General Sykes's servant was shot dead by guerrillas and some teamsters were killed by them not far from camp. During the war many stragglers were killed by guerrillas, being reported missing or perhaps as deserters. In my own company, two men who were supposed to have fallen asleep by the roadside during a rest on a night march were never heard from.

On this day it was the turn of the Fifth Army Corps to be in the rear on the line of march, and my brigade was the last in the corps, which made it quite late in the morning before we started on the road. It was the custom, when it could be done and when a large part of the army was marching on the same road, for the corps in advance to-day to be in the rear to-morrow. This rule applied also to divisions, brigades, regiments and companies of regiments, the leading company to-day being the rear company to-morrow.

We marched by fours, and if there were fifty thousand men or more in line they extended for many miles, and it sometimes happened that the troops in the advance went into camp before those in the rear started on their march. Reveille, however, was sounded at the same time in all the camps, irrespective of their place in line. The supply trains with their guards often followed the troops on the same road and were very late getting into camp. Rations were then issued at night to the waiting, hungry soldiers. When the roads were very bad and conditions made it feasible, an army corps remained at rest in camp for a day avoiding the overcrowding of the road.

Marching with a large body of troops is very tedious and very annoying, when you are far to the rear of the line and the troops in front empty the wells and springs along the road and roil the rivulets and ponds to the extent of making water unfit to drink. When a halt occurred we did not know whether it was for a rest or only for a moment; a halt of a few minutes at the head of the line miles away multiplied itself many times before it reached the rear. If a piece of road had to be repaired, a stream forded or a bridge strengthened or repaired for the safe passage of artillery and cavalry, we were delayed for hours. Those in the rear knew nothing of the cause and wondered why we did not go on, expecting every moment to hear the bugle sound the call "forward." When we halted we stood still for a few minutes waiting to go on again, and if there was no indication of it among the regiments immediately in front of us, we broke ranks without orders and unslung our knapsacks and sat on them or lay on the ground by the roadside if it was dry, the officers doing the same—for all company officers had to march on foot. If the halt continued for a while the men soon began to straggle off in search of water and wood; if it was evening, soon many small fires were burning along the road and many were making coffee in their tin cups; and perhaps before the coffee boiled the bugle would sound the command to "fall in." We could not afford to throw away the coffee, partly made, but carried the cups in our hands to the next halting place and built another fire. We had become wise and put swinging handles on our cups, if we could find any wire for that purpose, to carry them more easily. A short delay at the head of the column became a long one in the rear, if the men broke ranks, for it required a little time to sling knapsacks and to take your place in line—very much like a tie-up on a long line of street-cars, when it seems a long time after the first one has started again before the last one moves. On night marches the afore-mentioned difficulties were greater, for tired out men fell asleep by the roadside and did not always hear the command "forward." If we missed them when forming ranks, we delayed a little and searched for them; if we did not, they had a chance of being picked up the rear guard, or ran the risk of being captured by guerrillas.

We passed through New Kent Court House and reached Cumberland on the Pamunkey river long after dark. Sykes' division encamped on the heights overlooking the valley of the river, and there we saw a sight the grandeur of which can never be effaced from the memory of those who witnessed it. Below us on a great plain the entire Army of the Potomac was encamped, reunited for the first time since leaving Yorktown. Thousands upon thousands of camp fires were seen as far as the eye could reach in every direction. The sight was magnificent. We rested at Cumberland for a day and the army was reviewed by Secretary of State William H. Seward.

Our next march was to the White House, at the head of navigation on the Pamunkey. Here the river was crossed by a bridge of the Richmond and York River Railroad. The tortuous river was crowded with vessels, all loaded with supplies for the army, for the White House landing was to be our base of supplies while operating against Richmond, and the railroad partly destroyed by the Rebels was to be rebuilt to convey the supplies to the Chickahominy river. The White House was a large plantation, formerly the property of the wife of George Washington and at that time owned by the Lee family. General McClellan ordered safeguards to protect this estate from vandalism, but about a month later the fine mansion was destroyed by fire along with our supply depot, when the Union Army retreated to the James river. Our next camp was at Tunstall's Station, and two more short marches brought us to Gaines's Mill, north of the Chickahominy and about seven miles from Richmond.

All the way up the peninsula the country was deserted; about the plantations and farms no young men were to be seen, they had all joined the Rebel Army. Few negroes were visible; all but trusty house servants had been sent within the Rebel lines to prevent them from running away from their masters. Scarcely a horse or any other domestic animal was to be seen about the farms; they were either secreted or had been sent away.

During the first eighteen months of the war, orders against foraging or destroying any private property in the enemy's country were strictly enforced; in our division we were not even allowed to take fence rails for firewood, safeguards being placed at many of the more important plantations for their protection. After the invasion of Maryland by the Rebels in September, 1862, and the discovery that many of the houses along the route of the army harbored guerrillas who murdered our stragglers, the orders were no longer strictly enforced and but few safeguards were furnished. I believe it was twelve days or more from the evacuation of Yorktown before our advance troops reached the Chickahominy river, a distance of something less than fifty miles. The Northern papers criticized General McClellan very severely for his slow pursuit of the enemy; but there were few roads that this large army with its immense baggage and supply trains could travel; owing to constant and unprecedented spring rains they were in a horrible condition and had to be repaired in many places before the artillery and wagon trains could pass, and besides the bridges had to be rebuilt. The battle fought at Williamsburg caused a loss of two days also in our advance on Richmond.

The great stretches of pine woods on the peninsula made us familiar with a camp-pest we had not encountered before— the woodtick, a small bug which buried its head in the most tender parts of the skin of one's body, causing intense itching, swellings and sores. In the morning, while on the march, when the sun was shining, and we were in good spirits, some regiment would start up a song. I particularly remember that my regiment marched directly behind the "Duryee Zouaves" one morning when one of their fine singers started "The Mocking Bird," and presently the entire regiment, twice as large as ours, took up the chorus. It was beautiful, and it has ever since remained one of my favorite sings.

Gaines's Mill, where our camp was located, was a part of

a large plantation owned by Dr. Gaines, a bitter Rebel who resided on the property in a large house that was protected by a safeguard. My brigade was encamped along the edge of the mill-pond, a body of stagnant water which received all the drainage of the camp and which was our only supply for cooking and drinking. No precautions of any kind were taken to prevent contamination of the pond; the soldiers bathed and washed their clothing in it. We dug some deep holes along the shore and allowed the water to seep into them, hoping in that way to filter it, but without perceptible results, for our sick list increased and we had some fatal cases of typhoid fever.

The Army of the Potomac was presently separated into two parts; only the Fifth Army Corps and one additional division remained on the north side, or left bank, of the Chickahominy, all the other troops being on the right bank of the river and nearer Richmond. They formed the left wing of the army between the Chickahominy and the James rivers; while we formed the right wing, virtually cut off and liable to be outflanked by the enemy, for the Chickahominy was bordered by large forest trees and low, marshy bottoms which a single heavy rainstorm would overflow; all bridges had been destroyed and had to be rebuilt and a number of new ones constructed.

General McDowell with the First Army Corps and other troops, to the number of about forty thousand men in all, formed an independent command at Fredericksburg at this time, only a few days' march away from General Porter's Fifth Army Corps. General McClellan had most earnestly requested the authorities at Washington to allow General McDowell to form a junction with him to strengthen the right wing of the Army of the Potomac, but General McDowell did not receive an order to join until it was too late, and we had to pay a fearful price for the delinquency.

At this time there were no less than six independent commands in various parts of Virginia, and even the soldiers in the ranks could understand that the war in that state was being conducted from Washington; no important operations could be undertaken without the approval of the President, Secretary of War Stanton, or the Commander-in-Chief, Halleck. It was not until General Grant's time in 1864 that the commander of this army was given a free hand.

After we had been a few days at this camp it was discovered that two brigades of the enemy, estimated at twelve thousand strong, were at Hanover Court House, between McDowell's army and our own and were threatening our communications with the White House, our base of supplies. A division of the Fifth Corps, together with Warren's brigade and some cavalry and artillery, marched at daylight next morning and encountered the enemy. Next day there was a spirited engagement in which the Rebels lost about a thousand, killed, wounded and prisoners, and were obliged to retreat to Richmond, while the Union loss was less than four hundred. The two regular brigades marched to the field a day later as a support, but we were not called into action. The "Duryee Zouaves" took part in the engagement, sustaining only a trifling loss. The following day the Virginia Central Railroad with its bridges was destroyed by our troops as far as Ashland and we returned to our camp at Gaines's Mill.

We assisted in building approaches across the Chickahominy swamps to the new bridges erected by the engineers and sometimes we worked in mud and water all day. Occasionally the enemy fired some shells at us without much damage and were quickly silenced by some of our batteries posted in a commanding position to protect the bridge.

The Rebels had one very long range gun which they sometimes fired from the other side of the Chickahominy in the direction of our camp. We could not hear the report of the gun but heard the shell pass over us and explode far beyond. This gun was supposed to be of English manufacture—the best type of rifled cannon made at that time.

On one of these working parties we found in a field a tobacco barn in which there was a goodly quantity of dried leaf-tobacco, from which we abstracted as much as the small party in my charge were able to conceal and carry away without being discovered. Next day in camp we made cigars of the stogie shape and enjoyed smoking them.

On the thirty-first of May occurred the very severe battle of Fair Oaks on the right bank of the Chickahominy, in which the Fifth Army Corps took no part, but was kept in readiness to cross the river, if that could have been accomplished. The recent heavy rainstorms had caused such a flood that the bridges had been carried away and the unfinished approaches destroyed. The enemy knew this and no doubt counted on the fact that our army was separated by an impassable river and could not be united at that time. We heard the constant roar of artillery and infantry firing from noon until dark. It recommenced at daylight next morning and lasted for several hours. We learned later that our troops were driven back on the first day, but regained their position the following morning and drove the enemy two miles further in flight towards Richmond, only five miles away. It was a victory for the Union Army, but could not be followed up; the condition of the roads was so bad that artillery could not follow. The troops went back to their former lines and greatly strengthened them. The combined losses of both armies in this battle were upwards of twelve thousand, killed and wounded.

When the month had expired, during which I had been excused from guard and picket, I had to resume those duties again. The guard duty was easy enough as we only maintained a camp guard; but going on picket was a very hard task which happened once a week or oftener, at this camp. Our entire company would march out of camp near evening, leaving our tents standing but taking our knapsacks with us. We would then proceed for a few miles in whatever direction we had been ordered to go, until we arrived at the picket reserve whom we were to relieve. There we were divided into relieves for day and night duties and received our orders and special instructions from the officer in command. When darkness came on we marched out to the picket line in small detachments, were challenged by the sentinels and relieved them consecutively, being informed by the soldier relieved of any suspicious circumstances or points to be especially watched. Then began our lonely vigil through the night until relieved at daybreak, for when near the enemy we had to remain on post all night, or from dawn till dark, as relief detachments were frequently fired on, even though the opposing picket lines did not fire at each other by a sort of mutual understanding during the daytime.

Picket posts were generally within sight or hailing distance of each other; some had the protection of trees or bushes or rising ground, while others were out in the open fields without any protection or concealment. Although I was a corporal, I had to take my place on the picket line with my squad when conditions were such that the pickets could not be relieved at regular hours in front of the enemy. While the daylight tours were much longer at this season of the year, I found the night tours a greater strain on me and more exhausting. There was a continuous strain on the eye and ear, watching for the movement of dark objects or listening for noises; a bird or a small animal moving in the bushes might sound like the stealthy approach of a person; while to fire a shot or to give a false alarm without a good cause meant punishment. We kept our rifles at half-cock, but when hearing a suspicious noise I would stand still and bring mine to a full-cock, waiting until all was quiet again. It was very hard sometimes to fight off sleep. When I felt a drowsy feeling stealing over me, I resorted to all kinds of expedients to keep awake, even to rubbing tobacco into my eyes to make them smart.

I put in one particularly distressing day at one of the new bridges which we were completing across the Chickahominy. At daybreak I was sent from the main picket guard at the Rebel side of the bridge to post a line of sentinels about two hundred yards ahead of the bridge, to watch and give the signal should the enemy approach to interfere with the working party on the bridge. We had to wade through an overflow of the river for a long distance up to our knees and some of the sentinels had to stand in the water all day behind trees as they could not be relieved before dark. I took for my post the farther end of the line behind a tree, where I did not have to stand in the water. When it was fully daylight I noticed a large tree out in an open field about a hundred yards in front of me and soon made out that there were two Rebel pickets watching me from behind that tree. Sometimes a gun was poked out and pointed in my direction on one side or the other of the tree, which caused me to do the same; but as they did not fire, I was only too glad to keep quiet myself. During the forenoon a Rebel battery fired over our heads at the men working on the bridge. This drew a concentrated fire from some of our batteries which soon forced the enemy to desist. A heavy rain came on before noon and lasted all day, soaking us to the skin. I watched my two neighbors, but nothing of an exciting nature happened on this miserable, wet day. When I felt hungry I ate some boiled bacon and munched a few crackers. The day seemed interminably long. Just as soon as it was dark enough I left my post for the main picket guard at the bridge, picking up the sentinels as I went along, for at this time the guard retired to the north side of the bridge over night.

After the battle of Fair Oaks, offensive operations seemed to be suspended for a time on both sides. Incessant rains for a week or more had put the country into such condition that an advance movement could not be attempted; only artillery duels, small skirmishes and some picket firing took place. But about the middle of June there was some excitement in our camps caused by a report that a large force of Rebels were in the rear of the right wing, threatening the destruction of our base of supplies at the White House. This proved to be the much vaunted Confederate General Stuart's raid. General Stuart, with a cavalry force of about twelve hundred and a section of artillery, made a swift and complete circuit of the Army of the Potomac. His progress was so rapid that he met with but little opposition; there was no considerable cavalry force at hand and the infantry sent out in a hurry could not pursue him. He was unable to inflict any damage, except to tear up a small section of the railroad track near the White House, cut some telegraph wires, kill a few cavalry-men and some teamsters and burn a dozen army wagons. The most important result of this raid for the enemy was that it disclosed to them the weakness, location and difficult connection of the right wing of our army, with the main body on the south side of the Chickahominy,—a condition of which they took advantage presently, to our discomfiture. Things went on quietly for a little while after Stuart's raid, until on the twenty-sixth of June, 1862, the enemy attacked our right wing with a superior force at Mechanicsville, which was the first of the "seven days of battle" and retreat of McClellan's army in front of Richmond.

PART X.

THE SEVEN DAYS' RETREAT.
1862.

ON the morning of the twenty-sixth of June, 1862, everything was quiet in our camps; only the fire of an occasional gun was heard in the front of the main part of our army, on the other side of the Chicahominy. We were enduring a very hot period of weather and sought relief from the fierce rays of the sun under our little shelter tents which we opened on all sides for more air. Men who were not on duty smoked, played cards, chatted or discussed the conduct of the war and explained how it should be managed; they damned the cabinet and the politicians in Washington, who really managed the war and interfered often disastrously with the commanding generals in the field. They expressed indignation against the Copperhead (Rebel sympathizing) papers in the North and wondered why they were not suppressed. They made rough estimates of the enormous cost of the war which drew forth a remark from one of the party, that he thought many millions could be saved if the Government advertised for bids to put down the rebellion and awarded the job to some Napoleonic contractor.

About the middle of the afternoon we were suddenly startled by heavy firing in the direction of our right wing at Beaver Dam Creek near Mechanicsville, about three miles from our camp, where the third division of the Fifth Army Corps under General McCall was posted in a strong position. Presently the firing increased to heavy volleys, mingled with the thunder of artillery, and we realized that the long expected attack on our right wing had begun. The drummers beat the long roll and in a moment all was activity in camp. Tents were struck, knapsacks were packed, rations were issued and cartridge boxes replenished; the wagons were packed and all ready for a movement; we only awaited orders to march to the support of the third division. Then came a lull in the firing for an hour or more, only to be renewed about sundown with increased fury when Sykes's division was ordered forward. We took the road towards Mechanicsville and marched in quick time to within half a mile or so of the battle line, when we were halted for a while and then turned off the road into a plowed field on the right, where we were to bivouac for the night. It was getting dark but considerable firing was still going on and it was after nine o'clock before it ceased entirely. We stacked arms and sat on our knapsacks on the ground waiting.

From orderlies and wounded men passing to the rear, we learned that the enemy had crossed and were still crossing the Chickahominy by the upper bridges; and had made fierce attacks on the strong position of the third division on Beaver Dam Creek where they had been repulsed with great loss, while our loss was small; but that by morning the enemy would be in such overwhelming numbers that the position would be untenable. This information made it seem sure to us that there would be another battle on the morrow and that we would take part in it; and for the first time we experienced the peculiar feeling and mental condition of the soldier on the eve of battle, a condition that has been described in prose and poetry, as the "night before the battle." Heretofore our brigade had only been under artillery and picket firing, in which there had been but few casualties, but now we were to face more serious encounters with the enemy.

We all felt grave. Each man seemed to reflect. I heard none boast as to what they would do to-morrow. Intimate friends made known their wishes to each other, in case either of them should not survive. We spread our blankets on the plowed field. It was a beautiful moonlight night. I lay awake a long time looking at the starry heavens, thinking of my mother, who was my only relative. I believe that to a young soldier the anticipation and certainty of a battle for many hours before it occurs is one of the most trying parts of it. I suppose that I felt just like my comrades. I prayed and hoped that I might be spared, or, if I was to fall, that I might be killed rather than mutilated. At last I fell asleep and slept soundly until awakened at daylight next morning.

The events of the next few days made a stronger impression on my youthful memory than any other occurrence throughout the war, and it seems to me that at this writing, after a period of more than fifty years, I remember and can describe my feelings and actions, step by step, as though it had all happened but a week ago.

After a hasty breakfast without coffee, we stood to arms and waited. Some troops were marching on the road to the rear and we learned that General McCall's division was being quietly withdrawn from their defenses. Only some rambling shots could be heard. After a while we marched out into the road and in the direction of Cold Harbor, which was simply a traven at the intersection of two roads. On our way we passed our old camp and the mill and noticed that all our wagons had departed during the night and that quantities of provisions which they could not carry had been set on fire and were still burning.

We were halted several times and remained in line of battle for an hour or more before we went on again; sometimes we countermarched. The forenoon was well spent when we passed Cold Harbor and took the road leading to Turkey Hill and Woodbury's Bridge. When we reached the vicinity of the Adams house, where General Porter established his headquarters, we halted again and were ordered to pile our knapsacks in a field at the edge of the road where a small guard was left in charge of them, while we went on about a quarter of a mile further and took up a position on some high ground in a field on the road leading to New Cold Harbor where we found Warren's brigade and other troops who had preceded us.

It was past noon when we arrived here and sat or lay down on the grass by the roadside under a broiling hot sun and ate our dinner of boiled bacon and hardtack. I remember distinctly that it was bacon, for when I took my piece out of my haversack and unwrapped it, I found it had melted nearly half away from the great heat since early morning. We lay around and smoked our pipes trying to find a little shade from some low bushes that grew along the road, while we listened to an occasional cannon shot which seemed to be a long way off.

The position of my regiment was near the highest part of the road which at this point was about two feet below the general surface of the ground, thus forming a low breastwork. In our front were open fields bordered by woods three hundred yards or more away. Some distance to our left the fields were broken by a small stream in a ravine fringed with bushes and some trees. This stream crossed the road we were on about three hundred yards to our left and at a lower level. Beyond the stream the fields rose again to the edge of the woods. In our rear there was a gentle upward slope which reached a height of about a dozen feet above the level of the road and was within sight of the Watt house surrounded by fields. On this commanding but exposed position a regular battery soon appeared, unlimbered their guns and prepared for action, the cannoneers filling their sponge buckets with water, while others tore down the rail fence in front of the guns on the high side of the road.

From our position I had a good view of the open fields and the locality made such an impression on my memory, that I had no difficulty in recognizing it many years afterward when I revisited the scene. The road to the right and left of us was filled with troops of Sykes's division. I noticed that Warren's brigade, which I recognized by the Zouave uniforms of the Fifth New York, was posted in some depressed ground in front of the road in advance and at some distance to our left.

I think it was some time after two o'clock in the afternoon that picket firing became more frequent and kept on getting closer. We lined up against the rail fence watching the fields in our front anxiously. Presently I noticed a company of the "Duryee Zouaves" leave their regiment, deploy as skirmishers, and enter the woods opposite them; and in a little while we heard the crack of their rifles. Then we realized that the enemy was driving in our pickets and preparing to attack us.

Two pieces of woods formed almost a right angle about five hundred yards from our position and in the corner there was a wide gap through which I could see the country for a mile or more beyond. I noticed a great cloud of dust which seemed to be approaching, and when it neared the gap I could make out that there were horses, but was not sure whether it was cavalry or artillery from the dust they raised. My doubts about this were dispelled in a few minutes when I saw a sudden puff of smoke and heard the familiar sound of a shell passing over our heads. We heard the command to lie down and obeyed it promptly, throwing ourselves face down in the thick dust of the road. The shots now came in such quick succession that I judged a full battery of six guns was firing at our battery, stationed directly in the rear of my regiment only a few yards away, which lost no time in replying and whose guns roared with deafening effect close over our heads as we lay in the road. Amid all this noise and the bursting of the enemy's shells among and behind the battery, we could sometimes hear the groans of a wounded battery horse.

As I explained before, we had some protection from this fire, inasmuch as the road was sunk about two feet, and only one of the many shells fired burst directly over our heads, killing two and wounding three men of Company G., next to my company on the left. While this firing was going on, I think each man tried to make himself as thin as possible—I know that I did. Each time I heard the scream of a shell coming our way, I hugged the ground so close that I broke the crystal and hands of an open-faced watch which I carried in my pocket, and I felt a great sense of relief when I heard the explosion of the shell behind me. I ardently wished to be in some other place or that the firing would cease.

I do not know just how long this artillery duel lasted—to me it seemed an age—but it was probably less than an hour before there was a lull in the firing. We arose, and I looked at the two men who had been killed close by and saw that one had had his head blown clean off, leaving only a stump of the neck; while the other had a large hole in the side of his head. The sight was horrible; they lay in a great pool of blood. The three wounded men had been removed. I took a look at the battery in our rear and judged from what I could see that they had not suffered as much as I had expected.

The battle had now begun in earnest at several points along our line; we heard the heavy volleys of the infantry and the thunder of many guns. I stood at the fence and, amid much smoke, saw that Warren's brigade had become engaged with the enemy who were at the edge of the woods. Soon I noticed a large body of Rebels come out of the woods, apparently in our direction, when the command to lie down was again given and this time a warning from the officer commanding the battery that he was about to fire canister at the approaching enemy. Canister shot is a round tin can made to fit the bore of the gun. It is filled with bullets. When fired, the tin is blown to pieces and the bullets have a tendency to scatter. A few dozen rounds of canister from our battery drove the enemy back into the woods leaving their dead and wounded out in the field. While the canister firing went on a little incident occurred which under other conditions might have been humorous. A man in my company was hit by something in a very soft part of his body, covered by the seat of his pants, and let out a yell that he was wounded. When the firing ceased and an examination was made, only a large red spot could be found on his skin; he had evidently been hit by a piece of tin or solder from a canister which no doubt stung him hard!

My regiment now received orders to form ranks and we

immediately went forward down the road at a run, passing other regiments held in reserve who encouraged us with such remarks as "Go in, Second Infantry, and give them hell! Pitch into them, boys!" When we came to the little stream previously mentioned, we filed to the right and passed along for some distance, halted, closed up the ranks and fixed bayonets when I discovered that I had lost mine; it had slipped out of its scabbard while I was climbing a fence. We then crossed the ravine and brush and went up the incline in company front and found ourselves on the right of the Fifth New York Regiment of Warren's brigade, prolonging his line of battle. I distinctly remember seeing General Warren mounted on a gray horse at the right front of his line, a very conspicuous figure, watching the Second Infantry taking their place in line.

At this stage of the war neither the officers nor the soldiers had learned to take advantage of any inequalities of the ground, or in the absence of such, to dig a hole and throw up a small heap of dirt for protection, behind which the soldier lay and fired if the enemy was at some distance. They learned to do this very soon, however. In passing I noticed that most of the Fifth New York on our left had set up their knapsacks in front of them and were firing in a horizontal position.

Our colors were planted on the very brow of the rise and we dressed (aligned) to them as we did when on parade. This brought us in full view of and made us a conspicuous mark for the enemy who were plainly seen at the edge of a wood directly in front about two hundred yards away. As soon as they observed us they began firing, with but little effect at first, until some minutes after when they estimated the distance more closely. We lost no time in replying. The command was given to commence firing, to fire at will, and to sight for two hundred yards.

As soon as I began to fire at the enemy, I was inspired by very different feelings from what I had experienced while lying inactively in the road, being shelled by the enemy and unable to reply; this, I think, has a dispiriting effect on a young soldier. I now felt a strong desire to inflict all the damage I could on the enemy. I was cool and collected and took deliberate aim with every shot, as long as I could distinguish individuals, and when the smoke became thick I aimed at the flash of their guns and admonished my nearest comrades in the ranks do the same.

The bullets began to whistle spitefully about our ears now; some struck the ground in front of us, raising the dust, but the greater part of them went above our heads. A hasty glance to the right and left along the line showed me, however, that men were falling here and there, and presently my comrade on my right in the front rank pitched forward on his face to the ground, exclaiming with a groan, "I've got it!" He seemed in intense pain and clutched the earth with his fingers. I turned him on his back and found that he had been hit in the right thigh, and I am sure that in the din of battle I heard the bullet strike him and break the thigh bone. There is a peculiar sound or thud when a bullet enters a human body, different from that which it makes when striking other objects—a sound, once heard, not easily forgotten. I ordered two men to take the wounded man a few yards to the rear, down the incline, out of the line of fire, where they left him in the shade of some bushes and saw to it that he had his canteen handy, and then they took their places again in the firing line. When the wounded man was removed I picked up his rifle, took off the bayonet and affixed it to mine, thinking I might need it if we came to close quarters.

I will here digress in my story and relate what happened to this soldier whom we left grievously wounded on the battle field when we had to retreat, for the purpose of showing how the enemy often cruelly neglected our wounded. The man's name was Charles Rehm. He was company clerk at this time, and I had known him well ever since he joined my company at Fort Leavenworth, Kansas, in 1858. I met him about eighteen months after this battle, while on a short furlough in Washington. He related to me how, soon after being wounded, he seemed to have lost consciousness and remembered little until near the close of the following day—more than twenty-six hours after he was hit—when a Rebel surgeon attended him and he was sent to a hospital in Richmond that night along with many other wounded Union prisoners. There they wanted to amputate his leg, but he told them he would rather die than loose his leg. He was a young man about twenty-five, strong and vigorous. He recovered, but his right leg was much shorter than the left; he had to use a cane and limped badly. At the time he was employed as a clerk in the War Department.

To continue my story of the battle, after firing many rounds in our exposed position we were ordered to fall back a few paces and to fire kneeling or lying down. The rising ground in front of us now gave us a little protection. I fired a few rounds in a prostrate position, in which it was difficult to reload, until I saw a man a few files from me receive a horrible wound which opened his face from his forehead to his chin; then I arose and fired kneeling until I heard a sudden command to close ranks and fire by company. This command, I learned afterward, was given because the enemy seemed to form for a charge upon us. We arose and in close double ranks began to fire volleys all together, to the commands of "load!" "ready!" "aim!" and "fire!" which proved to be very effective, for the Rebels retired into the woods and for a little while their firing ceased; then it recommenced in a more feeble way, when we ceased firing by company and fired at will again. While the volley firing was going on, I received what seemed like a hard blow on the right side of my head which staggered me; but I immediately guessed the cause of it and turned around to my rear-rank man, who had to fire over my shoulder, and soundly berated and threatened him. He proved to be the stupid and excitable recruit, named Davis, whom I had drilled in Washington at times. My neck and ear were blackened with powder, and it was months before I regained perfect hearing.

Loading and firing the old style muzzle loading arms was slow compared with modern arms and metallic cartridges. Before the gun could be fired, we had to take a paper cartridge out of the cartridge box, convey it to the mouth, bite off the end and pour the powder into the muzzle of the gun barrel held vertically. Then we tore off the remaining paper to free the ball and inserted that into the muzzle; the ramrod was now drawn, turned around, end for end, and the ball rammed home without any wadding; the ramrod was then drawn out, turned and restored to its place. The gun was now brought to the right hip, full cocked, a percussion cap placed on the nipple, and was then ready to aim and fire. All this required many motions and much time.

The day was intensely hot, my clothing was saturated with perspiration, the bright barrel of my gun was so heated by the fierce rays of the sun and the firing that it seemed to burn my hands and I was almost afraid to reload it without giving it time to cool off. I think we had been under fire nearly two hours, and our forty rounds of ammunition were almost exhausted when a regiment of the Pennsylvania Bucktails (so called because each soldier had a buck's tail sewed to his cap) arrived to relieve us. We were ordered to retire into the small ravine behind us, passing through the ranks of the Bucktails who advanced to take our places. We left our dead and seriously wounded behind us where they fell, unable to give them any help, crossed the little stream in the ravine and formed ranks on the other side in a field—a much shorter line than it had been but two hours before.

We marched off in good order to the rear until we gained some rising ground, when a Rebel battery opened on us with grape shot which killed and wounded more of our men, among them Captain Richard Brindley who commanded the regiment at this time. He was instantly killed by a grape shot. We broke into double quick pace to reach lower ground and escape from the fire of this battery; then we turned to the right in the direction of the Adams house and halted about a half a mile back of our firing line, where we found some regiments from General Slocum's division, which had been sent by General McClellan from the other side of the Chickahominy to reinforce the Fifth Army Corps which up to this time had held more than double its number of the enemy at bay. The battle at this time was raging fiercely—nearly a hundred thousand men were engaged; from our position, however, we saw but little of it except some batteries on high ground behind us firing over our heads at the enemy.

We lay on the ground, tired and exhausted by what we had gone through, noting the absence of many of our comrades and relating to each other how we had seen this or that one fall. Three of our lieutenants we had not seen since noon-time; and we wondered what had become of our band and the drummers and fifers, whom we had not seen since morning, and who should have been acting as stretcher-bearers to carry the wounded off the field. There was no organized ambulance corps in our brigade at this time, and but few ambulances; and, unfortunately, the wounded soldiers who could not walk were left on the field where they fell. This sad state of affairs was much improved later on in the war.

Some ammunition now arived, but only twenty rounds could be served out to each man. The first sergeant of my company informed me that I had been selected to serve on the color guard. This was considered an honor, but it had its disadvantages, the killed and wounded being always greater in proportion on the color guard than in the companies. One of our two color sergeants had been killed and two of the color corporals wounded. I left the ranks of my company and joined the color guard. I expected to find the colors riddled with bullet holes from the fire of the enemy and was greatly surprised to find a bare half-dozen holes in each.

We remained in our position a while longer and saw many wounded men and stragglers making their way to the rear Presently larger bodies of broken regiments appeared and we realized that the Fifth Corps was being forced back by the overwhelming numbers of the enemy. Some loud cheering on the high ground about a quarter of a mile to the rear startled us, and, from the appearance of the troops of which some regiments wore straw hats, we thought they were Rebels who had broken into our ranks from the rear, but they proved to be parts of French's and Meagher's Irish brigades which had been sent to reinforce General Porter. They were sent too late, however, to be of material assistance.

It was nearly sunset when two officers from General Sykes's staff made their appearance and gave some order to Captain John S. Poland who was now in command, and immediately the order was given to fall in, then by the left flank forward at double quick. The two aides-de-camp were mounted and led the column to make a charge on the enemy by General Sykes's order; one of them was Lieutenant Thomas D. Parker of my regiment, the name of the other, who belonged to a different regiment, I do not remember. We rushed on for about two hundred yards when we halted for a brief space to correct the alignment on the colors in the center; then the command "forward, charge." was given and we rushed up a hill for a hundred yards or so, cheering and yelling like mad, the two aides-de-camp riding in front in the center waving their swords.

It suddenly came to me that we were about to attack the enemy with bayonets. I had been instructed in bayonet drill and had practised until I was considered proficient; but I think at this moment I had a secret wish that the adversary whom I might encounter would not be a bigger man than I. I looked ahead but could see no enemy until we reached the crest of the hill, when we suddenly received a staggering fire, from a Rebel regiment that seemed not more than twenty yards away. I saw both of the mounted officers fall at the first fire, Lieutenant Parker being killed and the other wounded. One of the horses dropped, while the other rushed madly through our ranks.

I do not know whether it was by word of command or by

instinct that we halted and instantly began firing instead of rushing on with the bayonet. I dropped on one knee and commenced firing as fast as I could; I aimed at their colors which were almost opposite ours. We were so close together that for a few minutes I could plainly distinguish the features and color of clothing of our opponents until the smoke obscured them. Suddenly their fire slackened and then ceased altogether; they seemed to have melted away down their side of the hill, and we could see only their dead and wounded on the ground where they had been in line. Why we did not pursue the retreating enemy puzzled me, for I thought we now had a chance to give them a good thrashing

I stood up and looked around on a sight still vividly impressed on my memory. We were on high ground overlooking a considerable part of the fields on which the battle now raged; the sun was setting and with its almost horizontal rays lit up a magnificent panorama such as I have never seen since. I could see masses of infantry engaged in deadly struggle, the flashing of the artillery, and I heard the terrific roar; but what fascinated me was the figure of a Rebel officer, mounted on a horse reared up until he seemed to stand almost straight on his hind legs. I could see the officer waving his sword over his head, apparently urging his command forward. At this moment the horse and rider, illuminated by the parting rays of the sun, appeared gigantic and towered above all else. It was a picture for an artist. I took all this in, it seemed to me, in a few seconds, when I heard a command given and dropped back into my place. The enemy had been so close to us, and I had been so busy loading and firing, that I had looked neither to the right nor to the left, but now I observed that we had suffered severely and that two corporals of the color guard had been wounded.

Suddenly we heard the Rebel yell and saw a mass of Rebel infantry rushing toward us. We began firing at them as soon as we saw their heads appear above the crest of the hill. They halted, short of their former line it seemed to me, and delivered their fire as we had done when we had rushed at them. Later on, when I had time to think it over, it seemed to me that these tactics were not in accordance with what I had supposed a charge to be. In this case both sides, finding that the party attacked was not inclined to run, halted and peppered away at each other rather than become engaged at close quarters.

Our condition now was rather serious. Our ammunition was running very low and I suppose there were no reinforcements close at hand. A German battery posted on some high ground behind us tried to aid by firing at the Rebels, but unfortunately their aim was bad and they did us more harm than they did to the enemy; a few of our men on the right being killed and some wounded in the back by the firing of this battery.

I had not fired many shots in the second encounter on the hill and was in the act of ramming a cartridge, when a command or shout caused me to look to the right and I saw that our right wing had broken and were running down the hill helter-skelter, and that we were being fired at from that direction, as well as from the front. I understood that we had been outflanked and that we would be taken prisoners. I yelled to my comrades of the color guard and started to run with them, not taking time to withdraw the ramrod from the barrel of my gun. There was a friendly piece of woods a hundred yards or more ahead of us to our right—a shelter we were all striving for, but which many did not reach for the enemy kept up a hot fire all the way. Twice I had to jump over men who had been hit and rolled over in my path. The enemy kept on firing volleys into the woods for a time but made no attempt to follow us. I got behind a tree and, like many others, fired off half a dozen catridges in the enemy's direction, retaining but two out of the sixty I had during the day. Darkness was coming on. For us the Battle of Gaines's Mill was over, but it still raged on other parts of the field as long as it was light, and I think it was nine o'clock before all firing ceased. I learned later that our last attack had been made on Turkey Hill, not very far from the position we had held at noon before the battle began. Therefore we had lost little ground.

Efforts were now made by our officers to reform our command which had become scattered throughout the woods; and with difficulty the remnants were gathered together and we made our way out of the woods to the road by which we had approached in the forenoon. Here we reformed ranks and took up our march in retreat.

We soon came to a place where the road was skirted by thick woods on the left and a high bank on the right with a free space between the bank and the road on which were piled hundreds of boxes of infantry and artillery ammunition. As we passed, a young and very indiscreet officer made frantic appeals to some of us to stop and help him set fire to the ammunition to prevent it from falling into the hands of the enemy. No attention was paid to him further than calling him a fool, for the road was crowded with retreating troops and wounded men making their way painfully to the rear. An explosion of the ammunition would have made sad havoc among them.

After a while we arrived at the point of the road where we had deposited our knapsacks. Here we were halted and told to pick them out in a hurry. It was dark by this time and the piles of knapsacks seemed to be mixed up in hopeless confusion. Very few of the soldiers got their own; I could not find mine nor even one belonging to my company. I had to grab one and rejoin the ranks.

We resumed our march in the direction of Woodbury's Bridge, and when we neared it, we were ordered to bivouac in a piece of woods on the left side of the road. I sought my company to bivouac with them, but could find only a few men. The first sergeant had a prisoner in charge, a Rebel lieutenant whom he turned over to me as I was the only non-commissioned officer of the company present besides himself. He told me to have him guarded during the night, but I resolved to guard him myself for a time and then turn him over to someone else. I talked with him for a while and gave him a couple of my crackers, and fortunately, he had a canteen of his own with some water in it, of which I was very glad, as I had but a swallow or two left in mine, having been unable to replenish it during the day. He lay down on the ground, after telling me that he was slightly wounded in the leg and apparently went to sleep. I tried hard to keep awake and for a while listened to our army marching on the road to the bridge; but I was so tired and exhausted by the trials of the day that, in spite of my resolution, I dropped to the ground and to sleep; and I think the heaviest cannonading could not have awakened me before daybreak. When, in the morning, someone shook me and I looked about, I found that my prisoner had escaped during the night. Nothing was said or done about it, and I was thankful that the prisoner had not harmed me, helpless as I was from fatigue.

On the morning of the twenty-eighth of June most of our stragglers and men who had lost their way in the woods the evening before rejoined us. The greater part of the army had crossed to the south side of the Chickahominy during the night, and it was left to Sykes's division of regulars to form the rear guard and destroy the bridges, which we did about an hour after daylight, unmolested by the enemy at the Woodbury Bridge where my brigade crossed. When we reached the other side we marched half a mile or more until we reached some higher ground, where we stacked arms and rested among some shrubbery beside the road.

Here for the first time in two days, I was able to boil some coffee which greatly cheered and refreshed me. I then opened the knapsack which I had picked up the night before and found therein the usual soldier's kit, and in addition thereto a neat and well-kept diary, in which the writer described how he had left his home in England and had come to Canada, where after a time he was employed on the estate of a gentleman as a horse-trainer; and how he got into some trouble with the female members of the family and was discharged, when he made his way into the United States and finally drifted into the army. Up to this point the diary was very complete and full of details; but of his army life there were only a few straggling entries made at odd times. No name appeared, neither was his company mentioned, but I found some initials on his clothing by means of which, after many inquiries, I found the company to which he belonged, but he had not been seen since our last fight with the enemy on Turkey Hill, where he was supposed to have been killed or taken prisoner. I left the diary with the first sergeant of his company to be returned to him if he ever came back. I made inquiries in regard to my own knapsack but could find no trace of it. The only things I regretted losing were a few letters and keepsakes.

Many of our wounded were transported to, or had gone on to Savage's Station, where there were thousands of them, but there were still a number of slightly wounded with us who kept our surgeon and hospital steward, assisted by a detail from the band, busy all the morning dressing their wounds. First sergeants of companies called the roll during the morning and, when they came to a name to which there was no response, those who had seen the man fall, killed or wounded stated it and the sergeant made note of it; of others, no one knew anything. Some of them may have been taken prisoners at Turkey Hill. In this way we learned approximately of our losses in this battle, which amounted to more than one-third of my regiment—a larger amount in proportion to our small number, only six companies, than any other regiment in our brigade. Our losses could not be computed accurately until sometime later. General George Sykes, in his report of the Battle of Gaines's Mill, mentions the Second and Sixth United States Infantry of our brigade, the Twelfth and Fourteenth of the First Brigade, and the "Duryee Zouaves" of the Third Brigade as especially conspicuous during the action.

All of the Army of the Potomac was now united on the south side of the Chickahominy nearer to Richmond than the greater part of the Rebel Army which was now divided by a river as we had been—Jackson's, Longstreet's and Hill's divisions under General Lee being on the north bank with many of the bridges destroyed by the Federal troops in their retreat. Even the rank and file knew this and we fully expected to be led on to Richmond with every chance of success in our favor; and when in the afternoon we heard some heavy firing on our side of the river, we thought our opportunity had arrived, but, as we learned later, it was only a minor engagement between a part of General Magruder's troops and General Smith's division of our Sixth Army Corps at Golding's Farm and was repulsed with small loss on our side.

We lay around in the hot sun all day, getting but little shade from some low bushes, were awaiting orders, but none came until evening. Ammunition was issued to us and one day's rations. Our supply trains to the number of about five thousand wagons, together with the reserve artillery, were on the way to the James river, where General McClellan had decided to establish a new base of supplies. Well on towards evening we received orders to "fall in," and marched off not knowing where we were going; but about dusk we arrived at Savage's Station on the Richmond and York River Railroad. Here many troops were in bivouac and thousands of wounded were gathered in hospital tents by the roadside, but the greater part of them lay around in the fields or woods without shelter of any kind. It was a sad sight for us to witness. There were not ambulances enough to transport the unfortunate victims and more than twenty-five hundred of them were abandoned and taken prisoners next day. We were halted here for sometime and noticed great fires burning up supplies and military stores of all kinds which left no doubt in our minds that we were retreating from Richmond.

We started on again and soon entered some dark and gloomy woods, through which the road led toward the White Oak Swamp. It was so dark in these woods that we could not distinguish anything half a dozen files in front of us. At a few places where the roads crossed, fires were lighted and guards were stationed to indicate the way. Owing to the darkness, mainly, and some rain, our progress was very slow and we had many halts of long and short duration, at some of these tired out, I dropped to the ground and fell asleep as soon as I touched it. During one of these short rests in the night, I was suddenly awakened by hearing shots fired close by me. I jumped up and in my confusion imagined that we were being attacked. I hid behind a tree on one side of the road, like many others, cocked my gun and listened. There was a noise which sounded like cavalry and a chatter like sabre scabbards, it seemed to us in our half-awake condition. Scattering shots continued to be fired, until it was discovered that the alarm was caused by an officer's pack-mule, that had escaped from his keeper and was running down the road among the sleeping soldiers, rattling the kettles and pans which were a part of his load. A number of shots were fired at him, but the mule bore a charmed life and was unharmed.

Soon after daylight on June twenty-ninth, we crossed the White Oak Swamp at what was known as Brackett's Ford, halting a short distance beyond, where we stopped to boil coffee and eat breakfast. The only water to be had was that of the swamp which was dark and stagnant. After breakfast we took up a position a little further on and remained in line of battle for hours, listening to the heavy firing behind us at Savage's Station, where General Sumner kept the enemy at bay until dark and then retreated during the night across White Oak Swamp.

The country we were in was a wilderness of woods, bush and swamps, and for two days we hardly saw a clearing, or a cabin. The enemy had repaired some of the bridges across the Chickahominy and we were in danger of flank attacks from both sides, the more so on our right, between us and the James river where the enemy followed us on a parallel road. Several times during the day in these woods, where the heat was almost insupportable and not a breath of air was stirring, we thought we were about to be attacked, and, with our rifles at full cock, kneeled on the ground peering into the thicket and silently awaited the foe. At different periods of the day some of our own troops marched along the road in the direction of Malvern Hill, but we remained until dark, only changing our position slightly a few times. After dark we resumed our march and put in another distressing night; the more so, as the guide for Sykes's division lost the road, causing us to countermarch for a long distance, so that we did not reach Malvern Hill where we were due in the early morning hours of June thirtieth until nearly noon next day. On this day a severe battle was fought at Glendale, which lay between the White Oak Swamp and Malvern Hill, by Generals McCall and Kearney against Generals Longstreet and Hill of the Confederates. This battle resulted in a repulse for the enemy and enabled our troops to retire to Malvern Hill during the night, where by daylight on July first the entire Army of the Potomac was assembled in a strong position selected by General McClellan.

Sykes's division, upon its arrival during the forenoon of June thirtieth was posted on the western edge of the large Malvern plateau, from the Malvern house toward the Crew house, except General Warren's brigade which formed the extreme left down on the river road in the bottom lands. Half a dozen batteries, including Tyler's battery of ten siege guns, were stationed at the edge of the plateau overlooking the steep slope and the fields in front, which ended with some woods about a thousand yards away. The regiments of Sykes's division were placed between the batteries for their support. My own was very close to the Malvern house, an old Colonial mansion built of bricks brought from Holland. General Fitz-John Porter made this house his headquarters. It was also used as a hospital during the battle and as a signal station, for it overlooked much of the country and the James river, where several gunboats armed with heavy guns were anchored. My regiment and another were placed between the siege-gun battery and a regular battery of six Napoleon guns.

The position occupied by the Fifth Corps was a commanding one and we hoped the enemy would attempt to assault it. We lay down in the hot sun, thoroughly tired out after our night's marching. There was water at the foot of the plateau and by details we replenished our empty canteens but were forbidden to build any fires to make coffee—besides there was no wood to be had near our position. Shortly after our arrival at Malvern Hill a gill of whiskey was served to each man who wished to take it, also three pieces of hard-tack. I suppose these were a part of commissary stores left behind, for our wagon-train was by this time well on its way to Harrison's Landing on the James river. We rested and slept during the afternoon, until rudely awakened by our batteries beginning to fire on the enemy down in the low ground in our front and near Warren's brigade. A sergeant of the Fourteenth Infantry, who had probably had a little more than his gill and was confused when tardily aroused by the firing, cried out, "Is it possible I'm in the hands of the enemy? I'm a British subject!"

The Rebels advanced some artillery from the woods to a position within eight hundred yards of us and opened fire, some of their shells passing over us, some dropping among Warren's men. By standing up, I could plainly see their batteries out in the field, as well as a large body of infantry at the edge of the woods supporting them. In a few minutes some three dozen of our guns on the plateau were firing at them, making a tremendous uproar, above which we could distinguish the sound of the large guns from the gunboats on the river and the explosion of their enormous shells among the enemy in the woods, the effect of which must have been terrifying. The position of the Rebel batteries and their infantry was invisible to the gunboats owing to intervening woods, so that their fire was directed by signals. The signal corps had built a platform at one of the chimneys on the steep roof of the Malvern House, from which I noticed two men making signals. Whenever one of the great two-hundred-pound shells, fired at great height, rushed through the air, it sounded like a train of cars in motion at high speed and the explosion shook the earth. Some of these shells fell short in the fields in our front; all did not explode— some spun around, threw up dirt and dug holes in which it seemed a horse could have been buried. The well-directed fire of our guns on the edge of the plateau destroyed the Rebel batteries in less than a half hour. Several caissons were blown up, the soldiers abandoned their guns in wild flight, and the infantry disappeared, making no further attempt to molest Warren's brigade on the river road that day.

After a short engagement, in which there were only a few casualties on our side, it remained fairly quiet on the left wing during the evening and throughout the night, and for the first time since leaving our camp at Gaines's Mill we had a night of unbroken rest, wrapped in our blankets. I was so weary that even the certainty of a battle the next day could not keep me awake, and I slept soundly until awakened at daylight.

The morning of July first broke bright and clear, and gave promise of a hot day. The Union Army seemed in excellent spirits; bands could be heard playing patriotic airs in the early morning on various parts of our line; our own band played for a time with a most cheering effect. Our gigantic and genial Drum-Major Lovell whirled his baton joyously and showed no disappointment because his daily prayer to the Lord to send him a million dollars remained unanswered. He hoped, as he explained to us, that some day He would get tired and say, "Let the poor devil have it and not bother me any longer." Later on the Lord was good to him, for he became one of the color sergeants of the regiment and remained in that capacity for eighteen months until the close of the war, without receiving a scratch; and he was the only color bearer in my regiment who served that length of time without death or injury. He remained in the army for many years after the war; but, alas! ended his days in the Soldiers' Home in Washington.

The enemy were massing under cover of the woods all the morning; we caught glimpses of them through some of the clearings. After ten o'clock in the morning they advanced a battery occasionally, feeling different parts of our line, but were always quickly silenced by a concentrated fire from our artillery. Some one of the batteries which we supported kept throwing shells into the woods where the Rebels were supposed to be massing, and the gunboats also fired an occasional shell. This artillery duel went on until about one o'clock in the afternoon, when heavy infantry firing took place toward the center of our line. This went on for some hours, spreading toward the right; then for a time it slackened, only to recommence with renewed vigor after five o'clock when the most desperate efforts were made to break our line, but without success.

During this time all the batteries in our vicinity kept up a tremendous fire, as did Tyler's siege-guns and the gunboats. It was estimated that at times, when nearly all the artillery on both sides were engaged, over two hundred guns were in action. The earth trembled and the roar of the many guns so close to us was deafening. I think it was the heaviest firing which I heard during the war. Again we were in a passive state, in a position prone to the ground to escape the shells from the enemy, unable to fire a shot, as the Rebel infantry made no attack on our part of the line; they deemed our position too strong to be assaulted and did not have artillery enough to make any serious impression.

During this great artillery duel two of the immense shells from the gunboats dropped short and landed among the siege-guns beside us. One of the shells exploded, killing and wounding several men. The gunboat fire was stopped for a time by signal, then recommenced in a different direction. The batteries in our vicinity suffered little loss and in my regiment only two men were wounded during all this firing. About sundown the heavy volleys at the center and right of our line ceased, the attacks of the enemy in masses had been repulsed and they had withdrawn with great loss, without penetrating our line at any point. The batteries we supported ceased firing, but a heavy, desultory infantry fire with occasional cannon shots warned us that the battle was not yet over.

Suddenly we received orders to form ranks and my regiment marched off by the Quaker Road in the direction of the Crew House, near the center of our line and about a mile away. Our band, led by the drum-major, was at the head and, by orders of Captain Poland, began playing. It was the first and the only time during the war that I heard a band play, while a battle was on. We marched as if on parade; the music was inspiring and drew cheers from the troops among which we passed. This was kept up until we turned off the road and some spent balls began to drop among us, when the band ceased playing and fell in behind.

We marched on toward the place we were to occupy and, when near it, we passed a curious little battery which was stationed alongside of a barn. They were busy firing. I had remarked this battery a few times when it passed us on the road, while we were marching up the peninsula. It consisted of a small gun-carriage and limber drawn by two horses; on the gun-carriage was mounted a single steel barrel, somewhat longer and heavier than an ordinary gun-barrel, but of about the same calibre; there was a cranked handle to turn and a hopper to receive cartridges. The soldiers named it the "coffee-mill battery." It really looked like a large coffee-mill mounted on wheels, except for the barrel. It required the services of three men to fire the gun—one to feed cartridges into the hopper, another to raise or depress the barrel and swing it right or left in a quarter-circle and to take aim, while the third man turned the crank which caused the explosion of the charges. I think there were six of these guns, and their pop-pop-pop was quite rapid and continuous as we passed by them. They were the elementary production of the later inventions—the mitrailleuse and gatling guns. They disappeared soon after that from the Army of the Potomac and I never saw them in action again.

When we reached our position along a wide and deep ravine, it was almost dark and objects at some distance could only be distinguished with difficulty. An irresolute fire was opened upon us from the opposite side of the ravine, to which we immediately replied, although all we could see of the foe were the flashes of their guns, which stopped in about ten minutes after which we received the command to cease firing. Half a dozen were wounded in this short engagement, but none killed. We remained silent in our position, awaiting a possible attack, hearing very plainly some of the commands given by the Rebel officers on the opposite side of the dark ravine. From the ravine itself, we heard groans and cries of wounded men who were evidently Rebels, for one among them, probably an officer, in his delirium sometimes cried out, "Charge, Ninth Georgia!"

The firing on other parts of the line of battle did not cease entirely for an hour or more, and then the enemy seemed to have retired, leaving us completely victorious. I think it must have been much later than ten o'clock, when the word was quietly passed along the ranks to quit our position and creep back as silently as possible. I did this a part of the way, then went the rest of the distance in a crouching position, until we were halted and re-formed our line. Then we marched a little farther, halted again, and sat on the ground, resting and wondering what these movements meant.

Later, the first sergeant of my company called me and conducted me to the adjutant, who ordered me to make my way to the Malvern house, where one of our lieutenants and a company of our men had been left as a guard at the general hospital, and to inform the officer to hold himself and his men in readiness to rejoin the regiment when it passed during the night or morning. Since we were in the field I had been selected several times for special duties, but I did not like this one in the least. I knew the general direction of the Malvern house, whence we had come, and if I could gain the

Quaker Road the rest would be easy. But to reach this road it was necessary to cross some fields and a piece of woods, and it struck me I had a good chance of being shot by some picket, or getting lost and being taken prisoner.

The sky was overcast and the night dark. I made my way cautiously towards the woods and just before reaching them passed over an elevated piece of ground, where evidently one of our batteries had been stationed during the day. I inferred this from a number of dead horses, some with their stiffened legs up in the air, and among them a few dark forms which I knew but too well were the bodies of artillerists. I hurried over this place and gained the edge of the woods—which I dreaded the most on account of pickets, but was not challenged. I halted a moment and listened, thinking I heard the clatter of accoutrements and the heavy tramp of marching men. I knew that this could only be some of our army and felt much relieved.

Presently I was among them on the Quaker Road, for the woods proved to be shallow. These soldiers belonged to another corps and were retreating very reluctantly toward the James river. There was much grumbling among them; they wondered why, after a victory and with a retiring enemy, they were ordered to leave a strong position. We learned later that some of the corps commanders had importuned General McClellan to hold Malvern Hill, but the General ruled against it, giving as his reason the difficulty of supplying the army in that location.

I reached the Malvern house a little before midnight and found a sentinel who directed me to the lieutenant in charge. He was fast asleep. I awakened him and repeated the adjutant's orders. He ordered some of the men to watch the road near the corner of the house and notify him when the regiment appeared. On looking around I saw that the house was brightly lighted and there was much commotion caused by officers and orderlies rushing in and out of General Porter's headquarters; it was also the principal hospital, and in the out-buildings and some tents I could see surgeons attending the wounded and performing amputations by candle-light, while the ground back of the house was covered with wounded soldiers.

I did not tarry long to look at this heart-rending scene, but made my way along the front of the house and the out-houses. I was hungry and was looking around to find something to eat. My haversack was almost empty; and I knew the necessity of saving something for the morrow, as we were not likely to get any rations until we came to our supply trains. As we had not been able to make coffee for some days, I had plenty of that and sugar, but I had no meat and only a few crackers, so I prowled around until I observed a half dozen soldiers near the corner of a fence where there was a heap of boxes and barrels, which proved to be commissary stores left unguarded and probably forgotten. I joined the group and found them dipping their tin cups into a barrel, of which they had knocked in the head, and filling their canteens with what I knew from the odor to be whiskey. This seemed a heaven-sent opportunity and one not to be neglected. I emptied my canteen of water and filled it with whiskey. Some boxes of hard-tack had been opened, from which I filled my haversack. There were still some barrels of whiskey, also barrels of pork, which the group decided it would be unsafe to break open on account of the noise it would make. I dipped my quart cup into the barrel once more and hurried away with it in my hand, returning to the guard with whom I shared its contents. I kept silent regarding my canteen, however. I did not dare tell my comrades where I got the liquor, for fear some of them would become intoxicated; so I was forced to invent a tale of having received it from one of the hospital stewards, who was a friend of mine. I took especial care to guard my canteen with its precious contents, then wrapped myself in my blanket and went to sleep among my comrades.

I was awakened at daylight when our brigade approached. We hurried to the road and waited until the regiment came along, then joined its ranks. Sykes's division was again covering the retreat of the army. The First Brigade, under Colonel

Buchannan, formed the rear guard while our brigade immediately preceded them. It was storming, as it generally did after a battle, and the rain soon came down in torrents, wetting us to the skin in a few minutes. It was a cold, chilly rain which lasted all day.

The army had been retreating from a defeated enemy on this road all night, again leaving many of our wounded behind. By the time we reached Haxall's and the bottom-lands, we found the road in a frightful condition. Cut up as it had been by thousands of wagons and artillery, it was now a liquid quagmire from the torrential rain. We tore down fences and crossed fields to avoid some impassable places. We waded through many ditches and small streams, often knee-deep, and had many halts and interruptions, often coming to a halt in a part of the road where it was impossible to sit down for a much-needed rest, unless we should sit in mud nearly a foot deep. My shoes were soon filled with gritty liquid mud which chafed the skin and made marching very painful and distressing. At one time I just saved myself from falling, while crossing a stream, and my rifle slipped from my grasp and was submerged in the muddy water. I doubt if I could have discharged it if I had needed to do so.

I cannot describe our misery and suffering on this day, the seventh of the retreat, and by far the worst of all. We had reached the limit of endurance, weakened as we were by battles, marching and want of food. We had become callous and cared little what became of those who dropped out from exhaustion or of small squads of wounded men who were limping painfully along the road, sometimes being knocked down and crying out in anguish for help. The rule of self-preservation had a deplorable demonstration on this awful day.

Several times we formed line of battle in the fields, ready to repel the enemy who pursued and harassed the rear guard just behind us. Stuart's Rebel cavalry and a light battery of artillery followed us all day and occasionally sent a few shells into our ranks. We also had cavalry with the rear guard who skirmished with the enemy, and a battery of regular artillery which more than once took up a commanding position beside the road and with our cavalry kept the enemy in check. During the forenoon, while at a long halt, I gave Lieutenant McLoughlin, who now commanded my company (and the only company officer present at this time, Lieutenant Kidd having been wounded) a drink of whiskey from my canteen and he declared I had saved his life. He laughed when I explained how I had got it, but remarked that I was lucky not to have been caught. I took a big drink myself which cheered me, wet and shivering as I was; the remainder I doled out to my comrades, as far as it would go, and for that day at least I was the most popular member of the company.

We reached Harrison's Landing while it was still daylight. Although the distance was not more than about eight miles, it had taken us twelve hours to make it owing to the state of the roads, the frequent halts and the forming of line of battle several times during the day. We halted at the edge of an immense wheat field which I think must have been a mile square. Only a small part of this field had been cut and stacked in sheaves. It still rained hard. My bunkie and I decided to put up our shelter tent for the first time in seven days. We gathered a thick layer of the wet sheaves and lay down in our wet clothing, sleeping soundly all night. We could not make any coffee, but were surprised and cheered by an issue of hard-tack and a gill of whiskey during the evening and the promise of some meat on the morrow; which was a great comfort to us in our despondent condition.

Next morning, July third, directly after reveille, a Rebel battery commenced throwing shells into our camp from a hill which overlooked it. We formed line of battle, advanced a short distance and remained under arms until the firing ceased in a short time, the battery being driven away and the hill occupied by a Maine regiment. This was the finish of the seven days' retreat, or "change of base," as General McClellan preferred to name it. No large body of the Rebel Army had followed us from Malvern Hill, where they had received such a crushing blow that they retired within the fortifications of Richmond to recuperate, leaving only small reconnoitering parties to observe us.

After the firing had ceased and while we were still standing in ranks, a private of my company stepped into the bushes just behind us and presently we heard a shot; and he came running out, holding up a bleeding hand and crying, "I am wounded. Take me to the hospital!" But he ran so fast, it would have been hard to catch him. We found his rifle in the bushes, apparently just discharged, which left no doubt that this was a case of self-mutilation, fortunately of rare occurrence, so far as I knew; but I heard of a few cases where the mutilation took place during battle. This soldier never rejoined his company, which was well for him. The fear of the contempt of his comrades is even more powerful a factor than discipline in keeping a timid or nerveless soldier in the ranks during battle.

As we looked at each other while in ranks, we were amazed at the shocking appearance both officers and rank and file presented after the strenuous week we had passed through. Our clothing was torn and shapeless and coated with sticky mud from head to foot; our faces and hands were grimy with powder and dirt, for few had had opportunity to wash themselves for a week. Several who were slightly wounded wore bandages. Our guns were rusty but serviceable. Some had lost their knapsacks and some a part of their accoutrements, and upon all the faces there was a gaunt and weary look which plainly told the story of our endurance. Of the great field of wheat which I had seen the evening before, scarcely any remained that had not been trampled down during the night by soldiers and horses.

The rain had ceased, but the sky was still clouded and the day cheerless. During the forenoon we marched to a point within about a mile and a half of Harrison's Landing and the brigade encamped on low ground on the border of a sluggish and boggy creek, where we were destined to remain for many weeks sweltering under the great heat of the summer.

TEN YEARS IN THE RANKS U. S. ARMY

The first advance upon Richmond had failed, as did also the second under General Grant two years later, when he operated on substantially the same ground against the same enemy reduced in number and resources. Military writers and historians have accused General McClellan of grave errors in the Peninsula Campaign; but some of them accuse the Administration at Washington, together with the Joint Committee of Congress on the conduct of the war, of graver errors and blame them as being the real cause for the unsuccessful termination of this campaign. That the Army of the Potomac, made up of as fine and intelligent soldiers as ever took the field, remained as true and loyal to its commander after this campaign as it had been before, proved beyond question that it had not lost confidence in him.

The "retreat" to the James river was not a retreat in the usual sense of the word; we kept our formation, all our movements were directed by General McClellan and there never was a rout. We fought daily battles in all of which, except that of Gaines's Mill, we were successful in checking the enemy and keeping them at bay until a new position was gained. We lost none of our artillery, except in battle, and we saved all of our heavy siege guns and our immense wagon-train preceded the army. All this was done in an unknown, swampy country with few roads upon which a great army could march and make any rapid progress, even if unpursued by a determined enemy. The enemy's losses in the seven days' battles were greater than ours by nearly four thousand men, according to authorities.

The battle of Gaines's Mill, although not ranking as one of the great battles of the war, was remarkable, being the one with the greatest disparity in numbers. When the battle commenced General Porter had only the Fifth Army Corps, consisting of less than twenty thousand men, to oppose double their number, and it was not until late in the afternoon that Slocum's division of seven thousand reinforced him. For four hours the powerful enemy tried in vain to break our lines and it was not until near sundown that, reinforced by General Jackson's troops, augmenting their numbers to more than sixty-five thousand, against our less than thirty thousand actually engaged, they succeeded in breaking our line in the center; and when darkness ended the battle they had only advanced as far as the ground previously occupied by our reserves. The losses of the Fifth Army Corps during the seven days were about seventy-six hundred, of whom forty-eight hundred were killed and wounded and twenty-eight hundred captured or missing. My battalion, consisting of six companies of the Second United States Infantry, about three hundred and fifty present for duty, lost two officers who were killed and four wounded; fourteen soldiers killed, one hundred and three wounded, and sixteen captured or missing—total, one hundred and thirty-nine, more than one-third of our number.

I had no clear idea at the time of the distance the army had covered during the seven days' retreat and I was astonished when twenty years later I made the trip with a friend from Richmond to Haxall's, following the route of the army in a single day, and had sufficient time to take a number of photographs. We had a carriage and a pair of good horses. The coachman was black, but his name was White. We remained on Malvern Hill until dark, when we went to Haxall's to spend the night, much to the relief of Charlie White, who showed great terror as we passed through the dark and gloomy woods on our route which he said were full of ghosts. He declared that "sodjer ghosts" marched on this road until daylight.

In my narration of events which occurred during McClellan's Peninsular Campaign I have tried to describe in detail a soldier's experience in camp, on the march, in battle and when retreating before a pursuing foe, as accurately as my memory permits after an interval of more than fifty years. I consider that campaign unsurpassed in hardship, suffering and endurance by any subsequent campaign while I was in the Army of the Potomac, unless perhaps it be the battle of Fredericksburg and General Burnside's "Mud-March," both of which occurred in winter time. I therefore deem it superfluous to burden the remainder of my narrative with similar details.

PART XI.

Harrison's Landing to Fredericksburg, Va.—1862-1863.

THE part of the camp at Harrison's Landing occupied by our brigade was, I think, the most unhealthy spot in which I had ever camped. The weather had become intensely hot and water fit to drink was difficult to obtain from a poor spring, at which crowds stood in line waiting for a chance to fill their canteens. The water of the boggy creek was soon contaminated and the sinking of barrels and cracker boxes at its edge had but little effect in purifying it. Nearly a third of our men were soon sick with miasma and swamp fever; the hospitals were over-crowded and the mortality high. Every morning and evening we heard the dead march.

Our second day in this camp was the Fourth of July, and General McClellan caused a salute to be fired at noon at each army corps headquarters. In the afternoon he reviewed us and his address to the Army of the Potomac was read to us on parade. A few days later President Lincoln visited the camp and held a review in the cool of the evening. He was enthusiastically cheered.

About this time I became very ill and had to report to the regimental surgeon, who wanted to send me to the hospital; but I did not want to go there among so many sick and dying men and remained for a few days in my tent, over which we had built an arbor, which was of little use, however, as the camp was exposed to the torrid sun. I became very weak. A kind comrade assisted me from camp to the creek, about a hundred yards away, where he spread my blanket and I lay there under the shade of a tree all day, until he helped me back to camp at night. It was better than remaining in the little shelter tent; but I was so miserable that I cared very little whether I lived or died.

The sick and wounded of the volunteers had a "sanitary commission," supported by the various states, which furnished nurses, supplies and delicacies that the army could not provide. The regulars, when in their own hospitals, received no such attention; they had to get along on soldiers' rations, if they could eat them. At this camp we had company cooks. My comrade brought me rice soup from our kitchen, and on that and some soft crackers and condensed milk, bought at the sutler's, I managed to keep alive. In about ten days I began to improve, but was greatly emaciated, and it was well towards the end of July before I could take my place in the ranks again.

One of our first lieutenants and two second lieutenants, all civilian appointees, who had not shown themselves at any of the recent battles the regiment had been engaged in, turned up at Harrison's Landing and were promptly arrested. They were tried by court-martial and cashiered on July twenty-first, 1862. I believe two of them succeeded in getting back into the army early in 1863, and one—the first lieutenant—redeemed himself by being killed at Gettysburg. I shall not mention the names of these valiant officers; they are recorded in the official Army Register of 1862-'63.

We had been in camp about a week when we were surprised by the reappearance of the captain of our company, whom we had left in Georgetown four months before with a medical excuse from field duty. He was more corpulent and his face was more florid than ever. He brought with him some cases, containing a variety of liquors, which he charged his servant to guard very carefully when he was absent from his tent— which was seldom, as he performed no duties. Few of our officers paid any attention to him or visited him in his tent, with the exception of the three lieutenants under arrest; they were his chums and boon companions from morning till night. My tent was within ear-shot of the captain's and when I lay there while sick or convalescent I could not help hearing their loud talk while they were carousing—a daily occurrence. They fought the seven days' battles all over again, the captain bewailing the ill health which had kept him from the active service which he so ardently desired. Had he been in charge of the brigade he would have formed an oblique square and in that form he would have charged upon the enemy at a double-quick. He demonstrated to the entire satisfaction of his auditors that the impact of the sharp corner of the oblique square could not have failed to break the enemy's center, while the two sides of the square would have brushed away their right and left wings and caused them to be annihilated by our fire. He admitted that such a bold movement could be successfully executed only with reliable troops like the regulars, if led by an officer who was a tactician able to conceive such a daring attack. At times the officers under arrest became maudlin and with tearful voices lamented their hard luck in being under arrest, when the captain would cheer them by saying, "Gentlemen, I know you are all brave men; trust in me, I will see you vindicated! What will you take now?"

This went on until the three officers were cashiered and left camp.

One night soon after the Rebels shelled the camp at Harrison's Landing and there were rumors of another advance on Richmond. The captain hastily departed with bag and baggage, leaving only the empty cases behind. This time we were rid of him for good; he was retired for disability (!) August twenty-seventh, 1862, and we never saw him again. John S. Poland now became captain of my company. He had been graduated from the West Point Military Academy and was a very efficient officer. The departure of our captain, the dismissal of the three lieutenants, a few transfers and some promotions from the ranks, left us with a better lot of officers—men whom the rank and file could respect.

We were much in need of clothing, particularly shoes, and these were issued to us while at Harrison's Landing; also the medical department ordered whiskey and quinine occasionally as a prevention against malarial fever, as had been done while we were on the Chickahominy. Most of the soldiers would have preferred to take this dose unmixed, dispensing with the quinine.

TEN YEARS IN THE RANKS U. S. ARMY

We had regular drum and bugle calls and bands played in the evening at this camp. Promotions took place among the soldiers—I was made a sergeant, the youngest sergeant in the regiment at that time.

Shortly after midnight on August first a heavy fire from field pieces on the south side of the James, which quickly aroused the entire army, was opened on our camps and the many vessels in the river. Our batteries at the river opened fire; so did the gun-boats. For more than half an hour there was a tremendous noise of guns and exploding shells, when the Rebel batteries suddenly ceased firing. None of the shells reached us, but ten men were killed and fifteen wounded in the camps nearer the river; the shipping received only trifling damage.

Next day troops were sent across the river, my regiment among them. We crossed on a steamboat, near noon; deployed as skirmishers on the other side; advanced up a hill through some woods and came upon a meadow where the Rebel guns had been placed, commanding our camp and the river, but screened by the woods. It was possible to locate the guns and count them. There were forty-one of them. Some artillery ammunition was scattered about and we noticed large holes in the ground near-by, made by shells from our gunboats.

The day was very hot. We lay in the shade of the woods and I was taking a nap when I was awakened and ordered to take six men and examine a piece of wood land on our right, for half a mile or more, and then return and report. I started with my little squad at a "trail arms," the guns at half-cock. There was much underbrush and we advanced cautiously for nearly half a mile, when I heard a noise and thought I caught a glimpse of a man in a gray uniform, trying to hide behind a tree only a short distance away. I made a sign to my squad to halt and advancing a little nearer brought the gun to my shoulder at full cock, when I challenged and was immediately answered, "Friend of the Sixth Infantry!" as the man stepped from behind the tree. He was dressed in a gray woolen shirt, having left off his blue blouse on account of the heat. I frightened him when I explained how near he had come to being shot on account of his gray shirt. He belonged to another party examining the woods from a different direction. I made my way back to my command, diverging somewhat from the way we had come. In a clearing we found six fine cows grazing which we drove towards our party. They were kept and turned over to the commissary later on. We noticed some Rebel cavalry on high ground a mile or more away watching us, but they did not venture any nearer.

The place where we had landed was called Coggin's Point. We were on part of a large plantation, the property of a prominent secessionist. There was a large house within view, called the Cole house, which was ordered to be destroyed and was set fire to by another detachment. We re-crossed the river about sundown and returned to our camp. General McClellan ordered Coggin's Point to be occupied and field works constructed to prevent a recurrence of a bombardment from the south side of the James.

About August fourth General Hooker made a strong reconnoissance in the direction of Richmond and drove a Rebel force from Malvern Hill. There were rumors of a campaign and the authorities at Washington and the Northern journals united in urging General McClellan to become active. The sick and wounded, more than ten thousand of them, were being shipped North as fast as water transportation could be provided for them, and we supposed that another attempt to capture Richmond would be made. We were disagreeably surprised when we learned later that we were to reinforce General Pope north of the Rappahannock river, whom "Stonewall" Jackson had hopelessly bewildered by his rapid movements.

The commands of Generals Freemont and Banks had been withdrawn from the Shenandoah Valley when "Stonewall" Jackson gave them the slip in June and by forced marches reached Richmond to take part in the seven days' battles. These two commands were consolidated with that of General McDowell to form the Army of Virginia, which was to operate between Washington and Richmond for the protection of the capitol. General Halleck called General John Pope from the West, with the approval of the President, to take command of the Army of Virginia, although he was out-ranked by both McDowell and Freemont. General Freemont, unwilling to serve under Pope, promptly resigned his command. When General Pope took command he addressed a proclamation to the Army of Virginia in which he expressed his contempt for certain phrases he found much in vogue, such as "bases of supplies" and "lines of retreat"—phrases which he enjoined his army to discard, as unworthy of soldiers destined to follow the leadership of one "who came from the West and had never seen anything but the backs of his enemies."

This bombastic and arrogant nonsense was a satire pointed at General McClellan. Alas for Pope! Less than two months after he took command the enemy saw his back and his heels as well. He was shelved to the command of an unimportant department in the West and cut no further figure in the war. The Northern papers made much of him and his proclamation, but the soldiers had a clearer insight into his character and ability as the commander of a great army. He became known among them by the sobriquet of "Headquarters in the Saddle."

The Fifth Army Corps was the First to leave Harrison's Landing. On the afternoon of the fourteenth of August Sykes's division received orders to strike their tents and prepare to march to Newport News, Virginia. We left our camp about six o'clock in the evening and marched all night, resting only about two hours at midnight. Some time during the forenoon of the next day we reached the Chickahominy, and crossing it by a pontoon bridge about a thousand feet long, went into bivouac. The following morning we started again at daybreak, and passing through Williamsburg and Yorktown, we reached Newport News on the fourth day, the eighteenth, remaining there for two days awaiting transportation. There we had salt water bathing in the James river, which was very refreshing after the hot and dusty march. We were hurried along and made rather long marches. I had not recovered my full strength after my illness at Harrison's Landing, but I managed to keep up by lightening my burden. I threw away my knapsack and part of my clothing, made a roll of the blanket and shelter tent, wrapping up in it a change of underclothing and socks, and slung the roll over my shoulder. I put on my newest shoes and threw the others away. All this made marching easier for me. Many of my comrades did the same.

On August twentieth we embarked on a steamboat along with other troops for Aquia Creek on the Potomac and had the usual overcrowded and uncomfortable experience. We arrived on the twenty-second and were a long time getting ashore by tugs. There was a railroad to Fredericksburg, less than twenty miles away, and we were tumbled into empty freight cars and upon platform cars and taken to Falmouth Station, near Fredericksburg, where we disembarked in the evening and bivouacked.

Next day, after receiving some rations, we started our march up the north bank of the Rappahannock in the direction of Pope's army. The other corps of the Army of the Potomac went up the Potomac river as far as Alexandria, which gave them only half so long a march to join Pope, as the Fifth Corps had had from Falmouth. General McClellan accompanied the main part of the Army to Alexandria.

Our march up the Rappahannock and along the line of the Orange and Alexandria railroad by the way of Bealton, Catlett's and Bristoe Stations to Manassas was a severe one. The heat was so excessive that a man in my company declared "the sun must be in the hydraulics!" Parts of the country seemed to be destitute of water, which caused us great suffering, and many were overcome and dropped by the wayside. We did not have the muddy roads of the Peninsula, but we had an intolerable amount of dust which hung in great clouds over the marching columns and betrayed the movements of the opposing armies. As we neared Bristoe Station, where a stretch of the railroad had been torn up by the Rebels, we began to hear cannonading.

On the morning of the twenty-ninth we started at daybreak for Centreville, passing Manassas Junction, where we saw the ruins of locomotives, cars and immense quantities of rations and military stores totally destroyed by fire a few days before when Jackson's army had slipped around the bewildered General Pope's right and got in his rear, between him and Washington.

We had only just passed Manassas when we were ordered to face about and march in the direction from which we had come on the Warrenton Pike towards Gainsville. Before reaching there some of Longstreet's troops were encountered about noon, concealed in the woods near the Manassas railroad. We took up a position near Bethlehem Church, massed in the rear of the First Division as a reserve. Later in the afternoon very heavy firing was heard some miles away to our right, where the battle of Groveton was being fought. We had a strong force of skirmishers out; so did the enemy. There was much firing between them until dark and some movements as though we were forming for an attack, with the object of preventing Longstreet from sending reinforcements to Jackson at Groveton, but nothing came of it and we remained in our position until daybreak, August thirtieth. The last issue of rations had been, I think, at Warrenton Junction; we were nearly out, in fact had lived on half-rations for the last day. During this night we received a small allowance of hard-tack and nothing else.

On the morning of the thirtieth we marched by way of the Warrenton Pike in the direction of yesterday's battle and took up a position about noon near the center in a cornfield not far from the Pike, my brigade forming the reserve in rear of the First Brigade. We were soon under a heavy fire of shells from the Rebel batteries which kept up with more or less vigor until the middle of the afternoon, when the real battle commenced with General Butterfield's attack on the enemy, strongly posted in a railroad cut towards the right. Historians have described this bloody battle and how, about sundown, our army was out-flanked and forced to retreat. It was about this time that Sykes's regulars were ordered to retreat and did so in good order towards the Henry house plateau, which commanded the road by which the army was retreating in some disorder, towards the stone bridge over Bull Run. Sykes's regulars assisted by some volunteer regiments checked Longstreet's pursuit.

Here for the first time on that day my brigade became engaged with the enemy at the edge of some timber through which they were advancing. For nearly an hour we held our ground, delivering heavy volleys until we were out-flanked, forced to retire, and the fight continued by other troops.

General Warren's Third Brigade, consisting of the Fifth and Tenth New York, about one thousand strong, had earlier in the evening, in an isolated position, sustained the first onslaught of overwhelming numbers of Longstreet's troops. In less than fifteen minutes this small brigade sustained a loss of more than four hundred killed and wounded, the Duryee Zouaves alone losing two hundred and ninety-seven men, a greater loss than that of any other regiment in this battle. During the two days my small regiment lost sixty-six killed and wounded and, singular to relate, only one officer and one private were killed outright; seven others, however, were missing and we did not know what had become of them. The first sergeant of my company, Rudolph Thieme, was among the missing, but no one had seen him fall. A small detail from my regiment, which under a flag of truce recovered Lieutenant Kidd's body, failed to find that of the sergeant, who was an old soldier and expected soon to be commissioned. The mystery of his disappearance was never solved.

When darkness came upon us and the firing ceased, except for a few shots here and there, the second battle of Bull Run was over. We marched by way of the Pike to the Stone Bridge, where we found an indescribable scene of confusion. Ambulances, artillery, army wagons, sutlers, wounded soldiers and stragglers were all crowding towards the narrow bridge, colliding with organized bodies of marching troops and destroying their formation. Slowly and with great difficulty we crossed and re-formed on the other side, taking up our march to Centreville and keeping off the road as much as possible to avoid the confusion there. To add to our misery a steady rain had commenced after dark and kept up all night. The retreat continued until daylight, when the bridge was blown up. We reached Centreville about midnight when, tired and exhausted, we lay on the wet ground and slept until morning.

Able writers and critics have pointed out the monumental blunders of General Pope which nearly caused the destruction of his army, and the advantageous opportunities he failed to grasp, particularly where Lee divided his army by sending Jackson to Manassas in his rear. They also show his vindictiveness towards the meritorious General Porter, who was cashiered after the Antietam campaign, but established his innocence after a struggle which lasted for many years and was restored to the army.

During the active part of this campaign General McClellan was detained, by order of General Halleck, at Alexandria and ordered to forward his troops as fast as they arrived from Harrison's Landing to join Pope's army. This he did and they had all joined us in time to take part in the battles of Groveton and the second Bull Run, except Franklin's and Sumner's corps, who were still on the march. General McClellan then found himself in the singular position of a commanding general stripped of his army, with nothing but a few orderlies and small camp guard. General Pope had sent a very favorably colored report of the second Battle of Bull Run to General Halleck; but the next day Colonel J. C. Kelton, A. A. G., was sent from the War Department to Pope's army, and upon his return on September second reported the true condition of affairs, which alarmed the President and Cabinet and terrified the city of Washington. Pope's army was ordered to retreat immediately within the fortifications of Washington for the protection of the city. The administration now turned toward McClellan again and placed him in command of the defenses of Washington and the troops of Pope's defeated army as they arrived within the fortifications.

The morning after the battle, August thirty-first, during a cold rain, we were marched within the old Confederate works

TEN YEARS IN THE RANKS U. S. ARMY

at Centreville and encamped there. The day was quiet, but toward night there was a rumor that a part of the Rebel army was on the move to turn our right and intersperse between us and Washington. Next morning two army corps were ordered to march in the direction of Chantilly, where that afternoon a severe battle was fought which resulted in a victory for the Union arms. Among our losses was the daring one-armed General Kearney, one of the bravest officers in our army.

It was a race now to see which army would get to Washington first. We could hear the firing at Chantilly and, while it was still going on the Fifth Corps received orders to proceed to Fairfax Court House in a hurry. After a weary night-march we arrived there on the morning of September second and went into bivouac. The following morning we resumed our march, taking the road towards Washington. The enemy was close on our flank and there was some skirmishing just after leaving Fairfax Court House. Late in the afternoon we saw the dome of the Capitol and kept on, weary with the long march, until after dark, when during a halt, we heard loud cheering in front. Soon word was passed along that General McClellan had come out to meet us, and the cheering was taken up by the entire corps. The General had only a very small escort of soldiers and one officer with him, but his presence cheered us and revived our depressed spirits. We felt that Washington was safe.

The Fifth Corps encamped for several days on Hall's Hill. While at this camp the skeleton battalions of the Second and Tenth United States Infantry were consolidated under the command of Captain Poland of the Second Infantry, the ranking officer, and henceforth we were designated as the Battalion of the Second and Tenth Infantry; company formations were not interfered with.

With the arrival of the army within the defenses of Washington the enemy disappeared and on the fifth of September were reported to be crossing the Potomac into Maryland. The cavalry of the Army of the Potomac was promptly started on the march and quickly followed by the artillery and infantry.

TEN YEARS IN THE RANKS U.S. ARMY

The Fifth Corps left on the evening of the sixth and crossed the Potomac on the Chain Bridge, then marched by way of Tennallytown, Rockville and Monocacy to Frederick City, where we arrived the twelfth of September. The roads were good, but very dusty; the country was well cultivated and we got some fruit and plenty of green corn on the way, roasting the ears at our camp-fires.

Next day our march was across the mountains to the Middletown Valley, where we encamped near the foot of South Mountain. We could hear the guns at Harper's Ferry, which was besieged by Stonewall Jackson. On the afternoon and evening of the fourteenth General Reno had a battle at Turner's Pass on South Mountain, part of which was visible from our camps. The Rebels were driven from the mountain and retreated toward Sharpsburg during the night. General Reno was killed near the close of this action.

On the morning of the fifteenth we crossed the Blue Ridge by the road across South Mountain leading to Sharpsburg, passing a part of the battlefield, where we saw a number of dead Confederates beside the road and in the fields where they had fallen the evening before. In descending the western slope of the South Mountain we had some fine views of the valley of the Antietam, the great fields of grain, orchards and farmhouses—a beautiful picture of peace and plenty, soon to be destroyed by the horrors of war. Our march was toward the Central Bridge over the Antietam on the pike leading to Sharpsburg, where we took up a position on the left of the road. The Rebels had batteries on the opposite side of the Antietam on high ground, which opened on us as soon as they saw us approaching; but they did us no damage and we were soon under cover where their fire was returned by two of our batteries.

The great Battle of Antietam, in which more than one hundred and fifty thousand men and some hundreds of pieces of artillery were engaged on the sixteenth and seventeenth days of September, is well described in histories and was decidedly a Union victory. General McClellan is severely criticized for allowing Lee and his army to escape across the Potomac on the night of the eighteenth, and General Burnside for dilly-dallying and delaying his attack on bridge number three, where he could not see his glorious opportunity.

Porter's Fifth Army Corps held an important position in the center of the line covering the reserve artillery and wagon-trains on the east bank of the Antietam. It was here, in the center, that General McClellan was most anxious that his line should not be broken, and he relied on General Porter for that. The Fifth Corps was not engaged as a body in this battle, but some brigades were detached from it at various times to reinforce other parts of the field. We were much exposed to the enemy's artillery fire and sharp-shooters at times. On the second day of the battle my battalion, the Second and Tenth, were ordered to cross the bridge about four P. M. to protect some light batteries on the opposite side of the Antietam. We deployed as skirmishers to the left of the road and while passing over a ridge were fired at by the Rebel sharp-shooters and by a battery with canister shot. We sustained considerable loss but kept on as far as a fence, where we halted and commenced a fire which soon caused the enemy's cannoneers to leave their guns; and although soon reinforced by a part of the First Brigade, we were not considered strong enough to charge and take this battery and were ordered by one of General Sykes's aides-de-camp to withdraw from our dangerous position to a place of cover, where we remained until sun-down and then re-crossed the bridge and returned to our former position. Our small battalion lost about fifty of its number, killed and wounded, in this engagement.

The day after the battle we remained quietly in our position. The Rebels, under flags of truce, were picking up their wounded and burying some of their dead, while squads from our army performed the same sad duties.

At daybreak on the morning of the nineteenth it was discovered that the enemy had departed during the night and the last of their rear guard was then crossing the Potomac at Shepherdstown ford. General Porter's Corps was ordered to the ford. On the way we passed through a part of the battlefield, which was still strewn with Rebel corpses. Most of them had turned so black that they looked almost like negroes and their heads and bodies had swollen to an enormous size. It was a horrible sight. We passed through the town of Sharpsburg and beyond that through some of the deserted Rebel camps, where fires were still burning and there was every evidence of hasty departure.

When we approached the ford there was much artillery firing from Rebel batteries posted on the hills on the other side of the Potomac, which was replied to by some of our batteries. Sharp-shooters were posted at the river-bank and canal, firing at the enemy opposite. Towards evening a regiment of the First Division and the sharp-shooters crossed the river by fording and found a lodgement on the other side, capturing a few guns.

Early on the morning of the twentieth our brigade and the Fifth New York of the Third Brigade were ordered to ford the river and make a reconnaissance on the Charlestown road. General Sykes himself accompanied the brigade. We deployed as skirmishers, advanced about a mile and halted in some woods, when it was discovered that a large force of the enemy was rapidly approaching with artillery. General Sykes ordered the brigade to fall back slowly to the bluffs on the river-bank. In the meantime Barnes's Brigade of the First Division of the Fifth Corps had also crossed the river to go to Shepherdstown, but General Sykes ordered them to take a position on the heights near where they had crossed, to our right, where their skirmishers soon became engaged with the approaching enemy and brought on a spirited engagement. General Sykes, who informed General Porter of the large force opposed to his two small brigades, was ordered immediately to recross all the troops. This we were enabled to do in good order by the aid of a number of our batteries, posted on the heights on the Maryland side. These batteries delivered a destructive fire over our heads which kept the enemy from the river-bank, or it would have gone hard with us while fording the river. Before night all our troops had recrossed the Potomac.

This engagement at Shepherdstown ended the Maryland campaign. The loss on our side was about five hundred and, with the exception of nineteen, was all in General Barnes's brigade. The loss in my battalion was one killed and two wounded. Later it was learned that the retreating foe had turned back nine brigades of infantry with artillery under Generals Early and Hill to oppose us at Shepherdstown. No doubt they over-estimated our numbers and thought we were an army corps instead of two weak brigades. We then realized what great peril we had been in.

A daring act was performed by First Sergeant Daniel W. Burke of Company B, as we re-crossed the Potomac. He voluntarily attempted to spike some abandoned Rebel guns near the shore under a withering fire from the enemy. He received a commission soon after and was retired in 1899 as a brigadier-general and medal-of-honor man.

The next day we established a permanent camp in some woods near Sharpsburg, where we remained for more than six weeks and received a detachment of recruits during our stay, which somewhat replenished our skeleton companies. Four companies of the Seventh Infantry also joined our brigade at this place. They were a part of the troops surrendered in Texas, who were paroled at the time and had since been exchanged.

A few days after we had settled down to our regular camp duties I was much surprised when the first sergeant of my company informed me that I had been detailed to report to Lieutenant Hawkins as brigade commissary sergeant. This was promotion to a post usually filled by an older and more experienced soldier. My comrades congratulated me and said I was in luck to get that position—one that was greatly desired. I was not much elated over it, however, and seriously considered whether I should not ask to be excused and remain with my company.

By this time the sergeant major and half a dozen of the first sergeants of the companies had received commissions as second lieutenants, and without exception they made good officers and gave the regiment a better character and standing than the inexperienced civilians that had been inflicted upon us at the beginning of the war, many of whom we had since got rid of. All of these sergeants were older than I and had been longer in the service; I had only just turned twenty-one and looked much younger. With the exceptions of our two musicians, I was the youngest soldier in the company, until some recruits joined us a while later. I had learned from the sergeant major that my name had been mentioned in the regimental report for good conduct in battle, along with those of some other non-commissioned officers.

I had spoken to a couple of our officers, who were most friendly to me, about applying for a commission, and was advised to wait until I should be first sergeant of a company. This seemed a long way off, as I was only the third sergeant of the company at the time. I realized that if I left the company on special duty, to act as brigade commissary sergeant, the man who remained in the ranks would get the preference in promotion, other reasons being equal. On the other hand the position offered many advantages and was less arduous than that of a company officer. No more marching—I would have a horse to ride; no more guard and picket duties; no more standing in ranks to be fired at for hours by the enemy. The worst that had befallen the army trains thus far had been guerrilla attacks and captures by the enemy. So far I had been so lucky as to escape without a scratch, but I had seen many of my comrades fall in battle while in the ranks, and it might be my turn in the very next engagement. I decided to hold the position and left my company to report to the acting commissary officer at brigade headquarters. There was no extra pay attached to the position. I was carried on the company's muster rolls as "absent on special duty."

First Lieutenant Hamilton S. Hawkins of the Sixth United States Infantry was acting as the brigade commissary and quarter-master. He was a West Point graduate and a gentleman—one of the finest officers I met in the service. He was very dignified, honorable and just, kind and pleasant with his inferiors in rank—one of Nature's noblemen. In after years he was called the "Sir Henry Havelock" of the American Army. In the Spanish War he was a major-general of volunteers and commanded the division that captured San Juan Hill. He retired in 1898 as a brigadier-general of the United States Army, and at his death (which occurred recently) he was the governor of the Soldiers' Home in Washington, D. C.

With Lieutenant Hawkins, as his chief assistant, was John W. Clous, quarter-master sergeant of the Sixth United States Infantry, who acted in the double capacity of brigade quartermaster and commissary sergeant. It was to relieve him of the duties of the latter that I was detailed. Sergeant Clous was a remarkable man and had a most honorable and successful career in the army. He was well educated—a student—he had served on the frontiers and was my senior by eight or ten years. He became a second lieutenant in December, 1862; and after the war he made a study of military law and became the professor of law, with the rank of lieutenant colonel, at the Military Academy at West Point. At the close of the Spanish War he was a brigadier-general and judge advocate of the commission which settled the affairs between the United States and Cuba. He retired as a brigadier-general in 1901 and died a few years ago. Much to my regret, I never had the opportunity of meeting either of these men after I left the army.

When I entered upon my new duties I found that I had much to learn, but I had a very capable instructor in Sergeant Clous. He was thoroughly familiar with all the rules and regulations of the commissary department and the many forms for accounts and reports which the admirable Government method of accounting for everything demanded. We had a wall tent which we used for an office when in a permanent camp, furnished with two small field desks and a folding table. When in camp Sergeant Clous and I slept in this tent; on the march we slept under the clear skies or in a wagon when it rained. Our little detachment included a clerk and three men to load and unload wagons and assist in issuing rations. One of these men was also the butcher who slaughtered the beef cattle when we had any, killing the cattle with a rifle and dressing the carcass. Another did the cooking for our mess and the third man took care of Sergeant Clous's horse and mine, besides his other duties. These men were all soldiers detailed for special duties, temporarily absent from their companies and, like myself, liable to be ordered back to duty in the ranks at any time. There was also a wagon-master who was a civilian, as were also most of the teamsters; he had charge of our supply train under orders from the commissary officer. When in camp Lieutenant Hawkins, who had a private servant, generally stayed at brigade headquarters, but while at Sharpsburg he had his tent for a time in a grove along with the officers of his regiment. I remember that his mother visited him there and remained for some days. She was a very fine, motherly lady who adored her son.

While the army was at Sharpsburg all of its supplies had to be hauled from Hagerstown, Maryland, about twenty miles away, which was the nearest railroad depot. There was a good turn-pike road all the way from Sharpsburg, which passed through the recent battle-field, on which the Dunkard church was a conspicuous mark. It was one of my duties to draw supplies at Hagerstown once a week or oftener. I was provided with the necessary requisitions, signed by Lieutenant Hawkins and countersigned by the brigade commander, given charge of as many wagons as were required and accompanied by the wagon-master. We generally made an early morning start so as to arrive in Hagerstown early in the afternoon, loading the wagons on the same day, then going into camp for the night, and returning to Sharpsburg the following day. This could not always be done, as the place was crowded with army wagons on the same business and it was a case of first come, first served. I always rode on ahead to get my requisition on file, and if we could not be attended to on that day, I rode back to meet my train and park them in some field on the outskirts of the town. It often took two days and a night to make the trip, sometimes more.

TEN YEARS IN THE RANKS U.S. ARMY

On one occasion, after the train had been parked, it became necessary for me to return to the town, and as my horse had cast a shoe, I had my saddle put on one of the teamster's riding mules. It was my first experience in riding a mule. I got along well enough for a short distance until I came to the ford of a small stream, where we were in the habit of watering our animals. I stopped to let the mule drink and then started to cross, but he was determined to go back to the train. I next tried to cross an adjoining bridge with the same result. I coaxed him, I dismounted and tried to lead him, I remounted and did all that could be done to a mule with a pair of spurs and strong language, much to the amusement of some soldier spectators, who advised me to build a fire under him. I could not make him go to Hagerstown, but he willingly went back to camp, to my discomfiture, and I had to borrow the wagon-master's horse to make the trip.

We were paid while in the Sharpsburg camp and I was able to buy fresh bread and other things for our mess while in town. The bread tasted mighty good after being on hard-tack for six months. I also regaled myself a few times with a real dinner in a tavern at the extravagant price of twenty-five cents. Nearly all through October the weather was delightful and I enjoyed the trips to town immensely; the days were warm, but the nights began to be cool enough for camp-fires.

President Lincoln visited the army on the first of October and remained with General McClellan for several days. Near the middle of October General Stuart of the Confederate Army made a swift raid with two thousand cavalry-men and a battery of horse artillery into Pennsylvania and around the Army of the Potomac, as he had done on the Peninsula. He was almost unopposed, as our cavalry—never equal to that of the Confederates in number—was at this time broken down, scattered and so reduced in numbers by the late campaign that not a thousand serviceable horses could be mounted. After Stuart's raid the road to Hagerstown was patroled by cavalry.

When not on the road I was kept busy in camp issuing rations and making up accounts. At this time the system was for the brigade commissary to issue rations to companies on the requisition of the officer commanding the company, approved by the commander of the regiment. Companies subdivided their rations among themselves. While in camp issues of rations were made about once a week, except fresh meat, which was issued on days when cattle was slaughtered.

Provisions for officers and their servants, according to regulations of the commissary department, could only be sold to them for cash and on their certificate that they were for their own use; for the Government sold commissary stores to officers at cost, less the cost of freight, but for their own use only. The rule of selling for cash only could not be enforced strictly in war times, but the commissary officer made himself liable for any credit he chose to extend. Sales to officers were made during fixed hours of the morning; money received and vouchers for same were turned over to the commissary officer daily. As commissary sergeant I soon found that I was really gaining the experience of a manager for a large grocery firm.

Issues of whiskey to troops, one gill per day, were only made on the order of the brigade commander in cases of excessive fatigue or severe exposure. Officers could purchase all they wanted, if they stated in their written orders to the commissary that it was for their own use and signed their names. Some good-natured officers who hardly drank at all, seemed to buy much whiskey, for they frequently gave one of their company sergeants an order which read something like this: "Let the bearer have one canteen full of whiskey for my use." Others more scrupulous omitted the words "for my use," knowing the order would not be filled in that case; but I suspect that in some cases the soldier added the necessary words to the order which he himself had written after the unsuspecting officer had signed it.

Sometimes stores became damaged or were received in a damaged condition, when a board of survey was appointed by the commanding officer to ascertain the amount of damage, for the commissary officer was virtually obliged to account for every cracker he received. There seemed to be no end to the many accounts we had to keep and reports to make out, but it was an instructive business experience for me.

On the sixth of October General McClellan received an order from Washington to cross the Potomac and give battle to the enemy or drive him South while the roads were good. At this time the army was in no condition to move for want of supplies which arrived very tardily, and it was not until the end of October, when bad weather had set in, that the first part of the troops re-crossed the Potomac. During all this time the authorities at Washington and the Northern papers were accusing McClellan of being dilatory and demanding his removal. The Fifth Army Corps left Sharpsburg on the thirtieth and crossed the Potomac next day at Harper's Ferry, while the train crossed on a pontoon bridge at Berlin, some distance further south. Riding a horse was a very agreeable change from marching in the ranks and carrying a heavy load. All I carried now on my person was a large Colt's revolver. To my McClellan saddle was strapped an overcoat and a canteen of water, while the saddle-bags held some cooked meat and crackers and a pipe and tobacco.

The roads were fairly good on the start until we neared the Blue Ridge Mountains. Being again in the enemy's country, the train had a guard of some infantry and a small detachment of cavalry. The chief quarter-master of the Fifth Army Corps was in charge of our train and directed its movements.

On November second we rejoined our brigade at the small town of Snickersville. That evening Sykes's division was ordered to occupy Snicker's Gap and make a reconnaissance to Snicker's Ferry on the Shenandoah. I was ordered to follow the troops with a couple of wagons and issue some rations to my brigade. The ascent to the top of the Gap where the troops rested for the night was steep and wearisome; the night was dark and cold, and when we arrived on the mountain-top, late, a strong wind was blowing. I snatched a little sleep in one of the wagons and issued the rations at daylight.

Part of the divison descended the Gap towards the Shenandoah in the morning but did not cross, and during the day an artillery engagement occurred between some of the Rebels on the opposite side of the river and the Sixth and fourteenth United States Infantry. After taking a long look at the beautiful and fertile valley of the Shenandoah at our feet I started back to our camp. On the way down the mountain we had a mishap; one of the teamsters struck a boulder and broke a wheel, which caused delay and we were obliged to cut down a small tree and rig up a drag to get the wagon back to the camp.

We remained in camp until Sykes's division was withdrawn from Snicker's Gap and resumed our march east of the Blue Ridge by way of White Plains and New Baltimore to Warrenton, where we arrived on the ninth of November. On our march to White Plains we had a wet snow nearly all day, which made the roads bad. At Warrenton we learned that General McClellan had been relieved from the command of the Army of the Potomac and Major General Ambrose E. Burnside placed in command. General McClellan's enemies in the Cabinet, together with Halleck, the bureaucratic general, had finally prevailed in their schemes to cause the President to relieve him. The following day, the tenth, that part of the army which was at Warrenton was drawn up along the turnpike and General McClellan's farewell address was read to them; then came hearty cheering, as the General rode down between the lines of the troops, bidding them farewell. The army was sad over the loss of a commander who had their affection and confidence.

Two days later the Fifth Corps had another sad parting scene when their old commander, Major General Fitz-John Porter, was relieved and ordered to report at Washington. Major General Joseph Hooker was now placed in command of the corps.

General Burnside did not seek—nor did he wish—to take the command of the Army of the Potomac, frankly declaring himself inadequate for that exalted position. In this he was prophetic, and in a month proved it to the mournful knowledge of the army and the entire country.

We remained about a week at Warrenton. General Burnside formed the six corps of the army into what were to be called the Right, Center and Left Grand Divisions, commanded respectively by Generals Sumner, Hooker and Franklin. The Right Grand Division was composed of the Second and Ninth Corps; the Center of the Third and Fifth, and the Left of the First and Sixth Corps, General Hooker being selected, as I have mentioned, as one of the Grand Division commanders. General Daniel Butterfield was appointed to command the Fifth Army Corps, which Hooker had commanded only for a few days.

We left Warrenton on the seventeenth and went by way of Warrenton Junction and Hartwood Church to the vicinity of Falmouth, near Fredericksburg, and parked the Fifth Corps train, establishing a camp near the Henry house on the twenty-third of November. This march was a very severe one, as we had a cold rain nearly every day and the roads were execrable. Wagons were stalled in the mud, teams had to be doubled to pull them out, the road was blockaded for hours at a time, and it was very late at night when we caught up with the troops, who were in bivouac long before our arrival.

It soon became very cold and we experienced the rigors of a winter campaign. The soldiers built little log huts and shacks, roofed them with their shelter tents, and built earth and stone fireplaces, the chimneys terminating in a flour or pork barrel which often caught fire. For an office and a place to sleep I had a wall tent with a camp stove in it. We fixed up a kitchen and, with the aid of tarpaulins, erected a few store-houses for the protection of the commissary stores, which were guarded by a sentinel. The railroad from Aquia Creek on the Potomac was quickly repaired and we drew our supplies at a railroad switch about two miles from the camp.

On evenings when I was at leisure I often visited my regiment to talk with my comrades. Some sat around camp-fires built in the company streets, others played cards in their little huts. Tricks were often played upon the card-players, such as covering the barrel chimney with a gunny-bag and smoking them out; or some more mischievous man would throw percussion caps down the chimney, or a few paper cartridges, which scattered their fire and broke up the game for a while. On some days when three or four inches of snow had fallen and then melted to a soft slush, the soldiers were in misery; and at other times they suffered from cold, which was very severe for that latitude.

As General Burnside had determined to cross the Rappahannock and attack the enemy at Fredericksburg, I was ordered on the tenth of December to issue five days' marching rations to the brigade and then to load all stores into the wagons and be ready to leave camp when ordered. On the morning of the eleventh, before daybreak we heard the booming of cannon in the direction of Fredericksburg, three miles away, where the engineer troops were preparing to lay pontoon bridges across the river. Shortly after daylight the Fifth Corps began its march towards the river and the train followed the troops. On our arrival at the river-bank the corps and train were massed behind the batteries on Stafford Heights, which overlooked the river, the town and much of the country beyond, although a heavy fog enveloped the town during the early morning hours and hid it from view. The engineers, engaged in laying the pontoons, were opposed by such a destructive fire from the Rebel sharp-shooters concealed in the houses and in rifle-pits on the opposite side of the river that they were obliged to cease operations and retire to cover, although some troops on our side of the river kept firing on the sharp-shooters.

About ten o'clock General Burnside ordered the one hundred and forty-seven guns on Stafford Heights to shell the town, which was done for nearly two hours. The noise was terrific. During this bombardment I made my way to the front, alongside of one of our batteries, where I had a good view of the effect of our terrible fire on the city about a mile away, until the smoke from bursting shells and burning buildings obscured the view. The Rebel batteries on the heights beyond the town made little attempt to reply to our fire; only a few long-range guns could reach us, and they did little damage in my vicinity. When our bombardment ceased it was found that it had failed to dislodge the sharp-shooters, as our guns could not be depressed enough for the shells to hit the houses on the riverbank.

It was after the shelling ceased that the Nineteenth Massachusetts and the Seventh Michigan regiments, which were at the river-front, volunteered to cross the river in pontoon boats and drive away the sharp-shooters. This they did in gallant style, under fire. Two bridges were completed at four thirty P. M. and troops began to cross, continuing all night and the following day. Sykes's division was held in reserve and did not cross until the afternoon of the thirteenth. Very few wagons were sent over besides ammunition wagons.

Lieutenant Hawkins sent me with a written message to brigade headquarters about sundown on the same day. I went on foot, past the Lacey house (which was Burnside's headquarters during the battle and was also used as a hospital) down the hill to the river and across a pontoon bridge. I found my brigade halted in one of the streets near the edge of the town, preparing to march out and relieve some of the troops on the front line. I delivered my letter to Major Andrews, the brigade commander, who returned the envelope to me marked in pencil with his name and time of delivery, as was customary.

On my way back to the pontoon bridge I had time to say a few words to my comrades in the regiment as I passed them. The streets were dark, but there was light enough to distinguish the effects of the bombardment and the burnt houses of two days before. I walked in the middle of the street while passing through some of the residence blocks, for the brick sidewalks were littered with chairs, sofas, bedding and all manner of household goods from the looted houses, which had been thrown out by some of our soldiers who had bivouacked in the street the night before. Some of the stragglers were still in the houses; in one of them I heard some soldiers playing a piano. We had been told that a number of women and children had remained in town, hiding in cellars, but I saw none of them, although I did see a number of corpses lying about on the sidewalks and in the streets, and wounded soldiers making their way to hospitals which had been established in the public buildings and many of the private houses. Nearer the river business buildings and stores had been looted and the contents scattered over the street. In passing through one of these streets I picked up a book as a souvenir and when I examined it later on in camp I found the name of Alexander H. Stevens written in it. He was the vice-president of the Confederacy. At the bridge I was stopped by the guard and was obliged to explain my business to the officer in command and exhibit my envelope before being allowed to re-pass the river.

The story of the Battle of Fredericksburg covers the saddest pages in the history of the war. From it we learn how Burnside planned this battle, then lost his head and followed no particular plan; how he stubbornly hurled division after division in a front attack on the impregnable position on Marye's Heights against the advice of his corps commanders; how thousands were sacrificed in this bloody and most useless slaughter of the war; the indescribable sufferings of the wounded to whom no help could be extended, many of whom were frozen during the winter nights. The rank and file themselves knew the hopelessness of the attack, and yet bravely made three more charges after the first had been nearly annihilated.

Sykes's division was not called upon to take part in the direct assault, but on the night of the thirteenth took up a position which at daylight proved to be in a depression so shallow that to raise a limb while lying down or to turn over, meant surely to be wounded; and some who tried to get to the rear for water immediately fell lifeless, pierced by many balls. No help could be given to the wounded—they were obliged to lie and wait until night, when the command was enabled to creep away. In our brigade eighty men were killed and wounded, mostly while hugging the cold earth all that day and having no chance to inflict any damage on the enemy except for a little while the previous evening.

The army was skillfully withdrawn on the night of the fifteenth during a violent rain-storm. The First Brigade of

General Sykes's regulars, and General Warren's Third Brigade covered the retreat. When these troops had crossed some time after daylight on the seventeenth, the engineers cast the pontoons loose and none remained behind in the death-trap into which Burnside had led the army, except the many thousands of our wounded, their surgeons and some prisoners. The army returned to its former locations and re-established its camps.

The morale of the army was much impaired by this battle; it had lost confidence in its commander which could never be restored, and for the first time the Army of the Potomac might be considered demoralized.

Christmas and New Year's passed, celebrated among the volunteers by the reception of thousands of boxes containing gifts and good things from their friends at home; but few of the regulars had any friends to remember them. The only exception to the usual routine on those two days was the issuing of a gill of whiskey by the commissary.

But we were not yet done with General Burnside. Once more he tried to surprise the vigilant enemy. On January sixteenth orders were issued to prepare to march on the eighteenth, then were countermanded and it was not until noon of the twentieth that the movement started—which gave the enemy plenty of time to learn of it through their spies and be prepared for us. The weather had been severely cold for some time and the roads frozen hard. We marched about five miles towards the Rappahannock in a direction to bring us above Fredericksburg at Banks' Ford, not fordable at this time, and halted for the night, when rain began to fall and continued throughout the night.

The next day when the movement was resumed, the storm was worse. Soon the roads were blocked by artillery and wagons stalled in quagmire; and pontoons were upset and laid along the road, the condition of which was appalling. It seemed as though the elements were determined that Burnside should not again lead the army into disaster. Before night the army was literally mud-bound and was unable to advance or retreat; large details of infantry tried to help pull the artillery and wagons out of the clayey and sticky roads, ineffectually; then thousands of men were put to work to fell trees to corduroy and to build new stretches of road. Though the rain ceased on the evening of the second day, men and animals continued to suffer greatly while trying to extricate the teams. Some of the horses and mules that dropped exhausted in their traces were drowned, so deep was the liquid mud in places. It took four days of Herculean toil to enable the army to return to their camps again. My train did not fare so badly as some others, for we halted at the end of the first day's march and remained there for three days. During that time we issued some rations of hard bread and sugar and coffee to replace what had been spoiled by the fierce rain in the men's haversacks. As the wagons could not move to get to the brigade, details of soldiers had to come and get these rations and carry them for miles on their backs to their comrades. This was "Burnside's Mud March," never to be forgotten by those who participated in it. The Rebel pickets on the opposite side of the Rappahannock in derision put up some large sign-boards marked, "Burnside stuck in the mud!" "This way to Richmond!"

On January twenty-fifth, directly after our return from the "Mud March," General Burnside resigned the command of the Army of the Potomac and was later on given a command in the West. There was no farewell parade, as there had been for Generals McClellan and Porter a little more than two months before. He had lost the confidence of the army and the support of the Administration, and had drawn upon himself the censure of the press and the people for his useless sacrifice of thousands of human lives.

General Joseph Hooker was now placed in command of the army, "Fighting Joe Hooker," as the soldiers called him, an officer fairly well liked in the army but not possessing the entire confidence of the corps commanders as to his fitness for the position. General Hooker made many changes. He did away with the Grand Division formation. In the Fifth Corps he made Major General George G. Meade the commander, in place of Butterfield, who became his Chief of Staff. We lost General Warren, the commander of our Third Brigade; he became the Chief of Topographical Engineers on General Hooker's staff. Distinctive corps badges were ordered to be worn on the cap or hat of each officer and soldier; headquarters of each brigade, division and corps had a standard with a device the shape and color of which indicated at a glance that part of the army they typified. The badge of the Fifth Army Corps was in the shape of a Maltese cross of red for the First Division, white for the second, blue for the third, and green when there was a fourth division. These badges proved to be very useful when arresting stragglers and returning them to their command. They were made of cloth, one and one-half inches square. We wore them to the end of the war.

After the "Mud March" the soldiers rebuilt their huts and made themselves as comfortable as possible under the circumstances; but the winter proved to be an unusually severe one for Virginia. We had much snow and some very cold periods. Many furloughs were granted, absentees returned, and recruits arrived. The commissary issued full rations, often including fresh bread which had been baked in Washington and could be issued within two days. Some regiments drew flour and baked their own bread.

After Fredericksburg there was much Confederate money in some of the camps which had been plundered from the banks and houses. It soon became widely distributed through poker playing and it was no uncommon thing to find games for large stakes going on in the tents at night. Expressions such as "I'll see you, and raise you a hundred dollars!" were often heard; some had thousands of dollars. Much of this money was sent away as souvenirs, much of it was lost or destroyed; some, in a spirit of bravado, lit their pipes with ten-dollar bills—much to their vexation, when later on a man came along, offering to pay three cents on the dollar for the Confederate money.

While in this camp Sergeant Clous was promoted, becoming

Second Lieutenant in the Sixth Infantry. He had instructed me so well in my duties that by this time I was competent to get along unassisted. I also lost Lieutenant Hawkins, who remained Brigade Quartermaster but was replaced as Commissary by First Lieutenant William F. Greeley of the Eleventh United States Infantry, a civilian appointee from New Hampshire. I got along very well with him and never had any trouble while he remained Commissary Officer; my only objection to him was that in many difficult situations he let me find my own way out of trouble without his advice or assistance. At this time I traded my rather large gray horse for a smaller dark bay, an intelligent and kindly-disposed animal of whom I became very fond. I called him Tommy, and among other tricks I taught him to push his head through the opening of my tent and beg for a cracker or sugar.

The winter seemed long and dreary. In April reviews were held and there was much drilling. By the middle of April the Army of the Potomac had increased in numbers to about one hundred and ten thousand infantry and artillery, and about eleven thousand cavalry, and was once more ready and eager for active service.

PART XII.

Chancellorsville, to Winter Camp of 1863-1864.

GENERAL HOOKER had conceived a corps formation of all the cavalry of the Army of the Potomac, instead of scattering it by details among the various corps and divisions where its usefulness was frittered away; and where it was generally out-numbered and beaten by the enemy, who had consolidated their cavalry forces long before.

The spring campaign of 1863 was opened on April thirteenth by the departure of General Stoneman with ten thousand cavalry for the upper fords of the Rappahannock which he was to cross, turning the enemy's left, destroying the railroads and severing his connection with Richmond. But the cavalry moved so cautiously, or leisurely, that they consumed three days in marching twenty-five miles to the ford, where they were overtaken by a heavy rain-storm, which swelled the river so they could not cross and did not do so until the twenty-ninth at Ely's Ford, along with infantry and artillery. Before the crossing was accomplished all chance of a surprise was lost and the large cavalry force was able to inflict only trifling damage on the enemy's communications.

I was ordered to issue eight days' short rations to the brigade, which the men were obliged to stow away in their haversacks and knapsacks as best they could, besides some extra rounds of ammunition in addition to that in their cartridge boxes. Thus, loaded up more heavily than ever before, without any wagon-train (except to carry ammunition and forage) and without any regimental baggage or tents for officers, the army began its march on April twenty-seventh. General Hooker had divided the army into two parts: the Fifth, Eleventh and Twelfth Corps marched to Chancellorsville above Fredericksburg, by way of Kelly's Ford on the Rappahannock and the Germanna and Ely's Ford on the Rapidan river: the First and Sixth Corps were to cross the Rappahannock below Fredericksburg; the Third Corps was held in reserve, but a few days later was sent to Chancellorsville where General Hooker himself was in command.

The Fifth Corps supply train remained in camp about three days longer and then was ordered to the United States Ford at the Rappahannock, where the wagons were parked on the high ground on the north side overlooking the river and pontoon bridge. The opposite side of the river was a mass of woods and tangled brush, a wilderness so far as eye could reach. We could plainly hear the firing on the other side of the river and sometimes observe the smoke of battle rising above the trees. We heard Jackson's onslaught on the unfortunate Eleventh Corps on May second, and General Sickles's midnight battle. The fighting on Sunday, May third, seemed near the river. The white canvas covers of our wagons must have been visible to the Rebels, for one morning at daylight I was awakened by shells from a section of a Rebel battery on the south side of the river, crashing through our train and exploding in the woods beyond. They struck only one of my wagons before they were quickly silenced by one of our batteries nearby.

On the morning of May fourth, I was ordered to issue a day's rations to the brigade, and as no supply wagons were allowed to cross the river, they were to be packed on mules. Neither Lieutenant Greeley, the wagon-master, nor I understood anything about packing mules. Fortunately we discovered a few men among the teamsters who had had some experience in that line; but we had no packsaddles. We used the teamsters' riding saddles, as far as they went, and on the remainder of the mules we strapped blankets. We selected three or four dozen of the most docile animals from the train and loaded each one with two boxes of hardtack weighing about fifty pounds apiece, slung across his back, one box on either side. Others we loaded with sacks of bacon and bags of coffee and sugar. But the mules were as green at the business as we were, and most of them resented their treatment vigorously. When we succeeded in getting the load on them, they tried to roll it off, which disarranged it so we had to strap it on all over again, a man holding each mule to keep him from lying down.

After hours of labor, ill temper and strong language, I was at last ready to make a start with a detail from the train guard, one man to lead each pair of mules and a few extra men—teamsters—who best understood the packing. It was an odd-looking procession, in front of which I rode down the hill towards the pontoon bridge over the river, amidst the laughter and mirth of the spectators, and I wished that Lieutenant Greeley were leading the procession instead of me. Before I had gone fifty yards trouble began again. Through bad packing, some of the loads shifted forward on the mules' necks when going down hill; some of the animals fell and would not get up again with their loads on; they seemed to prefer to roll down the hill the rest of the way. All this delayed me very much and it was well past noon when the troop had passed the bridge and entered the woods on the other side.

I was instructed to follow the United States Ford road until I came to an intersecting road about two miles or more away, near which the Fifth Corps was posted. The road was level and shady and I got along fairly well, until I reached a short piece of road which skirted a ravine, lined with our troops behind breast-works. Here my little train must have been observed by the enemy, as the road was higher at this point than the breastworks, for they opened on us with some guns, before we had all passed this exposed spot. There was confusion at once. The men leading the mules rushed into the woods with them on the right side of the road. Only a few shots were fired and no damage done; but it took me more than an hour to gather the train again and re-pack the mules that had stripped their burden in going through the brushwood. At last I found my command and issued the rations. It was an hour or more until sun-down, and I deemed it best to wait until dark to return, so as not run the gauntlet of the Rebel battery again, and sought out my regiment, which was stationed parallel to the Ely Ford road behind log breastworks which had been constructed the previous night. I learned from my comrades that Captain S. S. Marsh was the only man killed on May first and that twenty or more men had been wounded on that and subsequent days. Just about sun-down I saw General Hooker, followed by some of his staff, walking very slowly down the road behind the breast-works. The General had been injured the previous day (and could not ride a horse, I believe) at the Chancellor house from a contusion caused by a cannon shot which struck a veranda pillar near which he had been standing. He was a fine and impressive figure, walking slowly, bare-headed, carrying his hat in his hand. Shortly after, I returned with my train of mules and reached the camp without further trouble.

The next day passed with little firing heard at the front. On the following day, May fifth, all the supply trains were ordered to return to their old camps near Fredericksburg. We started on the return march in the afternoon. Towards evening a rain-storm came on, such as I have seldom witnessed; it seemed like a cloud-burst—the rain came down in sheets. In a few minutes my riding boots, which reached almost to my knees, were filled with water and were over-flowing. The storm still raged when we reached our camp. During this night the army retreated across the Rappahannock, Sykes's regulars again covering the retreat and being the last to cross about eight o'clock next morning, unmolested by the enemy. The pontoon bridges were immediately taken up under the menacing protection of our batteries on the hills, and for the third time the army marched back to its old camps.

Historians agree that General Hooker's plan for an offensive battle was masterly and skillful, and everything pointed to success until, on the first day of May, after he had advanced to within a few miles of Banks' Ford and had but two divisions of the enemy confronting him, he suddenly decided to fight a defensive battle and marched back to Chancellorsville to take up an inferior and more perilous position with one of his flanks in the air. From that time on, it is said, his conduct was faulty and feeble, and the corps commanders despised his generalship. The army was forced to retreat, not because it was beaten, as at Fredericksburg under Burnside—it had not even been all engaged at Chancellorsville—but through the weak and vascillating conduct of its commander.

Coincident with the return of the army from Chancellorsville, its numbers were considerably reduced by the expiration of service of a number of men who had been enlisted for two years only. Few recruits joined, enlistments in the Northern states had fallen off alarmingly, and the enforcemnt of a draft began to be talked of. This was the darkest period of the rebellion for the Union, and an exultant one for the Confederacy. Among the regiments which we lost in our Third Brigade was the Fifth New York Volunteers, known as the Duryee Zouaves. About two hundred of the men who originally left New York in 1861 were now discharged and had left for home, their departure much regretted by the regulars, with whom they had served so long and so creditably. General Sykes complimented them highly in the general order for their departure. The remainder of this regiment, composed of three-year men, was transferred to the One Hundred and Forty-sixth New York Volunteers serving in the same brigade, and the Fifth New York Volunteers ceased to exist.

The two armies confronted each other for weeks in their former positions and the dreary camp life went on without any interesting events. We continued watching each other, until General Lee took the initiative on the third of June by sending some of General Longstreet's Corps to Culpeper, preparatory to his contemplated invasion of the North. Our cavalry, much reduced in numbers and now commanded by General Pleasonton, was ordered to make a reconnaissance in that direction, and on June eighth had a successful encounter with the enemy's cavalry at Brandy Station.

All became activity again in the Army of the Potomac. The march began on the tenth, some corps leaving on different days and by divers routes. The Fifth Corps left on the fourteenth, following the familiar route by way of Bealton, Warrenton and Manassas on the Orange and Alexandria Railroad, which we had traversed the previous year on our way to reinforce Pope. Then we inclined toward the Blue Ridge, where the Rebel Army was marching north through the Shenandoah Valley, and at Aldie we began to hear firing, as our cavalry skirmished with the enemy at the mountain gaps of the valley. We passed Leesburg on our way to Edwards Ferry, where we crossed the Potomac on a pontoon bridge into Maryland and arrived near Frederick City about the twenty-seventh of June. The weather was very hot and we made long marches. I issued rations several times while on the march and re-filled the empty wagons at Manassas. The route of the train was not always the same as that of the troops and we did some night marching to make up for lost time at Manassas.

Some-one had given me a puppy, while in the winter camp near Fredericksburg, which I had raised. He was then more than six months old, and was much attached to me, following me on the march. When tired, he would beg to be lifted up and ride on the saddle in front of me. He hated to swim across streams which we forded and insisted on crossing them on horse-back. When we arrived at the Monocacy river, which we forded a few miles from Frederick City, our supply train, which had partly passed, was stopped to allow a battery of our artillery to cross ahead of the balance of the train. The river was several feet deep, had a swift current and a gravelly bottom. I sat on my horse on the river-bank, watching the battery cross, and listening to the crunching noise the heavy wheels made in the stony river-bed, when something about our train on the other side caused me to plunge in hastily and cross without paying any attention to my dog, who had his forepaws on my stirrup and was waiting to be pulled up. I heard him bark behind me, and when I had crossed I turned around and saw him swimming after me; but the current carried him toward one of the passing gun carriages. He disappeared for a moment among the wheels and then came up on the other side, emitting unearthly yells. He succeeded in reaching the shore, and when he left the water I noticed that all but a few inches of his tail had been pinched off. He gave me a reproachful look and started up a road like a streak. I galloped after him, calling and coaxing him, but he ran on howling and paid no attention to me. After chasing him for half a mile, he ran into a thicket where I could not follow. I never saw him again. I felt very sorry to lose him.

We remained at Frederick City for two days, receiving and issuing rations. There was some militia there, hastily called out and badly armed—some of them with shot-guns. The Seventh Regiment National Guard of New York City was also there for another thirty days' war experience, and was guarding Government stores at the railroad depot. They looked very jaunty in their neat and unsoiled uniforms, some of them wearing paper collars, forming a striking contrast to the bronzed and begrimed veterans of the Army of the Potomac, from whom the Seventh had to endure much good-natured chaffing in passing.

General Hooker, like McClellan in the Sharpsburg campaign, requested the then useless garrison of ten thousand men at Harper's Ferry to be added to his command in the pursuit of Lee's army, and was refused by the autocratic General Halleck, whose chief concern seemed to be the safety of Washington; and, finding himself generally thwarted in his plans by the authorities in Washington, he requested to be relieved of the command. On June twenty-eighth, while still at Frederick City, Major General George G. Meade of the Fifth Army Corps was appointed as the commander of the Army of the Potomac. General Hooker was sent to the West, where he gained some fame from his "battle above the clouds" at Lookout Mountain.

General Meade was a man of personal bravery and experience, highly respected, but not very popular in the army. However, the Army of the Potomac was loyal to him, as it had been to all its commanders, and the soldiers proved their loyalty by tremendous sacrifices. It has been said that this fine army was always better than its commanders, of whom General Meade was the fifth within less than two years. McDowell, McClellan, Burnside and Hooker preceded him; Pope had commanded only a part of the army at the second Bull Run. I have always held the opinion that, if the unfortunate Army of the Potomac could have had General William T. Sherman for its commander in its earlier days, the war would have terminated successfully for the North much sooner, providing he had been given a free hand to plan his own campaigns.

Although it was a delicate time to change commanders in the presence of the enemy, not a ripple occurred to disturb the harmony or movements of the army. General Meade was a favorite with General Halleck and took it upon himself to break up the garrison at Harper's Ferry, which had been denied to Hooker, and no notice was taken of his action at Washington. On June twenty-ninth the army, which had been chiefly concentrated at Frederick, was put into motion on several roads towards Gettysburg.

General Meade's promotion caused some changes in the Fifth Army Corps; General Sykes became the corps commander; General Romeyn B. Ayres commanded the Second (Regular) Division; Colonel Hannibal Day the First, and Colonel Sidney Burbank the Second Brigade. The Third (Volunteer) Brigade was in command of General Stephen H. Weed. All of these commanders were good and experienced officers, who had served in the army before the war.

The supply train of the Fifth Corps followed the troops as far as Westminster, about twenty miles southeast of Gettysburg, where there was a branch railroad, connecting with the main road from Baltimore to Harrisburg. An engagement with Stuart's cavalry had taken place at Westminster on the previous day, and some dead horses were still strewn along the road and the streets of the town. The train was kept at Westminster during the three days' battle at Gettysburg, it is said, because General Meade intended to fall back to the strong line of Pipe Creek, not far from Westminster, had he been unsuccessful. On the third day of the battle we could hear very plainly the firing of the two hundred and thirty guns, which preceded General Pickett's famous charge that afternoon. On the evening of the third of July the supply train left Westminster and, after traveling all night, arrived at Gettysburg on July fourth and halted in the rear of Little Round Top, as near to the Fifth Corps as we could get. Here I issued rations to our brigade and when that was completed I left my horse with the train and ascended Little Round Top to view the great battle-field. It commenced to rain hard soon after and continued to do so all day. My view was very limited, owing to the rain, but I could see burying parties at work in some of the places where fierce fighting had taken place.

When I found my regiment I learned that Lieutenant Goodrich had been killed, three officers wounded, five soldiers killed and about fifty wounded. The losses in the Fifth Corps had been very heavy on the second day's battle. The corps had arrived on the field early that morning.

The Fourth of July passed quietly, both armies holding their positions, but General Lee was sending his trains away; and on the morning of the fifth General Meade found that the Rebel Army had disappeared—the same thing that had happened to McClellan at Antietam. General Lee retreated rapidly by the shortest route to Williamsport on the Potomac, where he found his pontoon bridges destroyed and the river so high from recent rains as to be unfordable. General Meade pursued leisurely by a much longer route. This gave the Rebels at least four days' time to take up a strong position and fortify it, when they discovered that they could not cross the Potomac.

The Fifth Corps left Gettysburg on the afternoon of the fifth of July and moved by way of Emmittsburg and Middletown across the South Mountain range at Fox's Gap to Williamsport, where it arrived about the eleventh. Part of this route was familiar to us, as we had gone over it the previous year. General Meade directed a strong reconnaissance to be made on the morning of the fourteenth, which developed the fact that the enemy had slipped across the

Potomac during the previous night. The authorities at Washington were angry at the escape of the enemy without another battle; and the army, whose hopes had been raised to a high pitch by their victory at Gettysburg, grumbled audibly. General Meade wrote to General Halleck asking to be relieved of the command of the Army of the Potomac, but his request was not granted. Military critics claim that in allowing Lee to escape from Gettysburg and again at Williamsport, General Meade missed the greatest opportunity of the war to rout the Rebel Army and end the struggle nearly two years sooner.

My horse, which had become a great pet, grew fat while traveling through the rich farming lands of Maryland and Pennsylvania, where there was an abundance of the finest clover and corn. On night marches I often snatched a little sleep along the road by leaning forward in the saddle, resting my head on his neck and encircling it with my arms. Sometimes I fell asleep sitting up straight in the saddle when slowly jogging along, until awakened by a low branch of a roadside tree brushing my face or knocking off my cap. At such times the horse seemed to be asleep also, and moved along mechanically.

The people in this section treated the soldiers kindly; some women baked bread and biscuits to give away; others sold us bread, butter, eggs and pies at most reasonable prices. And how good that bread tasted! I remember reporting for orders at brigade headquarters camp one evening when the officers were having supper and overhearing the General remark that he would like to marry the woman who baked the bread he was eating, no matter what her looks might be. In some of the small villages and farmhouses the natives understood but little English and spoke only Pennsylvania Dutch.

General Meade put the army in motion on the fifteenth of July for Harper's Ferry, where we crossed the Potomac, and I had an opportunity to see John Brown's Fort. Some of the troops crossed at Berlin, about six miles below. We marched east of the Blue Ridge, over much of the same road McClellan had traveled the previous fall, while the Rebels passed down the Shenandoah Valley, guarding all the passes. At Manassas Gap the Confederates were overtaken and an attempt was made to bring on an engagement, which resulted in a lively skirmish until darkness came on, but next morning the enemy had disappeared. We resumed our march leisurely, by way of Warrenton, and about the sixth of August went into permanent camp at Beverly Ford on the Rappahannock, drawing our supplies from Culpeper on the Orange and Alexandria railroad.

While on this march, near Centreville, we noticed a horse in a field some distance off the road. His condition was deplorable, he hobbled most painfully, and I suppose the greater part of the army had seen him in passing, but no one cared to have such a lame and sorry-looking animal. One of my men was curious enough to go out into the field to look at him, and discovered that his foot was wedged fast into an empty tomato can; and when that was removed he was no longer lame. The horse was cleaned and fed and became a useful extra riding-horse. He was known by the name of "Centreville."

About this time we read in the papers about serious riots in New York city called the "Draft Riots." Congress had passed an act to enroll all available citizens of the loyal states for military duty, to enable the states to furnish their quota, when called upon for additional troops by the Government. Names were to be drawn by lottery, and each man so drawn was to serve in the army or furnish an acceptable substitute. This had to be done; all the two-year volunteers had been discharged and, after the defeats at Fredericksburg and Chancellorsville, there were few voluntary enlistments. The regulars were unable to obtain any recruits to fill up their skeleton regiments, owing to county and town bounties offered for volunteers. The riots in New York had been controlled for the time being, but there was much uneasiness in the city as to what would occur when the actual drawing of names began, for the Government needed soldiers and was bound to enforce the draft. It was therefore decided to send the two small brigades of regulars and a few volunteer regiments to New York city to report there for duty to General John A. Dix, commanding the Department of the East.

Accordingly on August thirteenth the troops destined for New York city, under the command of General R. B. Ayres, left their camps for Alexandria, some of the soldiers going on freight-cars from Culpeper, while others marched with the supply train to Alexandria. On our arrival there, after issuing rations, I was ordered to turn over all Government property to the depot commissary, make out transfers and take receipts for it for Lieutenant Greeley. It cost me a severe pang to part with my horse Tommy, to whom I had become much attached. He was so gentle that often after a hard march when he was unsaddled and fed he would lie on the grass and I would lie down with him, resting my head on his neck and we would both go to sleep.

My little staff of assistants was dispersed and sent to their companies; and so was I, but not to do duty with them, only to be accounted for. I was still brigade commissary sergeant and was to be at Lieutenant Greeley's call when needed. We had to wait for transportation in Alexandria, where my regiment was on a block in a private street. We stacked arms in the street, and in the daytime sat on the curbstone under the shade trees or loafed about the neighborhood. We did our cooking by little fires in the street and at night lay down on the brick sidewalks in front of the houses. This we did for two nights. Fortunately it did not rain. In the house before which my company was stationed there were some ladies who had a piano and they sang secession songs after dark; and we retaliated by singing all the Union songs we knew. They kept their blinds closed and we saw none but negro servants enter or leave the house while we were there. On the third day we marched to the wharf and embarked on a freight steamer—the worst old tub I was ever on! As usual, we were crowded and I prefered to remain on deck and camped near one of the masts. This steamer was a very slow propeller. The weather was fine and we got along fairly well down the Potomac and the Chesapeake Bay, until we passed the Capes and entered the Atlantic, when we discovered that she was a high-roller and hadn't ballast enough. Soon more than half of the command was seasick. The ship had no bulwarks, only an open pipe railing through which it would be quite easy to roll over-board. As I was not seasick I remained on deck, taking the precaution to tie myself to the mast in the night-time. We were a long time getting to New York, where we arrived in the middle of the day and landed at a dock at the foot of Canal Street.

Parts of our brigades, who were on faster boats, had arrived on the preceding day. The command was scattered throughout the city; some regiments encamped in Battery Park; others in Washington, Union, Madison and Tompkins Squares. Some companies were stationed on the upper part of Fourth Avenue along the New Haven Railroad tracks and elsewhere. My regiment and another encamped on the block bounded by Fifth and Sixth Avenues, Forty-eighth and Forty-ninth Streets. This block was vacant except for a row of four-story buildings on the Sixth Avenue side, still standing. The block had been filled in and graded fairly level a few feet above the street, and had a picket fence on the other three sides. There were few houses in the neighborhood; close by, on Fifth Avenue, were the foundations of St. Patrick's Cathedral which had just been begun. The nearest horse-car line was on Sixth Avenue, where we noticed an occasional car, smaller than the others and painted yellow, bearing a sign in large letters, on either side of the car, which read: "Colored people allowed in this car."

We left the dock at Canal Street during the afternoon and marched up-town by way of Hudson Street, up Sixth Avenue to our destination at Fifth Avenue and Forty-ninth Street, where the men were obliged to sleep on the ground without tents that night. I went to my home. We still had our band, though reduced in numbers. It played during our march up-town, and we had many spectators and the usual juvenile following. We did not look as pretty as the militia the people had been accustomed to see; we were sunburnt, dirty and ragged-looking; but, nevertheless, we received many cheers on the way. The arrival of the soldiers from the Army of the Potomac restored peace of mind to many people in New York and allayed their fears of rioting and destruction of property, while enforcing the draft. No disturbance occurred while that went on; if there had been, the rioters would have received a severe lesson, for we had no sympathy for them.

The next day was a busy one in camp; tents were received and put up; sinks were dug and a water supply arranged for; and guards were posted at the gates to keep the soldiers in and the overwhelming public out. Crowds of people, who seemed to have nothing else to do, lined the fence and crowded the sidewalks from reveille to tattoo, watching the soldiers. In the afternoons the nursery-maids with their baby carriages appeared, and were made love to by the soldiers on the other side of the fence and forgot their charges. At sunset, when dress parade took place and the band played, the sidewalks around the camp were impassable. At night such of the soldiers as were fortunate enough to possess any money and had not obtained a pass jumped the low fence where it was not guarded and remained away until the small hours. The commander was liberal in granting daily passes to a certain number to be absent from camp.

Lieutenant Greeley made a contract with one of the many caterers who supplied food to the conscripts, substitutes and recruits while they were in the city to provide cooked rations for three meals per day for our brigade for the Government money value of a soldier's rations, as computed in New York city. This proved unsatisfactory from the start, the food being poor and insufficient and often cold—being served by wagons, and at irregular times. In a few days the contract was cancelled and each company drew its rations direct from the New York commissary on Stone Street, and were furnished cooking utensils and fire-wood to cook their own rations in camp. This proved to be another very interesting item to the loiterers about the camp, watching the cooking and serving of meals for the soldiers. Lieutenant Greeley gave me the names and addresses of a few prominent bakers in the city, whom I was to interview with regard to obtaining fresh bread for the brigade. Among them I found one named Wall, at that time located on the lower part of Sixth Avenue, or on Carmine

Street, who agreed to give us eighteen ounces of good wholesome bread for the daily Government allowance of eighteen ounces of flour, or its money value—which offer was accepted. I now had no duties of any kind to perform, except to see that the baker kept up the weight of his loaves, and I was absolutely free to come and go, when and where I pleased, during our three weeks' stay in New York. I had some money with me, also some at home, where I had at times sent part of my pay. I took advantage of this short opportunity after the arduous field service to enjoy myself as much as possible.

The brigade's headquarters were in Madison Square, which at that time was enclosed by an iron fence set on a granite coping, and around this the crowds were even denser than in my own camp. Here the Fourteenth Infantry and some other troops were encamped. And here Lieutenant Greeley, to whom I reported almost daily, had his tent. The proprietors of the Fifth Avenue Hotel, opposite Madison Square, generously furnished meals for the officers in this camp free of charge during their stay. Sergeant William J. Milligan of the Sixth Infantry, who was acting as brigade quartermaster sergeant, and who was an old bunkie of mine at Governor's Island, had his tent here, where I slept much oftener than I did in my own camp. The tent was under a large tree, facing the main entrance of the hotel, and I believe that I can still point out the tree.

The drawing for conscripts to fill New York city's quota for the Government's call for troops was completed without any trouble, and one morning in September, after a three weeks' stay, we were ordered, much to our regret, to strike tents and prepare to return to the field again. A paymaster appeared in camp very early and gave us four month's pay, which was due us, and which, I believe, had been purposely withheld until the day of our departure. As we were not to leave until sometime in the afternoon, I had plenty of time to say good-by at home and farewell to my friend, Sergeant Milligan, for his regiment, the Sixth Infantry, was ordered to Fort Hamilton in New York Harbor and did not go to the field again during the war.

All of the old infantry regiments—the Third, Fourth, Seventh and Tenth—all mere skeletons, were retained in the forts around New York. For some reason the Second Infantry, consisting of six companies, not half full, had to go back to the field again, along with the newer and larger regiments, the Eleventh, Twelfth, Fourteenth and Seventeenth Infantry.

We sat around, ready and waiting for the order to start, but it was well along towards evening before we left camp and marched down Sixth Avenue to Canal Street, the way we had come. Only about one-half of our officers marched with us; the others were probably having farewell dinners and knew that the steamer would not leave until daylight next morning. Many of our men did not have a cent when they arrived. The four months' pay was burning holes in their pockets, and they were tempted to have a little fling before going back to Virginia. The streets were packed with people and it was quite easy to dodge into the crowd and disappear quickly through the open door of some corner saloon without attracting the attention of the officers. By the time we reached Canal Street it was dusk and many slipped away before we reached the dock. When the roll was called, it was discovered that more than forty men were missing, among them the drum-major, Lovell, and one of the color sergeants, named McConnell, who had the regimental colors with him. A detail was sent out to round up the absentees; but after a search of several hours, they had only captured half a dozen. As many more came back of their own accord, in a more or less muddled condition, and when the steamer sailed in the morning about thirty men were still missing. All but two or three of these men rejoined the regiment about a week later in Alexandria. When they finished their spree, or their money gave out, they reported to the provost-marshal, who held them and sent them on. They had a hard time on the steamer with a disreputable lot of conscripts and substitutes, who were thievish and quarrelsome. The drum-major related that he was awakened on deck one night by a man going through his pockets. He said to the thief, "Friend, if you can find anything there, you are welcome to it!" Our colors remained for two days in a hotel on Canal Street, but were brought safely back. My regiment had to submit to a lot of jollying from the other troops about losing one of our colors in New York; but we never lost them to the enemy, neither did any other regular regiment in the Army of the Potomac. It was supposed that these men would all be tried by court-martial for absence without leave, but directly after our return to the field in the latter part of September, General Lee attempted a flank movement which kept our army very busy marching for some time. These were all good and faithful soldiers, and instead of a court-martial a general order was issued fining each man a month's pay.

The return trip of the regiment to Alexandria was uneventful. We had a better boat and made a quicker trip than we did going up to New York. The two regular brigades remained long enough in Alexandria to be refitted with a supply train and other necessities. I resumed my former duties under a new commissary officer, First Lieutenant James B. Sinclair of the Fourteenth United States Infantry. Of my former detail I had but one, all the others being new men. I could not get my old horse back and had to take another which was not nearly so good. The two brigades then joined the main army near Culpeper, about the time when the Eleventh and Twelfth Corps were withdrawn from the Army of the Potomac to serve in the West. The Rebel Army had also been reduced during the summer by sending Longstreet's corps to Tennessee.

When General Lee learned of the departure of two of our Army Corps, he put his troops in motion to turn our right flank and rear. This was the beginning of a campaign of manoeuvres between Generals Meade and Lee, like the moves in a game of chess. We crossed the Rappahannock and for about two weeks we marched and counter-marched along the familiar line of the Orange and Alexandria railroad, the supply trains along with the troops, until by forced marching we reached Centreville ahead of the enemy, where General Meade offered battle. General Lee retreated, however, south of the Rappahannock, destroying the railroad and burning the stations from Bristoe to the Rappahannock.

For some days we were prevented from following him by a heavy rainstorm which made Bull Run unfordable and pontoons had to be sent for. During these marches in the latter part of September, 1863, we passed one morning through the almost deserted small town of Brentsville, the county-seat of Prince William County, Virginia. The street in front of the court house was littered with books or records and bundles of papers which had been maliciously thrown out through the open door and windows, probably by some of our stragglers, or "coffee-coolers," as they were also called. I dismounted and examined some of the books which I found to contain mainly records of wills and transfers of property. Some of these books and papers were being carried off by passing soldiers who, when they examined them at the next halt, either threw them away or built fires with them. I picked up a few bundles of the papers and carried them with me until I got to camp, where I examined them. The greater part of them proved to be written consents from masters for his slaves, "Caesar and Dinah" or "Rastus and Lucy" to get married. No surnames seemed to be used for the slaves. Among the papers there was one, however, which interested me and is still in my possession. It is a writ for the arrest of William Murphy, as follows:

> George the second by the grace of God of great Britain, France & Ireland, King Defender of the Faith & .c. To the sheriff of the County of *Prince William* Greeting. We command You that You take *William Murphy*................ if *he* be found within your Bailivic and *him* safely keep so that you have *his* Body before our H Justices of our said County at the Court house of the said County on the *fourth monday* ..in..*July*....next to answer....*Benjamin Grayson Gent of a plea of Trespass upon the Case, Damage ten pounds*........ and have then there this writ witness Peter Wagener Clerk of our said Court at the Court house of aforesaid the *XXIII* ......day of *June* in the *XXVIth* year of our reign *1752*
>
> P. Wagener.

On the reverse side of the paper is this endorsement:

> Not to be found within my Precinct.
> John Crump

This paper, yellow with age but well preserved, is five by six inches in size. It is a coarsely executed pen blank with the words in italics inserted in fine clear penmanship. John Crump's endorsement is written in a good plain running hand.

* * * * * * * * *

The army now took up positions along the north bank of the Rappahannock, where we encamped for two weeks or more, while the railroad was being repaired; and during that time we had to haul supplies from Bristoe Station until the repairs brought them nearer. A number of skirmishes took place during the two weeks of manoeuvring, but no battles were fought.

While at this camp I witnessed the impressive sight of a military execution. A man from one of the new regular regiments had been sentenced by a general court-martial to be shot for desertion. Near sun-down the brigade was paraded and formed three sides of a square on a level field outside of the camp. At the open end of the square was a rude coffin and a newly made grave. Soon the prisoner and provost-guard approached, preceded by a band playing a dead march, passing through the square towards the coffin. There the prisoner, whose bearing was firm and steady, was blindfolded and made to kneel on the coffin. A firing party of eight took position in front of the condemned man at about ten paces. There was a breathless silence for a few minutes, then suddenly were heard the provost-marshal's commands, "Ready! Aim! Fire!" and the man fell forward over the coffin. A surgeon examined him and pronounced him dead; the brigade marched back to camp, and the man was buried in the grave prepared for him.

On the seventh day of November General Meade again put the army in motion to force the passage of the Rappahannock. At Rappahannock Station, where the Rebels were intrenched, there was a spirited engagement, when the Sixth Corps charged the works and captured about sixteen hundred prisoners with small loss to themselves. The Third Corps was also successful in forcing a passage at Kelly's Ford and capturing some four hundred prisoners. The Confederates, taken by surprise, retired during the night beyond Culpeper.

Next day the supply trains crossed at Kelly's Ford and the army went into camp from there to Brandy Station. The railroad had to be repaired as far as Brandy Station, and an important railroad bridge crossing the Rappahannock rebuilt, which consumed considerable time. We supposed that this was to be our winter camp, as the weather grew very bad and cold, as the season advanced, and the road became worse, but it was not to be so. The authorities at Washington, unmindful of the disastrous ending of Burnside's winter campaigns the previous year, urged upon General Meade to continue offensive operations. Accordingly General Meade on the twenty-sixth of November, after a severe storm, broke up the camps and started the army on its march to the fords of the Rapidan.

The Fifth Army Corps crossed the river on a pontoon bridge at a place called Culpeper Mine Ford on the same day, all of the supply trains, except some ammunition wagons, remaining on the north side of the river. On the twenty-eighth it was discovered that a surprise was out of the question, the enemy having concentrated all their forces in a strong position on the west bank of Mine Run.

General Warren, who had commanded the Second Corps since General Hancock had been wounded at Gettysburg, was ordered to make the main attack on the morning of the thirtieth. He made an early examination of the enemy's works and had the moral courage to suspend General Meade's order to attack, sending him word to that effect. This brought General Meade to make a personal examination, after which he agreed with General Warren as to the hopelessness of the attempt. The men of the Second Corps realized that they were to attack a position as hopeless as that at Marye's Heights at Fredericksburg and knew that few would escape. The night before the attack was to be made each man wrote his name, company and regiment on a piece of paper and pinned it to his clothing.

On the same night I was sent across the river with a few supply wagons and reached the front early in the forenoon, when I issued the rations and rested a few hours. I had a good view of a part of the Rebel position, which appeared very formidable, in front of the Fifth Corps. On my return march in the afternoon a cold rain-storm came on, turning to sleet; then it became so cold that my saturated clothing was frozen stiff before I reached camp. The sufferings of the soldiers before the enemy was dreadful. The next day General Meade decided that the campaign was a failure and began to withdraw the army, which recrossed the Rapidan unmolested and, thanks to General Warren, without a useless slaughter, as in the Burnside campaign of the previous winter.

This ended active operations in the Army of the Potomac for 1863. The troops established winter camps; the Fifth Corps guarded and was encamped along the line of the Orange and Alexandria railroad, by brigades stationed at intervals from Fairfax to Brandy Station. The headquarters of my brigade were at Noakesville Station, a small place no longer on the map. Colonel Burbank, who commanded the brigade, and staff occupied a large farm-house situated a few hundred yards east of the little station on a hill. A small two-story out-house was assigned to the brigade commissary and quartermaster departments. A few regiments of the brigade were encamped in the immediate vicinity, where they made themselves comfortable in their winter huts. I rigged up a store-house and, together with the quartermaster sergeant and our assistants, used the little two-story house as an office and for our sleeping quarters. The house had a good roof, a fireplace and chimney. There was plenty of wood and we were warm and comfortable. My horse was stabled along with the brigade staff horses in one of the farm stables.

The commissary depot for the Fifth Corps was at Catlett's Station, about five miles from our camp. I was sent there once a week with a wagon-train to draw supplies for the brigade, and was always accompanied by an infantry escort, as there were guerrillas about. One morning as I was starting off with my train, Captain Samuel A. McKee, of my regiment, and Lieutenant Edwin E. Sellers, of the Tenth United States Infantry, who, with an orderly, were going to Catlett's Station, asked me to ride with them in advance of my train. They soon began to ride very fast and I found that my horse could not keep up with theirs; frequently they were out of sight and I was a quarter of a mile behind in the lonely woods. Then I thought of the guerrillas, but we arrived safely at the station. About a week later, April eleventh, 1864, Captain McKee, accompanied by an orderly, made the same journey and was shot dead on his way to Catlett's; his body was found lying on the road, stripped of his arms and valuables and most of his clothing. The orderly escaped.

About this time many brevet ranks were conferred on officers—the greater part of them for gallantry in the field; others for efficiency in various lines of duty; and some for no particular reason that anyone could discover. So generous was the War Department in distributing brevet ranks that they seemed to lose dignity and sometimes became a joke. The army mule was dubbed a "brevet horse" and the camp follower became a "brevet soldier." Some officers were advanced several grades above their lineal rank by supplementary brevets. It was no uncommon occurrence to find a lieutenant who was a brevet major or colonel; and I know of a few cases where first lieutenants held the honorary rank of brigadier-general.

Lieutenant Sinclair, the commissary officer, was an easygoing, very pleasant man, much liked by both officers and soldiers. He was a first lieutenant and brevet major—a very brave officer, who had the peculiar experience of being wounded in the same leg in three different engagements, but never very seriously—each time able to resume his duties after being discharged from the hospital. He remained in the service for some years after the war. Lieutenant Sinclair was a New Yorker. He had been with the Singer Sewing Machine Co. before the war.

During this winter and spring a large number of recruits joined the Army of the Potomac, among them many conscripts and substitutes, who as a class were not the equals of volunteers of 1861 and 1862. The armies needed still more men and on February first President Lincoln ordered a draft for five hundred thousand men to be held on March tenth, and another on March fifteenth for two hundred thousand more, to be held April fifteenth, 1864. Recruiting for the regular army almost ceased, owing to the large bounties paid for substitutes, and the fact that the enlistments among the volunteers were only for three years, or the duration of the war. I had a short furlough at this time and spent four days very pleasantly in Washington with comrades of my regiment, who had been detailed as clerks in the War Department or were employed as civilians after their discharge from the army.

On March twelfth, 1864, Lieutenant General U. S. Grant was made commander-in-chief of all the armies of the United States, deposing General Halleck, to the great satisfaction of many of the officers and the rank and file in the armies. General Grant visited the Army of the Potomac for a few days in March, consulting General Meade, its commander. Soon after many changes and consolidations were ordered. The five corps were reduced to three, viz: the Second, Fifth and Sixth, commanded respectively by Generals Hancock, Warren and Sedgwick. The Fifth Corps lost its old commander, that sterling old soldier, Major General George Sykes, who had commanded the regular brigade at the beginning of the war and had risen to the command of the Fifth Army Corps. We lost him with profound feelings of regret, which were only compensated by the confidence we had in Major General Gouverneur K. Warren, who had long been a brigade and division commander of the corps. Skeleton companies and regiments were consolidated, brigades and divisions were enlarged. All of the regular infantry soldiers who remained in the field at this time were placed in the First Brigade of the First Division of the Fifth Corps, along with four regiments of volunteers; the One Hundred and Fortieth and One Hundred and Forty-sixth New York and the Ninety-first and One Hundred and Fifty-fifth Pennsylvania, which when combined, outnumbered the regulars considerably. Brigadier-General Romeyn B. Ayres, an old regular artillery officer, commanded the brigade.

General Meade remained in the immediate command of the Army of the Potomac, now increased to ninety-nine thousand, four hundred and thirty-eight officers and enlisted men present for duty, equipped; while General Lee's army, composed of the corps of Longstreet, Ewel and Hill, with Stuart's cavalry, was estimated to number about sixty-two thousand.

General Grant arrived on April twenty-sixth and established his headquarters at Culpeper; with his coming preparations for a forward movement were begun; there was bustle and tumult in all the camps, and a week later, May fourth, the Fifth Corps crossed the Rapidan with the Second Division in the lead preceded by a division of cavalry.

PART XIII.

IN GRANT'S CAMPAIGN—1864.

A FEW days before the breaking up of our winter camp on the Orange and Alexandria railroad an order was issued from corps headquarters to discontinue our brigade commissary department and turn over all property to the commissary of subsistence of the First Division, Fifth Corps. Lieutenant Sinclair was ordered to rejoin his regiment as soon as the transfers were completed, and I expected to be sent back to my company to shoulder a musket among my comrades once more. I was busy for a couple of days in making out the transfer papers. When they were completed Lieutenant Sinclair sent me to Captain M. R. Came, the division commissary officer, to obtain the necessary receipts and acknowledgements. Captain Came was an elderly man and very peculiar. He glanced at the papers and in a drawling voice with a strong "down-East" accent asked me if I had made them out and if I understood them, to which I replied in the affirmative. He then slowly and carefully put on a huge pair of spectacles and taking another short look at the papers, turned to me and said. "Young man, your threes and your fives, your sevens and your nines I can tell apart, which is of great importance; but I have seen better writing."

Then without further examination he signed the receipts on his camp table and I saluted and departed.

On my arrival at camp I made preparations for my return to my company on the following day, and was greatly surprised when that evening I was ordered to report to Captain Came the next day as acting division commissary sergeant. When I reported for duty the following day he seemed to be pleased to see me. He asked me to sit down in his tent and talked with me about the duties I was to perform, telling me to keep a daily journal for his private use of the marches we made, when and where we drew supplies or issued them, and of all incidents worthy of note. Then he told me to go and make myself comfortable and become acquainted with his "boys," as he called his assistants, of whom, he said, I was to be the "boss." I kept the journal for the Captain during the time I served with him and also a copy of it for myself. When I left him to serve elsewhere I continued the journal as long as I remained with the Army of the Potomac and I still possess it. I have often regretted not having kept a diary all through my war service, which would have made the task of writing this book much easier than relying upon my memory, after the lapse of half a century.

The Captain's "boys" consisted of a civilian clerk, a relative of his, to whom the Government paid seventy-five dollars per month and the allowance of one ration. He was a genial, careless young man, who hated work and passed his on to an assistant, a soldier of a Pennsylvania regiment, who was a bright, smart fellow, detailed as a clerk, and very efficient when he could not get any whiskey. Between the two they kept the "old man," as he was called, in trouble on account of delays in rendering reports and accounts to headquarters, and in having them returned for correction, with which the Captain himself was not very familiar.

Fortunately my duties did not include the keeping of accounts; I was to attend to the drawing of supplies from the depots and the issuing of them at the front and I was also to have a general supervision of the supply train, under the orders of Captain Came. There were also four or five soldiers detailed to do the heavy work, and a cook. All of these men were volunteers; I was the only regular. The "boys" showed very little respect for the "old man," who familiarly addressed them by their Christian names. They seldom saluted him and never stood at attention when he gave them his orders, unless some strange officer was present. The cook was a good one. He belonged to a Massachusetts regiment and was an artist on baked beans. He would dig a hole in the ground and keep up a fire in it all day, and at night put in an army camp-kettle filled with salt pork and beans, cover it over with earth, and next morning dig it up with every bean just done to a turn and none of them burnt.

Captain Came was a native of the State of Maine. He had joined the volunteer army as a commissary of subsistence and had not served with any regiment. He was a man over fifty, of medium stature and heavy build. He wore a grizzled, ill-kept beard and had long gray hair, which together with his carelessness in dress, gave him the appearance of a hard-working old farmer. When in camp he wore a soldier's blouse without any shoulder straps to indicate his rank which, along with an old felt hat, caused him to be mistaken at times for one of the teamsters and to be addressed as such by soldiers who did not know him.

He was an eccentric man, stubborn, but still kind and good-hearted, especially to negroes in distress, for whom he seemed to have a special tenderness. He always spoke of them as "colored boys," and would not tolerate having them called "niggers." On the march we were sometimes pestered by "contrabands"—negro men, women and children—slaves—who had run away and followed the supply trains. These he would care for and feed for days, instead of turning them over to the provost-marshal. One day I saw the Captain almost shed tears while listening to a tale told by a sleek, fat wench, who seemed to be the spokesman for a large party to whom he gave permission to ride in the heavily loaded wagons, and from which they were presently ejected, to the Captain's great regret, by Captain Thomas, the division quartermaster.

He had a negro servant, a lazy, worthless, lying rascal, who imposed on his kind master shamefully. Often when called, though close by, he paid no attention; then the Captain left his tent to go in search of him, calling out "Aleck! Aleck! Alexander Tyler, I want knowledge!" which was one of the peculiar expressions he used when he wanted information about anything. If he found "Aleck," and sometimes gave him a mild reproof, the rascal always had a lying excuse and only grinned at the old man. We wondered sometimes whether the Captain bossed the negro or the servant bossed the Captain, for he slept in his tent and helped to drink his whiskey.

The Captain was rather fond of a little whiskey himself and always kept it in his tent and carried a flask in the holster of his saddle when on the march. He was very free with it when officers visited him and on those convivial occasions he sometimes had me called to his tent on some pretext of wanting "knowledge," and when he dismissed me I could overhear him say, "This is my regular." He seemed to be pleased to have a regular sergeant as one of his assistants. The Captain was an early riser and on fine warm mornings stepped out of his tent dressed only in his undershirt and slippers. In one hand he carried a tin cup containing his "toddy"—whiskey, some sugar and a little water—which Aleck prepared for him every morning; in the other hand he held a stick with which he stirred the toddy, while gravely walking about the camp in his bare shanks and talking to us until Aleck had his breakfast ready. I never saw the Captain unfit for duty; he was always attentive to that. The principal effect that drink had on him was that it made him cranky and ill-tempered at times. The laxity of discipline in Captain Came's department was to me astonishing with the training I had had, and I so expressed myself to my comrades, who cared little about it and were always somewhat jealous of me.

The supply train, heavily loaded with ten days' rations, in addition to the five days' rations issued to the troops just before starting on their march, crossed the Rapidan at Culpeper Mine Ford on a pontoon bridge on the afternoon of May fourth and proceeded a few miles on the other side, where we encamped for the night. The train was guarded by a greater number of cavalry and infantry than I had ever seen employed for that purpose.

The next morning we marched in the direction of the Wilderness until well along in the forenoon, when we halted and remained in that spot for two days; then we made a night march in the direction of Spottsylvania Court House. From our position we plainly heard the firing which opened the battle of the Wilderness of May fifth and sixth, which was the beginning of a series of battles, marching, and almost continuous fighting which lasted for forty-two days, until we had arrived at the James river. General Grant, regardless of tremendous losses, had sent a despatch to Washington in which he used the noted phrase, "I propose to fight it out on this line if it takes all summer." He continued his movements to the left to outflank Lee, who met him on ground of his own choosing and fought a defensive battle.

Of the great battles of the Wilderness, Spottsylvania, North Anna, Cold Harbor and the historical minor engagements I saw but little, for my issues of rations at the front were sometimes made at night or during a lull in a battle, if in daytime. I was always hurried away quickly, for the white covers of the wagons, if noticed, drew the fire of the enemy's artillery and on a couple of occasions caused the loss of some of the wagons and the wounding of some teamsters. Only at Spottsylvania and at Cold Harbor, while waiting for darkness before returning, was I enabled to see my regiment in the breastworks and something of the battle-field and to hear my comrades' storics of the fight. After the battle of the Wilderness the Army of the Potomac was reinforced by General Burnside's Ninth Army Corps, numbering about twenty-two thousand men, mostly newly raised troops, of whom but a third had ever been in the field.

While the troops were at Spottsylvania the supply train was parked on Stafford Heights, overlooking the town of Fredericksburg, near a large spring of fine water which supplied the town; but there was no fire-wood to be had except by tearing down old and unoccupied houses. From this place, about midway between the front and Belle Plain on the Potomac, the new supply depot where we drew rations, we supplied the troops until they advanced to Cold Harbor. Captain Came was very energetic in trying to keep up his supplies. He nearly always accompanied the train to the depot, of which fact I was very glad, as he could obtain better attention from the officers in charge than I. The depots were busy places. The rule of "first come, first served" was not always observed; favoritism was shown, and sometimes when alone I was unjustly detained for many hours, or an entire day, before I succeeded in getting my wagons loaded. When rations were to be issued at the front the Captain remained in camp with the main part of the train, which sometimes moved before I returned and I had to follow it up—with great trouble at times.

On our first trip to the depot at Belle Plain the Captain and I rode ahead so as to arrive early and get our requisition on file. The Captain rode a large horse named "Ned," to whom he gave commands in a voice loud enough for a squadron of cavalry: "Halt! Forward! Trot!" etc., which caused much laughter as we passed through the streets of Fredericksburg, among the soldiers and citizens, who vainly looked for a squadron to follow him.

Belle Plain was crowded with shipping, arriving troops and wounded soldiers, awaiting transportation, as well as prisoners. A long dock, only wide enough for a single line of wagons, led out to a small wharf, where there was room for but two boats at a time and little room to unload; beef cattle were made to jump overboard and swim ashore. It was after midnight when our last wagon was loaded and we drove off a short distance and rested until daylight. On this occasion we lost two lead-mules, who fell off the narrow dock in the darkness and were drowned.

Reinforcements for the army were being forwarded rapidly. On the way to Belle Plain we passed the First Massachusetts, First Vermont, Second and Eighth New York, all heavy artillery, serving as infantry, and the Thirty-sixth Wisconsin Infantry, full regiments on their way to the front.

Late on the afternoon of May nineteenth the Rebel General Ewell passed around the right wing of our army and made a dash for the supply trains. He captured twenty-seven wagons on the Fredericksburg road, but they were all re-taken. General Ewell was repulsed and his entire command came near being cut off from Lee's army, when darkness afforded him a chance to escape.

Our next supplies were drawn from Port Royal on the Rappahannock river. On May twenty-second the train was at Bowling Green, a fine village, almost deserted except for slaves, who were mostly women. We were now out of the Wilderness in a fine part of the country containing large plantations, which had not been visited by the ravages of war. From Bowling Green we went by way of Milford Station to Chesterfield, crossing the Mattapony river on the way. This river takes its name and is formed by four small rivers, named the Ma, Ta, Po and the Ny.

From Chesterfield I was sent with a part of the train to supply rations to the division at Mount Carmel Church, which the Fifth Army Corps was to pass during the night of the twenty-sixth. It had rained most of the day; the roads were bad, but I reached the place and waited for hours before the division arrived near midnight and halted until rations were issued, when they resumed their night march. The mules were fed but not unhitched, for at daylight I started on the return march. When I arrived at Chesterfield, where I had left the supply trains, I found that they had been ordered away, and I had to make a march of thirty miles that day over bad roads to catch up with them that evening near New Town.

I was kept exceedingly busy during this campaign; every three or four days the troops had to be supplied and six days' rations had to be kept in the wagons. This kept me on the go all the time, to the front or to the depots, which were often far apart. Much of the marching was done in the night-time, and often the only sleep I got was dozing in the saddle or snatching a few hours in an empty wagon when almost exhausted from fatigue.

We had much rain during the month of May and the early part of June. The roads—some of them bad enough in dry weather—were in a horrible state. At Spottsylvania I lost two loads of hard bread—the wagons upset in a deep puddle and one of them we were unable to extricate and had to abandon. The horses and mules, ill-fed, hard-worked night and day, and often suffering for water, sometimes succumbed. There were times when we did not dare to lose time to let them drink while fording a stream, no matter how they suffered. Often they were hitched up for forty-eight hours at a time and my horse did not have his saddle removed.

When the army reached Cold Harbor, the base of supplies was changed to the White House Landing on the Pamunkey river, a locality familiar to us in McClellan's time. On our march we passed through Dunkirk, Aylets, Newcastle and Old Church, a fertile region with many plantations. In passing through this section many contrabands abandoned the plantations and joined our train. A few times we took down fences and parked the train in a great clover-field, which was a rare treat for our hungry animals.

On our route we encountered General W. F. Smith's four divisions of sixteen thousand men, of the Eighteenth Army Corps, from General Butler's Army of the James, whence they had come to the White House in transports and were marching to reinforce Grant's army at Cold Harbor. We also met strong regiments of heavy artillery, withdrawn from the defenses of Washington, marching to the front. The authorities at Washington had given General Grant a free hand, which no former commander had had, to recruit his great losses in this campaign.

While the opposing armies faced each other at Cold Harbor for a period of twelve days, I made frequent trips with supplies from the White House depot to the front, and on my return journeys, which generally took place at night, we drove to the field hospitals and filled the empty wagons with the less seriously wounded and took them to the White House depot. This was also done at the Wilderness and at Spottsylvania, the supply of ambulances being inadequate to remove the great numbers of wounded men. The roads being bad during rainy weather, and the army wagons having no springs to lessen the hard jolts, the poor fellows suffered intense pain and I often heard them cry out in agony as I rode past the wagons. It was pitiful to hear them. When I was in charge of the train I made frequent halts to rest them, but this was all that could be done. Sometimes one or two of the unfortunates died during the night, the body remaining in the wagon among the living until we reached our destination. Upon arriving at the White House, the wounded were delivered at the general hospital, where thousands of wounded soldiers were cared for and rested for a few days in large hospital tents, before being shipped in especially adapted transport vessels to Northern hospitals or convalescent camps.

The great depot at the White House was a busy place. The narrow river was congested with vessels of all kinds, including some gun-boats. Great quantities of stores for the army were discharged and newly arrived troops came ashore. Departing vessels carried away wounded soldiers and Rebel prisoners, many of whom seemed pleased at the prospect of getting enough to eat; for they had been ill-supplied all through this campaign, as they informed us.

On June ninth we learned that a change of base to the James river was to take place. On the following day we loaded the wagons with all the supplies they would carry and by way of Tunstall's Station proceeded to the vicinity of Cold Harbor, over ground familiar to us. Some of the conflict at Cold Harbor took place on the battlefield of Gaines's Mill, only the position of the two armies was now reversed. After supplying the division the train left camp at three P. M. June twelfth, an exceedingly hot day, for the James river.

After dark on the same day the Army of the Potomac was withdrawn from the trenches at Cold Harbor, where they had such a deplorable experience that General Grant himself in his Memoirs says: "I have always regretted that the last assault at Cold Harbor was ever made; no advantage whatever was gained to compensate for the heavy loss we sustained."

On the fifteenth of June the Army of the Potomac crossed the James on a pontoon bridge at Wilcox's Landing, just six weeks after crossing the Rapidan. It had failed to capture Richmond or to destroy Lee's army, and the campaign ended at the James, as in 1862, but with an immensely greater sacrifice. Conservative historians compute our losses at 7,289 killed,

37,406 wounded and 9,856 missing; a total of 54,551. Others claim that these figures do not include the losses in Burnside's Ninth Army Corps and make the grand total upwards of sixty thousand,—a loss on our side nearly as great as General Lee's entire army at the opening of the campaign. None of the authorities place the Confederate losses over twenty thousand, or about one to three. This sanguine campaign, its awful sacrifices without any advantages, caused mutterings of discontent and had a gloomy and depressing effect, not only in the army but throughout the North. The army had lost thousands of its most capable officers and veteran soldiers, who could not be replaced, and it no longer seemed to be the same army.

When Generals Grant and Meade, whom I encountered a few times, appeared among the troops there was but feeble applause, and the hearty cheers received by some of our former commanders were no longer heard. At this period of the war the only bright spot was the masterly strategy and successful campaign of General Sherman against the Confederate General Joseph E. Johnson in the West from Chattanooga to Atlanta. In the Histories of the Wilderness,—Cold Harbor campaign, written after the conclusion of the Civil War by officers still in the service or on the retired list—histories most carefully written—there is an absence of criticism of the military strategy in this campaign. When all participants have passed away, some future historian will write an unbiased story of the war and its strategy.

Anxiety as to the safe withdrawal of the supply trains was felt, but they were well protected. So skillfully was the withdrawal of the army and its trains accomplished that General Lee was unable to determine for two days whether the objective point of the Army of the Potomac was the investment of Richmond or a movement to the James river. Except for some cavalry skirmishes, the march was unmolested.

The train arrived at the Chickahominy on the morning of the fourteenth and encamped at Wilcox's farm until the following day, waiting for the pontoon bridge and approaches to be completed, for an insufficient number of boats had been provided, causing twenty-four hours' delay. The river is wide and deep at that point. We crossed on the afternoon of the fifteenth. I counted forty-four large wooden pontoons and sixteen smaller canvas pontoons, all of which appeared to be spaced at greater distances apart than usual.

We halted at some distance on the opposite side and resumed our march at seven P. M., reaching the vicinity of the pontoon bridge over the James at Wilcox's Point before midnight. We were halted there to allow the Ninth Army Corps to cross before us. The train commenced crossing about two o'clock on the morning of the sixteenth of June. It was a beautiful, clear, moonlight night and I had no difficulty in counting the one hundred and one pontoons composing the bridge over the James, more than two thousand feet wide at this point. It was daylight when we parked in a cornfield on the other side, and men and animals were glad to get some rest. The teams were not unhitched, for we were liable to be ordered forward at any moment.

All day long the road was crowded with marching troops and trains coming across the bridge, and by midnight of the sixteenth the entire army with all its artillery and trains had reached the right bank of the James. After sun-down our train was ordered to pull out on the road, and after proceeding a few hundred yards it was halted and did not go on again until eleven P. M. After that we moved by fits and starts and at daylight had accomplished only about three miles on the congested road.

After daylight on the seventeenth we made better progress; we passed through Prince George Court House and halted after noon-time in an oat-field a mile square, which was destroyed in a few hours. There we fed the animals, after a twenty-four-hour fast, and unhitched them for a few hours— they had not had their harnesses off for two days. I also issued two days' rations to our division, which was halted close by. We plainly heard cannonading in the direction of Petersburg during the afternoon.

About six P. M. we resumed our march and for the third night in succession we were on the road until daylight. On the morning of the eighteenth we encamped within about two and a half miles from City Point on the road to Petersburg. All the supply trains of the army, commissary, quartermaster and reserve ammunition were encamped in this vicinity about six miles from the front at Petersburg; all except what was called the "Fighting Train," composed of ammunition wagons, which always followed the troops and supplied ammunition when required, in camp or during a battle. The supply trains were destined to remain in this camp for many months, while the long and tedious operations of the siege of Petersburg went on.

But I was not to remain in camp. A short time previous some further changes and consolidations had been made and my regiment was again placed in the Second Division of the Fifth Corps, and three days after our arrival I was ordered to report at the front as acting ordnance sergeant. The regulars formed the First Brigade, along with the Fifth, One Hundred and Fortieth and One Hundred and Forty-sixth New York Volunteers, under the command of Brigadier-General Joseph Hayes. When I learned of this change I knew that I would have to leave my detail in the First Division and expected to be ordered to join my company; being appointed ordnance sergeant was a complete surprise to me and I never learned to whom I owed the appointment. I left Captain Came on the morning of June twenty-first and I think he was not well pleased at losing his only "regular." He told me to come and see him when I could, and to call on him for anything I needed in the commissary line. For my part I was glad to leave the kindly old man, for during my stay of eight weeks I always felt annoyed at the manner in which my assistants performed their duties.

First Lieutenant Richard H. Pond, of the Twelfth United States Infantry, was the acting ordnance officer of the Second Division, Fifth Corps, to whom I reported at the front. Lieutenant Pond had been appointed from the ranks in May, 1862, and he understood and performed his duties very well. He was a pleasant man, with a taste for literature and spent much of his time in writing.

The ammunition train was encamped close to General Warren's headquarters, in rear of some of the captured redoubts and breastworks, and near the Norfolk and Petersburg railroad. With this train was a permanent detail of a sergeant, a corporal and eighteen privates, whose duties were to guard the train and to assist me in caring for, receiving and distributing the infantry arms and ammunition for the Second Division. There was also a soldier named Ballard, detailed as ordnance clerk, a very staid, pious man, much older than I, who read his Bible when not otherwise occupied. Ballard and I had a wall tent for our use; the ammunition guard had shelter tents, and the wagon-master and teamsters slept in the wagons on the ammunition boxes. I was provided with a riding horse and accoutrements. I did not like the horse and soon swapped him for a better one at the corral where extra horses were kept.

My duties, while the siege went on, were much easier than in the commissary department, and the reports and accounts, which dealt only with arms, accoutrements and ammunition for infantry, were more simple. Every morning I sent a wagon loaded with twenty thousand rounds of cartridges to the front, a short distance away, accompanied by a file of the guard and sometimes I went with them. This wagon remained at the front until dark, supplying ammunition when needed; and when returning to camp, left a supply for the night.

Artillery firing was going on at some part of the long line all day, sometimes furiously. Picket firing was almost constant along the line in the rifle pits, and at night when the pickets were being relieved, the firing occasionally was increased by the men behind the breast-works on both sides, also by the artillery, until it sounded like a battle. This sometimes kept up for more than a half hour, when it suddenly ceased and only pickets' shot were heard. There were some mortars along our line, firing shells into Petersburg. I watched them at night, when I could distinguish the burning fuses in their curved course through the sky like rockets and could hear the shells burst. After a while I became so accustomed to artillery firing at night that it no longer awakened me, even if close to our camp. The enemy's longer range guns sometimes fired a few shells over our camp, invisible to them, and over General Warren's headquarters close by, without doing any damage.

The troops manned the breast-works and constructed redoubts, bomb-proofs and covered ways by brigades and were relieved by other brigades every few days. When relieved, they retired some distance to the rear, near division headquarters, a short distance in advance of the ordnance train's camp. Lieutenant Pond had his tent with the division staff, where I reported to him every evening about sun-down for orders, unless absent on other duty.

The weather had become intensely hot, and no rain had fallen since June fifth. The heavy cannonading failed to bring it on, as it generally did; with the exception of a few drops from a cloud early in July, there was no rain until July nineteenth—a period of forty-three days. At first we got water from a small stream a long distance from camp, but it soon dried up. We then resorted to wells, as the troops had to do from the beginning of the siege. Five or six feet below the porous surface soil, there was clay containing water. We dug pits and put down barrels with the heads knocked out. As the drought was prolonged, we were obliged to deepen our wells, digging ten to twelve feet or more in depth to get a sufficient amount of water for men and animals. The dust was many inches thick on the roads where, ground into a fine powder by passing troops and trains, it hung in great clouds so dense that often a teamster was unable to see his leading mules. This, and the absence of water along the roads, caused much suffering to man and beast.

The old Petersburg and City Point railroad was repaired for the required distance and a new road, called the United States Military railroad, was connected with it and finally extended south as far as the Weldon and Petersburg railroad. Very imperfect grading and ballasting was done in the hasty building of this road. The soldiers declared that it made them sea-sick to ride on its cars; nevertheless, it proved to be of great service to the investing army.

Once or twice a week I had to go to City Point, about ten miles away, to the ordnance depot with some wagons to replenish the supply of ammunition for our division. By starting early I was generally able to make this trip in a day, if no great delay occurred at the depot, returning in the evening, thickly covered with dust.

We presumed that General Grant would order a bombardment and assault on the enemy's works at Petersburg on July fourth but with the exception of firing a national salute at his headquarters at City Point, the day passed without special incident.

A few days later it was discovered that the Rebel General Jubal A. Early had slipped away and was marching up the Shenandoah Valley, well on his way to Maryland. The Sixth Corps was hastily embarked on transports for Washington and arrived there on the eleventh of July in the nick of time to save the city. General Early had arrived before the northern defenses of the city at an earlier hour on the same day and, finding the works but feebly defended, contemplated an assault on the following day which was frustrated by the timely arrival of the Sixth Corps, which forced him to withdraw.

Shortly after the arrival of the army at Petersburg, City Point assumed the appearance of a large and busy town. Great store-houses and other temporary frame buildings were erected and the wharf extended. General Grant's headquarters were there, the commissary, quartermaster, ordnance and medical depots; the general hospital with its many large tents near the banks of the Appomattox river; undertaking and embalming establishments, conducted by enterprising civilians; and a rapidly increasing grave-yard for the many sick and wounded soldiers, who died in the general hospital. The sanitary and the Christian commissions, sustained by the generosity of the Northern people, had large establishments. The two commissions were of incalculable benefit in helping the

Government in the care of sick and wounded soldiers and saved many lives. Many sutlers had tents or booths near the bank of the James, which looked like a market-place. It was not until some time later that regimental sutlers were permitted at the front. The river was so full of vessels that it resembled a great shipping port.

One day, after loading my wagons, I went to one of the sutler's booths to buy some crackers and cheese for a lunch before my ride back to camp. As I stood among a crowd of soldiers, waiting to be served, I heard one of them demanding something in a voice that sounded familiar to me. I soon discovered that he was a former drummer of my regiment, in fact one of the two boys who had accompanied me from Governor's Island to Carlisle. He was now a bugler in Captain Haxamer's New Jersey Battery. I was glad to see him again. We conversed a while and then rode together towards the front, his battery being stationed about a mile to the right of the main road to Petersburg. He told me he had a fine flute which he had found in a knapsack on the field of Cold Harbor, which he desired to present to me, having no use for it himself. At the parting of our ways he requested me to wait, while he rode to his camp to get it. He soon returned and handed me a package which I found, when opened, contained the first two joints of a flute and a music book. The third joint, usually made in two sections, was missing. He thought he must have dropped it out of the carelessly wrapped package, when he mounted his horse in camp to return to me. He promised to make diligent search for it, and did find the upper section of the third joint, where he thought he had lost it, and brought it to me. More than a month later, I met him again. He had recovered the last section of the third joint and the flute was finally complete. It appeared that a soldier of his battery had found this part in camp and kept it for weeks in his haversack as a curiosity, until one day my friend recovered it. I have treasured this flute which came to me so curiously in installments; the key on the last joint shows plainly the imprint of a horse's hoof.

Captain Came's camp was close to the City Point road. I called on him a few times, when he invited me to his tent and asked me to take a "little mite," as he expressed it. He seemed pleased to see me, or was pleased at the excuse I afforded for an extra drink. We chatted, and he urged me to stay and have dinner with his "boys." On one of my trips, I fortunately missed by a few hours the explosion of a boat with a cargo of ordnance stores, at the wharf where I loaded my wagons. It killed and wounded about a hundred of the negro stevedores and other persons near-by, demolished some ordnance wagons, and did great damage to the wharf and adjoining vessels. The cause of the explosion remained unknown, but it was surmised that Rebel spies were to blame for it.

Some change in the position of our division caused the removal of our camp nearer to the Jerusalem Plank road. This caused the digging of more and deeper wells to obtain a sufficient supply of water, during the great heat and drought. General Burnside's Ninth Army Corps was on the right of the Fifth and there I saw the first colored troops join the Army of the Potomac, observing the arrival of a new regiment of negroes with their white officers on the road from City Point. Many of them had taken off their shoes and carried them slung on their bayonets while trudging bare-footed along the hot dusty road. In the evening I went to their camp and heard the roll-call of one of the companies. There were so many Jacksons and Johnstons, that the first sergeant numbered them as high as "Johnston number five." They appeared to be very proud of being soldiers and serving with white troops.

There were rumors, late in July, that a mine was being dug at a point in front of the Ninth Army Corps, where the field fortifications of both armies approached the closest. On the night of July twenty-ninth, I was awakened by an orderly who brought me an order from Lieutenant Pond to have the ordnance train ready to move at three o'clock next morning. An hour later the order was changed to have forty thousand rounds of ammunition at the front at daylight. I supposed that the mine was to be blown up under the enemy's works and that a general bombardment would take place.

It was just daylight, when I arrived at the front with one wagon containing the ammunition. I waited, expecting to hear an explosion at any moment. It was a beautiful morning and all was quiet. I must have waited for an hour, when suddenly I felt the earth tremble as the mine was fired, and I heard a dull heavy thud in front of the Ninth Corps close by. The report had not yet died away when our batteries, mortars and great guns opened a tremendous fire on the Rebel works which shook the earth.

An intervening strip of woods prevented me from seeing anything except the great cloud of smoke which arose over the batteries. The teamster and two guards were busy trying to keep the mules from running away, while I endeavored to quiet my horse, which was trying to break the halter by which I had tied him to a tree. I think it was ten minutes or more before there was any reply from the Rebel batteries and longer than that before their fire became general. Occasional shells now began to fly over us and one of them—a twenty-pounder—landed within a few yards of me, kicked around and scattered dirt over me, as I threw myself prone to the ground; but fortunately it failed to explode. The artillery fire was kept up for more than an hour when it slackened, but was vigorously resumed for a time about nine o'clock By noon it had ceased and I was ordered to return to camp.

We learned later that the springing of the mine was a success, although it took place an hour later than intended, owing to a damp fuse which failed about half way into the mine and had to be replaced. The explosion blew a small Rebel fort, with all its inmates and guns, about two hundred feet up into the air and made a crater in the ground about one hundred and fifty, by sixty feet and twenty-five feet deep, which caused consternation and surprise among the enemy.

It has been conceded that General Meade's plan for a general assault on Petersburg was skillful and should have been a success, had his orders been fully obeyed. General Hancock's Second Army Corps had been sent across the James on the twenty-seventh to make a diversion, which resulted in General Lee's weakening his defenses by several divisions; while the Second Corps was to return on the night of the twenty-ninth to take part in the general assault on Petersburg, which failed to take place. Owing to deplorable delay and mismanagement of the division of the Ninth Corps, which advanced after the explosion of the mine and became huddled in the crater, the attack was doomed to lamentable failure, which caused the loss of nearly four thousand men. Some historians have termed this event "the mine fiasco." A week later General Meade ordered a court of inquiry to investigate the cause of the failure. This court, after the conclusion of its sessions, promulgated its opinion as follows:

That General Burnside had failed to prepare his parapets and abatis for the passage of the assaulting columns and had not given them proper formation; that he had neglected General Meade's order for the prompt advance to the crest and had not provided engineers, working materials and tools, etc., etc. As General Burnside remained at his headquarters, more than a mile away, during the assault, he had no personal knowledge of what was taking place. Brigadier-Generals J. H. Ledlie, commanding the white, and Edward Ferrero, commanding the colored troops of the assaulting columns, were found not to have pushed their divisions forward promptly, according to orders; nor did they accompany them, but remained in the rear in bomb-proofs most of the time and did not know the position of their troops. Two other brigade commanders were less unfavorably commented up. Six months later the congressional committee on the conduct of the war made a more searching and exhaustive inquiry into the "mine fiasco."

Unremitting picket firing and occasional cannonading went on during the sweltering first half of the month of August. On the night of the fifteenth, the Fifth Corps was relieved from duty in the trenches by the extension of the Ninth Corps to the left. General Grant had decided to destroy the Weldon railroad, an important means of supply for Lee's army, some miles to our west, and, if possible, to make a lodgement there and extend our investing lines to that point. The Fifth Army Corps was selected for this movement and was to march on the morning of the Seventeenth, but a torrential rain-storm on the night of the sixteenth had put the roads into such a condition that it was impossible to move artillery the next morning.

Just before midnight on the seventeenth some Rebel batteries opened fire on the Union lines and soon all the guns and mortars on both sides seemed to be engaged. It was the most furious midnight cannonading since the beginning of the siege. All the mortars were firing shells, which made the sky look as though there were a display of fireworks. It lasted for an hour and a half, when the firing slackened and then suddenly ceased on both sides, as if by an agreement.

A few hours later, at four o'clock in the morning on the eighteenth, General Warren started the Fifth Corps on the march to the Weldon railroad. At daylight we broke camp, loaded the wagons and were soon ready to follow the troops, but remained stationary awaiting orders. About noon we heard firing from the direction which General Warren had taken, and by two o'clock the firing had increased enough to indicate a considerable engagement. The day was very hot, although a heavy rain was falling. At five o'clock in the afternoon Lieutenant Pond ordered me to start immediately with nine wagons, loaded with ammunition, for the Weldon railroad and report to Colonel Fred T. Locke, the Adjutant-General of the Corps. I started promptly, taking along half of the guard, mine being the first ordnance train on the road and keeping in the lead all the way. The roads were in a bad condition from recent heavy rains. One of the teamsters broke a wagon tongue but there was no time to improvise a substitute and, as the stalled wagon could be passed, I left it sticking in the deep mud and hastened on.

I arrived at the Weldon railroad at nine P. M., where I halted the train and reported to the adjutant-general at the

Globe Tavern on the Halifax road, which runs parallel to the railroad. A lieutenant was ordered to guide me. He directed me to follow him with three of the wagons and led me up the road, nearly a mile, to a point between our line of battle and our pickets. There I supplied the picket reserve with ammunition. Sharp picket firing from the Rebel side began, as they heard the noise of my wagons, but it was raining and the night was pitch-dark and we escaped without damage. I next supplied the different regiments of the division and at daylight was ordered to retire and park the wagons half a mile to the rear and to be in readiness to move at any minute. I sent my empty wagons back to the old camp; and during the afternoon the remainder of the ammunition train joined me, also the wagon I had abandoned in the mud. Lieutenant Pond had remained behind, sick. I did not see him again for nearly a week.

Attempts to break our line were made soon after daylight on the nineteenth and at intervals during the day. About five o'clock in the afternoon the enemy turned our right flank and enveloped a part of our division, capturing Brigadier-General Joseph Hayes and some hundreds of prisoners. I saw much of this engagement, but when the enemy got in rear of our division, I was ordered to fall back hurriedly to save the train from capture. Reinforcements arrived at this part of the line and at dark the enemy had been repulsed.

It had rained nearly all day, the roads were now impassable for wagons, but ammunition had to be supplied. I was furnished with a large detail of men and, with much trouble, made three trips to the front during the night with pack-mules loaded with ammunition. About three o'clock in the morning, I took the saddle off my horse for the first time in two days and nights, and lay down in a wagon in my clothing, soaked for two days with rain. I was exhausted, and succeeded in getting two hours' sleep.

All day on the twentieth we were kept on the alert. The troops on both sides held the positions they occupied, after the close of the two days' fighting. The mules had not been unharnessed since we had left camp three days before and the horses were kept saddled. It had stopped raining, and our troops were busy strengthening their breast-works, while the pickets kept up firing. I made one trip to the lines with pack-mules after dark, and about eleven o'clock reported at General Ayres's headquarters for orders.

The division headquarters were in a small farm-house. Some officers' and orderlies' horses were tied to the picket fence in front of the house. When I had tied my horse and was stepping aside, one of the other horses landed a kick on my right thigh which sent me sprawling into the muddy road. Strange to say, I was very little hurt by this kick, which must have been delivered at too short, or too long, a range. I considered myself fortunate to escape so easily. Only a week before one of the teamsters was kicked by a mule and died on the same day. When I picked myself up and looked around for some means to clean my hands and clothing, I noticed a kitchen extension behind the house with a light in it. There I found the general's soldier-cook, who knew me. Besides being dirty, I was half famished; and he fed me substantially and gave me hot coffee, which I had been without for three days. A drink of the general's whiskey and one of his cigars concluded the most satisfactory and enjoyable feast I think I ever had, and I still remember the general's cook most gratefully.

The loss of the Weldon railroad was of such importance to the enemy that General Lee largely reinforced his line of troops, while to our force was added the Ninth Army Corps, which took position on our right, closing up a gap towards the Jerusalem Plank road. On the morning of August twenty-first, a bright sun-shiny day, the enemy made an attack on our right and center and were repulsed, mainly by our well-served artillery. At a later hour in the morning, a more vigorous attempt was made on our left near the Globe Tavern, of which I had a close view, my train being parked at the edge of the same woods, beside the tavern. A part of the enemy charged through a gap in our lines, but were almost surrounded and more than five hundred men and six flags were captured. The Rebels, repulsed at all points, retreated to their lines and the battle was over at noontime.

When the firing had nearly ceased, I was ordered out with two loads of ammunition. My division was stationed behind breast-works, which were at right angles to and across the Halifax road, nearly half a mile north of the tavern. As I neared the breast-works, the white covers of my two wagons were perceived and the enemy's pickets concentrated a lively fire on the wagons, although they could only hit the tops and not the mules, owing to the height of the log breast-works. The teamster of the leading team jumped off his saddle, dropped his lines and threw himself flat on the side of the road. I seized the bridle of one of the lead-mules and guided the team off the road to some depressed ground, followed by the other wagon. There the ammunition was issued, and I was preparing to depart when the teamster returned, somewhat shamefaced, saying he was a citizen employee and did not want to be shot. On our return to camp, we ran the gauntlet of the pickets at a gallop and were quickly out of range.

The losses in the Fifth Corps, during the three days' battle, were about thirty-six hundred in killed, wounded and captured. On the night of this day I got a fair amount of sleep and felt much refreshed the next morning. The enemy had retired for some distance and our pickets were advanced a mile beyond our breast-works, leaving us in possession of nearly all the ground they had occupied.

Lieutenant Pond, who had reported for duty, ordered me outside of the breast-works during the afternoon of this day with wagons and a large detail of men to collect the abandoned arms on the battle-field. The wounded had been removed and the dead buried; only dead horses remained. After dark I was sent out again to the picket line on the ground of the first day's battle. There we collected a large number of arms, remaining until approaching daylight warned us to depart and avoid drawing the enemy's picket fire. On the following night this was repeated under a heavy, soaking rain. I collected upwards of fifteen hundred fire-arms, of which more than half were those of the Rebels. There were rifles, muskets and carbines; also bayonets, swords, belts and cartridge boxes. The arms were rusty from having lain on the field during several days' rain.

It was necessary to classify these arms, make a report of them and turn them over to the ordnance depot at City Point. This work kept me, with the assistance of the ammunition guard, occupied for several days. Arms that were charged had to be fired, or the charges withdrawn, which was difficult in their rusty state. This work proved interesting to me and coincided with my own observations when in the ranks with my company in battle. I found that the ram-rods were missing from a considerable number of discharged guns, and a greater number had failed to be discharged on account of defective caps, or a befouled nipple. Some were doubly charged, and an occasional one had three, or even four, cartridges in the barrel, indicating that the soldier continued to load without noticing that his piece had not been discharged. Others were bursted at the muzzle, showing that the tompion had not been removed before firing. There were some with stocks broken by violence, probably by cool-headed men taken prisoners, who thoughtfully rendered their arms unserviceable. Such of the guns as had more than one charge in the barrel were fastened to a tree and, after fresh priming, we pulled the trigger with the aid of a string, at a safe distance. A few that could neither be drawn nor discharged, we buried in the ground. It has been said that it takes a man's weight in lead for every soldier killed in battle. I am inclined to almost believe that, from my own observations and from the amount of ammunition I knew to be expended on the battle-field of the Weldon Railroad, where I noticed innumerable bullet marks on trees standing on level ground, at height that could only endanger birds.

For the next few days the troops were occupied in further strengthening their positions and in destroying the railroad north and south, as far as our picket lines. This was accomplished in sections, by stationing a few hundred men close together on one side of the track and lifting the rails at the word of command, some with fence rails for levers, others with their hands, and tossing them over with the sleepers clinging to them. Huge fires were then made with the sleepers and the rails were laid over them. When the rails were sufficiently heated in the middle they were bent by their own weight. When there were trees near-by, the heated rails were twisted around them to make the rails still more unserviceable.

Although we had made a successful and firm lodgment on the Weldon railroad, the enemy could still use the road beyond our left as a line of supply and reach Petersburg in one day's hauling by wagons. General Meade ordered General Hancock with two divisions of the Second Corps and some cavalry to extend the destruction of the road as far as Ream's Station, or further. At Ream's Station General Hancock was met by a superior force of the enemy on the twenty-fifth, and after a disastrous engagement, in which he lost about twenty-four hundred men, was obliged to retire.

Next day some shifting of troops took place to secure our left and rear; the ordnance camp was shifted about half a mile away from the Globe Tavern. After the middle of August the long drought of midsummer was replaced by a rainy season, which lasted until the end of the first week in September and made life miserable in the breast-works and in camp.

As the result of recent drafts, many recruits now joined the army; they came uninstructed and without being disciplined. A few of them were volunteers, but the greater part were drafted or substitutes. All had received bounties—some of them a thousand dollars or more. This had a bad effect on the veteran volunteer regiments. In many cases the recruits out-numbered the veterans of high reputation, and changed the character of the regiment, to its disadvantage. Many of these recruits intended to escape at the first opportunity and some deserted to the enemy.

August thirty-first was muster day; six months' pay was

due us, and though the army was not very far from Washington and the United States Treasury, payment to the soldiers at this period of the war was very infrequent.

Throughout the month of September nothing occurred in front of the Fifth Corps except picket firing, and but little cannonading. I made some trips to City Point for ammunition and arms, until the extension of the United States Military railroad to the Globe Tavern on the Weldon railroad made that no longer necessary. On the night of the twenty-ninth, after midnight, I issued ammunition at the division headquarters, so as to furnish every man with sixty rounds, forty of which could be carried in his cartridge box, the remaining twenty rounds in his knapsack or in his pockets. The ordnance train was ordered a short distance further to the rear, near the Gurley house, to be in readiness to move at a moment's notice. An attempt to gain possession of the Southside railroad on our left was to be made. Our works were largely stripped of troops for this purpose and, for safety, nearly all other supply trains, except ammunition, were sent to City Point.

We remained hitched up all day and all night. During the night it rained and turned cold and continued to rain next day. I turned into one of the wagons, together with the teamster, to get some sleep. During the night I was awakened by the mules starting off with the wagon, and the voice of the teamster who, with his head out of the back of the wagon, was calling to the wagon-master, "Oh, Charley! I'm damned if my mules with tongue and all ain't gone." It appeared he had neglected to lock the wheels and, in his confused state, mistook the back of the wagon for the front.

The next morning, October first, I was ordered away with three loads of ammunition for the division. I passed Poplar Spring Church on the way and went on to the Squirrel Level road, where General Ayres had his head-quarters in a house near a redoubt and breast-works, which the division had taken from the enemy the preceding day. I arrived there about noon and was ordered to leave two of my wagons at head-quarters and proceed with the other to the front line about a mile in advance. There I began to serve out ammunition to the details sent for it. I had selected a position which I thought would screen the wagon from the enemy's picket line, but presently an occasional bullet struck the wagon cover, fired probably by sharp-shooters, posted in high trees. A man of the detail received a serious wound in the shoulder and I withdrew to a less exposed position, where I was able to complete my task unmolested and then returned to head-quarters.

Next morning early there was some firing at the front where our troops were driving the Rebel pickets further back. A large house, fired by our skirmishers, was burning; it had harboured Rebel sharp-shooters, who had done much damage the preceding day.

I was sent out to the lines again at noon and remained there until evening. My station was next to one of our batteries, which fired an occasional shell into the enemy's lines without provoking any reply. A wagon-load of muskets were picked up on the field, which I took back to head-quarters.

The losses in the Fifth Corps, in what was known as the battle of Poplar Spring Church, amounted to upwards of six hundred. After a feeble attempt by the enemy to assault our position on the evening of October first, the two opposing lines held their position for about three weeks. Our men strengthened their breast-works and the engineers built some redoubts. The balance of the ordnance train arrived and we established a camp. My tent was put up and our duties went on, as they had at the Globe Tavern. During the latter part of September and the first week in October, we again had an inordinate quantity of rain after the long summer drought, which made camp life miserable, the more so as the nights were getting cold.

In compliance with General Grant's order to extend the left of our army and gain possession of the Southside railroad, another important means of supply for the enemy, preparations for the movement were begun on the twenty-fifth of October. On that day I issued ammunition to the division; also arms to some newly arrived soldiers. On the morning of the twenty-seventh the movement commenced; the ordnance and other supply trains were ordered back to the Globe Tavern, there to await orders. As the troops marched off at daylight, a heavy rain fell which bade fair to continue. For nearly three weeks we had enjoyed beautiful weather and the roads were dry and dusty, until this movement started. The enemy's right was encountered about nine A. M. and spirited engagements took place during the day, but the attempt to gain the Southside railroad was a failure at this time. During the night of the twenty-seventh, and the morning of the twenty-eighth, the divisions of the Second and Fifth Corps, engaged in this attempt, were withdrawn to their former lines at Poplar Spring Church. The losses in the Second Corps were more than fourteen hundred, while those in the Fifth were two hundred and seventy-nine.

On the same day I was ordered to return to our camp at division head-quarters. While at this camp, I saw much of my company which was doing duty as provost guard at General Ayres's head-quarters. After the arrival of the army at Petersburg, the six skeleton companies of my regiment were consolidated into two. Company D, in which I had served for more than nine years, ceased to exist, and I became a member of Company C. These two companies, together with the remnant of the band, then did duty at division head-quarters.

On the thirty-first of October, General Grant ordered that all of the regular infantry, serving in the Fifth Army Corps, proceed at once to New York City and there report for orders to Major General Dix. This was cheering news for us. We presumed that we were to go there to keep the peace at the coming presidential election, for which Lincoln and McClellan were the candidates, and that we might be detained there for a while before returning to the field. I was kept busy for two days in transfering ordnance stores and making out the necessary papers, then I rejoined my company. Next morning, November second, 1864, at an early hour, all the regular infantry boarded a train composed of box and flat cars, waiting for us on the United States Military railroad, which conveyed us to City Point. Transports were ready for us, and by noontime we were under way down the James river on the voyage to New York.

PART XIV.

DEPARTURE FROM THE FIELD AND LAST DAYS OF SERVICE 1865.

THE voyage to New York was uneventful. We had the usual transport discomforts with some rough and cold weather and, on the second day before the election, we reached New York Harbor. The small battalion of the Second United States Infantry, consisting of half a dozen officers, about seventy-five men and a dog, landed at Fort Hamilton dock, along with about half the other troops on board. The remainder, as well as those on another transport, were distributed among various forts in the vicinity of New York. We marched to the fort with flying colors, but we had no band; the few remaining members of our band were doing other duty and Sergeant Lovell, the big drum-major, had been one of the color sergeants for more than a year. My company was quartered in one of the damp and gloomy casemates which had but a single window, or porthole, overlooking the bay.

On election day we were not allowed to go outside of the fort. Extra ammunition was issued and a thorough inspection of arms was held. A large ferry-boat remained at the dock the entire day to transport us to the city in case of a serious riot which, however, did not occur.

A few days later several soldiers in the company, including myself, secured passes to visit the city. We had to walk a long distance before reaching a horse-car line to take us to one of the ferries from Brooklyn to New York. While on this leave I visited my old friend, Sergeant Major Milligan, who was ill with consumption at his mother's house. The hardships of field service had been too much for his somewhat delicate constitution. It was the last time I saw him. He died within two weeks, much beloved, and his death greatly regretted by his comrades, who erected a modest but appropriate monument to his memory in New York Bay Cemetery.

During our short stay at Fort Hamilton, we performed regular garrison duty. I was sergeant of the guard a couple of times and one of these occasions I am not likely to forget. We mounted a strong guard and had sentinels posted all around the fort and the adjoining redoubt. The guard-room and prison were in casemates on the east side of the fort, on each side of a sally-port. At that time nearly fifty prisoners were in confinement—the toughest element I ever saw in the army. Some were general prisoners undergoing sentences— they wore a ball and chain; others were awaiting trial for various crimes; and there were, also, a small number of ordinary "drunks." It was customary to parade and call the roll of the prisoners in the morning when the guard was changed, and again at retreat in the evening, before they were locked up for the night.

A few of the prisoners had escaped at times, which made a young and inexperienced lieutenant, who was officer of the day on my first tour of guard, so nervous that he ordered most extraordinary and unwise precautions against a recurrence of escapes. He ordered me to turn out the guard and all of the prisoners at eleven o'clock at night and at three o'clock in the morning—hours at which the sentinels were not relieved. The officer of the day was present at eleven, when I called out the two relieves of the guard, not on post, and formed ranks in the sally-port. Then with a corporal and two files of the guard, we started to turn out the prisoners. They objected strenuously at the unusual proceeding and cursed and swore dreadfully. It took a long time to turn them all out and count them, by the aid of a lantern. They were left standing in the ranks, half clad and shivering, while the officer of the day ordered me to accompany him for an inspection of the prisoners' quarters. More than half an hour had been consumed in the parading of the prisoners.

At three o'clock, when we turned them out for the second time, there was almost a riot. Some swore they would kill the lieutenant, others refused to get up and I had to bring in more help to drag them from their bunks and push them into the ranks, with only a blanket to cover them. They yelled and shouted and began to throw things at the guards in the semi-darkness—the only light being from a few lanterns. The lieutenant drew his sword and threatened to run it through the body of any prisoner who refused to obey orders, but he prudently remained outside the doorway. Now all this trouble was needless. A sentinel was posted outside the prison door and another at the only window. The prisoners' chances of escape by slipping away in the darkness, while outside, were better than when locked up. When the post commander heard the next day about the turning out of the prisoners in the night-time he ordered that it should not be repeated, and it may be assumed that the over-zealous lieutenant was admonished to use more discretion in the future.

About a week after the election, my company (C) received orders to be ready next morning in full marching order and proceed to Governor's Island to escort a detachment of Rebel prisoners from there to Elmira, New York, where the Government had established a large prison camp. As the other company remained at Fort Hamilton, we supposed that we would return there when our duty had been performed. We embarked on a steam-boat and soon arrived at the Governor's Island dock, where about two hundred ragged and hungry "Rebs," who had been confined in Castle Williams for a few days, were awaiting us. Each prisoner, as he stepped on board, received a loaf of bread and a piece of boiled beef to which he immediately did ample justice. The boat started for Jersey City where we put the prisoners on the cars of the Erie railroad. It was a special train, made up of emigrant cars, which made but few stops. I had charge of one of the cars in which every seat but four for the guard was occupied by a prisoner. With me were six privates as guards. I stationed three at each end of the car with their loaded rifles. When the train halted, one of the guards was stationed outside on each side of the car, and I also descended.

At Goshen and some other stations where we halted for a brief time, some of the citizens gave the prisoners fruit, cigars and tobacco, which we allowed to be passed to them through the car windows. It was quite late at night when we arrived at Elmira and turned our prisoners over to some guards, who marched them to the prison camp two miles or more away. The company passed the remainder of the night in some freight sheds, while the captain and lieutenant put up at the nearest hotel.

Next morning we were vexed and disgusted at learning that we were not to go back to New York, but were to remain at Elmira to guard prisoners. The general desire was to go back to the field and see the close of the war, of which a part of the Second Infantry had seen the beginning. We had made up our minds that the end was near; prisoners at the front had told us of the dire straits of General Lee's army for food and clothing and the rapidly diminishing forces. We felt angry with the authorities who had condemned us to such an inglorious duty, after our long and faithful service in the field, where we had lost more than a third of our number. But there was no help for it. As soldiers, we had to obey orders. We were not the only ones thus treated. The companies of the Twelfth and Seventeenth Infantry, who had left the field at the same time, had arrived here a few days before and were then doing duty. Subsequently we learned that the First Battalion of the Eleventh and the Second Battalion of the Twelfth were returned to the Army of the Potomac, where they remained to the end and were present at the surrender of General Lee's army. The company left at Fort Hamilton, together with our small "field and staff," was sent to Newport Barracks, Kentucky, there to recruit and reform the Second Infantry for future service.

The company marched from the Elmira depot a long distance beyond the suburbs of the town to the prison camp, near which we encamped, alongside of other troops. We put up "A" tents and raided some hay-stacks for bedding. It was cold, and as wood was furnished for cooking purposes only, we crowded around the kitchen fire, which had no shelter, to warm ourselves. All the troops, except the recently arrived regulars, were sheltered in temporary barracks.

The force guarding the Rebel prisoners, who were all of the rank and file, was composed of a battery of artillery, nearly a thousand regular infantry, several regiments of the Veteran Reserve Corps and a few others. The Veteran Reserve Corps was a new organization, something like Home Guards. It was composed of men considered unfit for field duty. In its ranks were a considerable number of men who had for a time served at the front. The active soldiers named this organization "The Invalid Corps." Colonel Moore of the Veteran Reserve Corps, the ranking officer, was in command of all the troops of the prison guard.

The prison camp near Elmira was established in July, 1864, and, at the time of our arrival, contained upwards of ten thousand prisoners. They had been in tents all summer but were then in barracks, within a stockade enclosing about forty acres. The main front with the principal gate and guardhouse was close to and faced the road leading into Elmira; the back was near the Chemung river. A platform, from which the sentinels could overlook the prison yards and dead line, surrounded the entire stockade.

The site was badly chosen, there was a swamp within the enclosure and much of it was liable to be overflowed by the Chemung river. A great amount of sickness prevailed—at times five hundred were inmates of the prison hospital and as many more sick in quarters. More than ten per cent. of the prisoners died, while this prison existed; two thousand, nine hundred and seventeen were buried at the base of the hills about a mile from the prison. The greatest mortality was during the hard winter of 1864-'65, when often a dozen or more died every day and were removed every morning to be buried in trenches without any ceremony.

The Government allowed a soldier's rations for each prisoner, but that was considered too much for men who had practically no exercise, and it was left to the discretion of the prison commander, as to how much of the ration was to be issued. The saving was to constitute a fund for building quarters, hospitals, clothing, bedding and other supplies for the prisoners. At Elmira the prisoners received about two-thirds of a ration, served to them in two cooked meals daily. This kept them somewhat hungry, but they were far better off than our starving and shelterless prisoners in the South. When the inhuman treatment of our soldiers in the Southern prisons became known in the North, there was a hue and cry for retaliation; but I think none of it was practised in the Northern prisons. The suspension of the exchange of prisoners during 1864 by our Government caused increased suffering and many deaths of our soldiers in the Southern prisons.

Opposite the prison pen, on land not leased by the Government, several open-timbered observation towers had been erected by citizens. They were about forty feet in height with a flat deck on top, which had stairs leading up to it. From the top of these towers a good view of the interior of the prison and its teeming inmates could be had for the payment of ten cents admission fee. On clear days, and especially on Sundays, many of Elmira's citizens availed themselves of this opportunity to see the Rebel prisoners. The lower part of these structures were enclosed and used as groggeries, mainly patronized by soldiers. These places and some others along the road to town made trouble for the provost guard and provided inmates for the guard-house.

On the second day after our arrival, Colonel Moore ordered that one of the regular sergeants be detailed to act as post sergeant major. I was selected for the position and ordered to report to the post adjutant for duty. The adjutant's office was in a temporary building near the prison gate. It consisted of one large room, furnished with a number of desks and a stove. There were three clerks employed, all of whom belonged to the Invalid Corps. I performed the duties of a sergeant major at the guard-mount parade every morning which was no small affair, as the daily guard numbered more than two hundred. After guard-mount, Colonel Moore and the adjutant spent a few hours at the office, while the clerks and I were busy consolidating the morning reports of the troops and making out guard details from rosters for the following day. In the afternoon I was generally free to do as I pleased, go to town or to my cold camp, for I had to mess with my company and sleep in my tent. I had a standing pass to go anywhere about Elmira; but when the weather was bad, I usually remained in the adjutant's office until it closed in the evening. The hot stove there had an attraction for me.

One night there was a noisy disturbance and fighting among the soldiers in one of the groggeries. The provost guard arrested every one there, including Quinn, the proprietor. Next morning a boy came into the adjutant's office and handed Colonel Moore a dirty, crumpled piece of paper on which was scrawled in pencil—

> Kurnell Moore sir i am in the gard hous sir and i dunno for wat sir im a sitisen sir and me name is Patrick Quinn sir.

The Colonel was an elderly man with a good sense of humor; he was much amused by this note and pinned it up on the wall over his desk where he often called some of the visiting officers' attention to it. As for "Patrick Quinn sir" he had to be released, as he had a city license and was not located on Government ground.

On Thanksgiving Day, the ladies of Elmira provided a turkey dinner for all the soldiers. We marched by detachments to a temporary hall, neatly decorated for the occasion. There was a band and an abundant dinner served by the ladies themselves. At its close we gave thanks to the ladies of Elmira in speech and in rousing cheers.

After Thanksgiving Day we had deep snow, and it became so cold that we suffered greatly in our camp. Temporary quarters were being erected for the regulars, but they were not ready until the first week in December. My company did not occupy them; we were sent to Barracks No. 2, which was on the opposite side of the town, on the outskirts, more than three miles from our camp. Owing to this move I lost my position of post sergeant major, which I had held for only three weeks. At Barracks No. 2 we were fairly comfortable. We had stoves and bunks in the quarters. A few other companies were quartered there, but no Rebel prisoners. We did the ordinary garrison duty and had much spare time to walk around the town, going sometimes to a theatre, when a troupe came to town. The shows were held in a hall on the second floor of a building on the principal street. I particularly remember a piece called, "The Sea of Ice," in which, owing to the limited height of the pasteboard icebergs on the stage, the actors were forced to stoop low when trying to conceal themselves from the bloodthirsty Eskimos.

During the winter, which was severe, the first sergeant of my company reenlisted, receiving a two months' furlough, and in his absence I acted as first sergeant. I have still in my possession the company roll, as I then daily called it. Only ten names of soldiers, who had served on the frontiers, remained; all the others were the names of men who had joined during the war. Of the officers, there were but seven in the regiment who had seen frontier service, all of them serving elsewhere at this time. Not one of these seven officers belonged to the regiment at the outbreak of the war, they had all been promoted into it. Captain William F. Drum was in command of Company C, but left us during the month of February to become the colonel of the Fifth New York Veteran Volunteers, then serving in the field in the Fifth Army Corps under General Warren. Captain Drum, whose esteem I possessed, told me before his departure that, after he took command of his regiment, he would apply to Governor Fenton of New York for a commission for me as he desired to have me serve with him after my discharge, which was soon to take place. A few weeks later he wrote me, saying he had made the application.

About the middle of March, 1865, we left Barracks No. 2 and again went into camp near the prison pen, on the same ground we had occupied previously. The ice in the Chemung river had broken up and melting snow raised the river until it overflowed its banks and inundated a part of the prison barrack buildings, causing much suffering among the inmates. In a few days the first sergeant returned from furlough; but as I had not many more days to serve, I was excused from guard duty. At the request of the company commander, Brv't. Captain William Falk, I devoted the last days of my service to putting the company's books and papers in thorough order.

On the twenty-fourth day of March, 1865, I received my discharge from the army for the second time, by no means certain that I would not rejoin again. I put on my best uniform and disposed of my little belongings among my comrades. I received my final statements, which I handed to a paymaster, permanently stationed in Elmira, who paid me in full. That evening with a few special friends I had dinner at a hotel in the town, and at about nine o'clock bade them farewell at the depot. I boarded a train, spent the night on a seat, and arrived in New York next morning.

I had a letter to Colonel Richard I. Dodge, who was the chief mustering and disbursing officer in New York city, with the principal offices at 23 and 25 St. Marks Place. Colonel Dodge employed me at once as a clerk at seventy-five dollars per month. In a few days I entered upon my duties under Captain Henry A. Ellis, in whose office there were half a dozen other clerks, all but one being discharged soldiers, some of whom I had known in the field. Our duties consisted in making discharges and final statements for individual soldiers, regulars and volunteers. Later on, when the army disbanded, we made out the muster rolls and final accounts for many volunteer regiments, who were mustered out of the service in New York.

General Grant had put the Army of the Potomac in motion, and on the first day of April, the battle of Five Forks was successfully fought, which indicated the end of the Confederacy. All this time I was anxiously awaiting the arrival of my commission for I ardently wished to be present at the final stage of the war. General Lee surrendered on the ninth of April to General Grant, and General Johnston to General Sherman a week later. Peace was soon declared. The grand review of Grant and Sherman's veteran soldiers was held in Washington on May twenty-fourth and, by June first, the Fifth Army Corps had ceased to exist.

I received the commission from Albany early in June but I wrote to Colonel Drum informing him that, in as much as the Fifth New York Veteran Volunteers were likely to be mustered out of service within a month, I had decided not to be mustered in to join the regiment for so short a time. I have since regretted that I did not serve as an officer, even for so short a time. The fact of not having been mustered in debars me from becoming a member of the Loyal Legion according to its rules, no matter how much service I had in the field.

We were busy during the summer mustering out troops, and opened a branch office at the south-west corner of Broome and Elm Street where, under Lieutenant Netterville of the Twelfth United States Infantry, I remained for a few months. In the fall I was returned to the main office, where I continued until the month of January, 1866, when the mustering and disbursing office was ordered to be closed. This proved to be my final service for the Government, in or out of the army. Henceforth I was to be a citizen.

REFLECTIONS.

I SOMETIMES ask myself the questions—Was my army service a benefit or a detriment to me in after life? Would I have attained a better condition and standing, if I had not been in the military service? These are questions hard to answer in my case, as I had to struggle for a living and had no one to give me a helping hand to gain a higher plane. When I left the army I was not yet twenty-four and totally inexperienced in earning a livelihood in civil life, which was rendered more difficult by the fact that a million young men were released from the army at the same time, all seeking new careers outside of military service. An element of luck and some of the habits I had acquired in the army were beneficial to me. The military training taught me responsibility, promptness and self-control, which I found useful in my long business career and as an employer. The out-of-door life for ten years fortified me in health, which has lasted to the present day and for which I am most grateful. I have much to be thankful for and little to regret.

I believe that a three years' term of army service would be beneficial to most young men of good character and habits. To-day soldiers of the United States Army enjoy many advantages and comforts that were unknown to the older army in times of peace; the soldiers' pay, food and clothing are better, and the discipline is less strict. I have visted a number of home garrisons and those in Honolulu and Manila, in all of which I found the quarters comfortable, clean and sanitary. There are libraries, schools and club-rooms; and separate beds with sheets and pillows are provided for each soldier, a luxury formerly unheard of in garrisons. I have seen British soldiers serving in India and those of other nations on foreign service in various parts of the world; but I think the American soldiers now receive better care and more liberal treatment than those of other nations. It has always been a soldier's habit and privilege to grumble. I suppose there is as much grumbling to-day in the army as there was in former times.

AUGUSTUS MEYERS,
Sergeant, Second U. S. Infantry.

November 17, 1913.

ADDENDA.

On a recent tour of the northwestern states I visited Sioux City. There, in September, 1913, I found a large and prosperous city with many fine buildings, where there had been only a wilderness in 1855. The riverfront was unrecognizable to me. The early houses that once clustered there had been replaced by a railroad yard.

I had the good fortune to meet Mr. J. M. Pinkney, a congenial business man who had lived in Sioux City almost from its foundation. He was well informed and we had a long and interesting conversation about the early days when the city was a mere frontier settlement. Mr. Pinkney introduced me at the office of the Sioux City Journal where I was courteously received. I found the Journal to be a large up-to-date newspaper such as one would expect to find only in a great metropolis.

I was seized with a strong desire to revisit Fort Pierre, although I had no pleasant recollections of it. To me it brought only thoughts of suffering. I left Sioux City on a late night train and arrived at Pierre, the capital of South Dakota, in the middle of the next afternoon. Pierre, built mainly on hills overlooking the Missouri River, is a city of only about three thousand inhabitants, but boasts a large and magnificent capital building surpassed by few in the western states. There is also a modern fire-proof hotel, a government post office, a Carnegie library and other buildings worthy of note. A substantial railroad bridge crosses the Missouri.

The smaller town of Fort Pierre, the county seat of Stanley County, South Dakota, is directly opposite on the west bank of the river. A small motorboat makes hourly ferry trips, communication by way of the railroad bridge being infrequent.

I boarded the motorboat next morning, September eighth, to go to Fort Pierre, where I had arrived fifty-eight years ago in the same month. I found the Missouri River just as muddy and treacherous for navigation as of yore. A large sandbar made a long detour necessary to reach the channel on the western side of it. The boat ran aground several times, and finally it was caught so hard and fast that we had to wait for the other ferry to haul us off on its return trip.

There were two other passengers on the boat beside myself, one a white citizen and the other a full blooded young Sioux who had been educated at Carlisle School. I learned from them that the old stockade fort no longer existed. It had been a few miles further up the

TEN YEARS IN THE RANKS U.S. ARMY

river, but they could not tell me its exact location. They offered to take me to the office of Mr. Stanley Philip, the owner of a large ranch near the site of the fort. Mr. Philip was out, but they introduced me to Mr. C. H. Fales, a prominent business man of the town, who kindly volunteered to show me the site of the old fort.

As we were preparing to start, Mr. Philip arrived in an automobile and invited both of us to go to the place in his machine. He soon set us down at the site of the old stockade about two and one-half miles up the river. Not a stick remained of the old fort. It had left no mark save a depression in the ground where a cellar had been. I recognized the contour of the low hills on the west and of the higher hills across the river. There was the same bleak prairie extending back to the foothills with its colonies of barking prairie dogs, who appeared to me to be somewhat bolder than of old.

The Indian burial place had disappeared, but the island in the river below the fort was still there. The most noticeable change was in the river front. The channel was much further out, and a wide strip of bottom land, covered with willows and brush, had formed at what was once an abrupt bank. As I gazed upon this changed scene, I thought of the time when I had seen the plain dotted with the tepees of thousands of Indians who had assembled at that very spot to sign a treaty with General Harney.

After a while we went about a mile up the river to Mr. Philip's large ranch where he has thirteen thousand acres fenced in for a buffalo preserve. There are more than three hundred of the animals roaming at large among the hills and the number is being increased by the annual addition of some dozens of calves.

Much of the ranch on the high bottom lands along the shore of the Missouri is under cultivation and is yielding good crops. All this great estate I had seen as a wilderness that I was glad to get away from. In those days I would not have taken the whole county as a gift had I been required to live there. Mr. Philip, who manages his own ranch, is a young man. His father, a Scotchman, lately deceased, was one of the early settlers and accumulated the property.

On the way back to Fort Pierre, which is a neat little town of about one thousand people, with wide streets and cement sidewalks, my companions told of the discovery on February 17, 1913, of a lead plate on a hill back of the town, where it had been buried by French explorers in 1743. It is now the property of Mr. William O'Reilly, a resident of Fort Pierre. Mr. O'Reilly kindly presented me with a photograph of the plate and a translation of its inscription. He also took me to the bank where it is kept in a safe deposit vault and allowed me to examine it carefully. It is of thick sheet lead about six by seven inches in dimensions and but little corroded. On one side is the seal of France above an inscription in Latin. Both are deeply

TEN YEARS IN THE RANKS U. S. ARMY

stamped in the lead and quite legible. A translation of the inscrption follows:

> In the twenty-sixth year of Louis XV's reign, in the name of the King, most illustrious sovereign, for the Governor, Marquis of Beauharnis, in 1743 Peter Gaultier de la Verendrie deposited this plate.

On the reverse side is scratched rather irregularly the following inscription in French:

> Deposited by the Chevalier of Laverdendried (Witnesses) Louis La Louette, A. Miotte. April 30, 1743.

In a Fort Pierre book store I was able to procure "A Brief History of South Dakota," written in 1905 by Doane Robinson, Secretary of the State Historical Society. In this interesting book Mr. Robinson says:

"The first white man that we know certainly to have visited South Dakota was a young man named Verendrye (de la Verendrie on the plate), in the year of 1743. He claimed the land for the King of France, and on a hill near the camp planted a plate engraved with the arms of France and marked the spot with a pile of stones. To unearth that plate would be a rich find for some enterprising young South Dakotan. Taking into account the direction traveled and the time spent in making the trip, it is most likely that this plate rests within fifty miles of the state capitol."

The book contains many items of special interest to me. On one of the maps is shown the location of the winter cantonments of "Harney's troops in 1856." There is a good picture of "Old Fort Pierre in 1855 and vicinity," also a ground plan of the fort drawn to scale, showing all of the buildings within it. This plan shows the fort to have been three hundred by two hundred and fifty feet square, somewhat larger than I judged it to be from memory. The names of some Indian chiefs and their pictures printed in the book bring the originals back to my thoughts.

In the afternoon I bade farewell to the two gentlemen who had been so courteous to me. I was the only passenger on the ferry when the boatman vainly tried to make her start. He finally went up the street to get some dry batteries and returned with another man. They installed new batteries and took much of the machinery apart and put it together again. Still the boat refused to budge. Nearly an hour had been lost and I was beginning to get apprehensive about catching my train, when another boat arrived from the east shore. The boatman aboard her soon found what the trouble was and we started for the other side which we reached without mishap save grounding twice on the sandbar.

TEN YEARS IN THE RANKS U.S. ARMY

A reporter of a local paper caught me there, but I had time to give him only a very short interview. I caught the train for the east with little time to spare. A state fair was being held at Huron, S. D., four hours' ride from Pierre, and many persons got on at the intermediate stations. Among them were a few Indians and their squaws. To see an Indian mount the steps of a car, carrying a suitcase, seemed extraordinary to me. Surely the Indian as I knew him no longer exists.

THE AMERICAN MILITARY EXPERIENCE

An Arno Press Collection

Brown, Richard C. **Social Attitudes of American Generals, 1898-1940.** 1979
Erney, Richard Alton. **The Public Life of Henry Dearborn.** 1979
Koistinen, Paul A.C. **The Hammer and the Sword.** 1979
Parrish, Noel Francis. **Behind the Sheltering Bomb.** 1979
Rutman, Darrett Bruce. **A Militant New World, 1607-1640.** 1979
Kohn, Richard H., editor. **Anglo-American Antimilitary Tracts, 1697-1830.** 1979
Kohn, Richard H., editor. **Military Laws of the United States, From the Civil War Through the War Powers Act of 1973.** 1979
Arnold, Isaac N. **The Life of Benedict Arnold.** 1880
Ayres, Leonard P. **The War with Germany.** 1919
Biderman, Albert D. **March to Calumny.** 1963
Chandler, Charles DeForest and Frank P. Lahm. **How our Army Grew Wings.** 1943
Collins, James Potter. **Autobiography of a Revolutionary Soldier.** 1859
Elliott, Charles Winslow. **Winfield Scott.** 1937
Gould, Benjamin Apthorp. **Investigations in the Military and Anthropological Statistics of American Soldiers.** 1869
Grinker, Roy R. and John P. Spiegel. **War Neuroses.** 1945
Hunt, Elvid. **History of Fort Leavenworth, 1827-1927.** 1926
Leahy, William D. **I Was There.** 1950
Lejeune, John A. **The Reminiscences of a Marine.** 1930
Logan, John A. **The Volunteer Soldier of America.** 1887
Long, John D. **The New American Navy.** 1903. Two vols. in one
Meyers, Augustus. **Ten Years in the Ranks U.S. Army.** 1914
Michie, Peter S. **The Life and Letters of Emory Upton.** 1885
Millis, Walter. **The Martial Spirit.** 1931
Mott, T[homas] Bentley. **Twenty Years as Military Attaché.** 1937
Palmer, John McAuley. **America in Arms.** 1941
Pyle, Ernie. **Here is Your War.** 1943

Riker, William H. **Soldiers of the States.** 1957

Roe, Frances M.A. **Army Letters From an Officer's Wife, 1871-1888.** 1909

Shippen, E[dward]. **Thirty Years at Sea.** 1879

Smith, Louis. **American Democracy and Military Power.** 1951

Steiner, Bernard C. **The Life and Correspondence of James McHenry.** 1907

Sylvester, Herbert Milton. **Indian Wars of New England.** 1910. Three vols.

[Totten, Joseph Gilbert]. **Report of General J.G. Totten, Chief Engineer, on the Subject of National Defences.** 1851

Truscott, L[ucian] K., Jr. **Command Missions.** 1954

U.S. Congress. **American State Papers.** 1834/1860/1861. Four vols.

U.S. Congress. **Military Situation in the Far East.** 1951. Five vols.

U.S. Congress. **Organizing for National Security.** 1961. Three vols. in two

[U.S. Bureau of Labor Statistics], U.S. Congress. **Wartime Technological Developments.** 1945. Two vols. in one

U.S. Congress. **Report of the Board on Fortifications or other Defenses Appointed by the President of the United States Under the Provisions of the Act of Congress, Approved March 3, 1885** and **Plates to Accompany the Report.** 1886. Two vols. in one

U.S. President's Air Policy Commission. **Survival in the Air Age.** 1948

U.S. Selective Service System. **Backgrounds of Selective Service.** 1947. Two vols. in four

White, Howard. **Executive Influence in Determining Military Policy in the United States.** 1925

Winthrop, William. **Military Law and Precedents.** 1920